THE FUTURE OF
LEADERSHIP

"The authors have clearly connected the role and power of leadership to the state of change that is accelerating for all global businesses. This book will help us better understand the basic tenets of leadership necessary in the world of the future."

Mike L Burns, VP Human Resources & Total Quality Culture,
Goodyear Tire & Rubber Co.

"*The Future of Leadership* and the white water metaphor powerfully capture the essence of business today. I'm afraid that today's business climate is not for those who wish to go "canoeing in the pond." This book is an outgrowth of personal experiences and philosophies that should be essential reading for all agents of change."

Maxine Fechter, VP Human Resources, Coach Leatherware

"*The Future of Leadership* dots the i's and crosses the t's on the latest thinking around leadership whilst, through practical examples, shakes up the alphabet and starts to create a new language for the future."

Anita Roddick, founder and chief executive of The Body Shop

"*The Future of Leadership* is tremendously insightful and must reading for effective leaders in the 21st Century. Learning, growth and change are the essence of this new age of leadership. Evolution, uncertainty, tumultuous rapids – not calm seas – are the future. To survive and prosper in this new age will require new skills and perspectives. *The Future of Leadership* provides the guide for understanding this new era and the skills necessary for success as we ride the rapids into the next millennium. Congratulations to Randy White and his colleagues for another cutting edge study of leadership."

Myrna L Bair, PhD, Senate Minority Leader, Delaware
Director, Women's Leadership Program, College of Urban Affairs & Public Policy,
University of Delaware

"An absorbing insight into the new corporate reality and the challenges facing tomorrow's leaders."

Sandra Harris, Editor, Business Life

"The authors put forth a critical challenge – overcoming our fear of ambivalence, ambiguity and uncertainty in order to face the demands of the future. Leaders will find *The Future of Leadership* curiously comforting and decidedly challenging. It reminds us that the hard questions are the ones that are worth asking."

Stephen J Wall, President, Manus and author, "The New Strategists"

"*The Future of Leadership* identifies the core competencies leaders of the future must have to enable their business to thrive in the future. This book reaches way beyond the obvious and focuses on the abstract."

Colleen Stenholt, Director Human Resources, Northwestern Mutual Life

About Ashridge

Ashridge is independently recognized as one of the world's leading centers for management and organizational development. Established in 1959, it has acquired an outstanding international reputation for helping improve managerial and business performance through its executive education programs – including a world-renowned MBA program – and its management research and consultancy activities.

Ashridge's clients include some of the world's leading international companies, as well as large organizations in the public sector and many small and medium-sized enterprises. Ashridge works in partnership with other institutes around the world in delivering its services, and has representative partners in several other countries including Hong Kong, Germany and the Czech Republic.

Ashridge is located 50 kilometers northwest of London, just outside the town of Berkhamsted in Hertfordshire. Set in a large country estate surrounded by peaceful woodlands, its imposing historic house, with its excellent residential facilities, provides an unrivaled environment in which to learn and develop.

THE FUTURE OF
LEADERSHIP

Riding the Corporate Rapids into the 21st Century

RANDALL P WHITE
PHILIP HODGSON
AND
STUART CRAINER

Ashridge

PITMAN
PUBLISHING

London · Hong Kong · Johannesburg
Melbourne · Singapore · Washington DC

PITMAN PUBLISHING
c/o National Book Network
4720A Boston Way
Lanham
Maryland 20706
USA
Tel: (+1) 301 731 9516
Fax: (+1) 301 459 2118

A Division of Pearson Professional Limited

First published in Great Britain by Pitman Publishing in 1996

This edition published in the United States of America in 1996

© Pearson Professional Limited 1996

ISBN 0 273 62206 4

British Library Cataloguing in Publication Data
A CIP catalog record for this book can be obtained from the British Library

10 9 8 7 6 5 4 3 2 1

Printed and bound in the United States of America

The Publishers' policy is to use paper manufactured from sustainable forests.

To Katie, Jane and Ro, who give
support and inspiration.

To our children – Logan, Jessica,
Erik and Heidi; Joanna and
Peter; Dan, Ryan and Ceira,
who give purpose.

Left to right: Randall P. White, Philip Hodgson and Stuart Crainer

About the Authors

RANDALL P WHITE: as President of RPW Executive Development Inc in Greensboro, North Carolina, Randy consults with organizations in the areas of executive development, leadership education and succession planning. He was formerly with the Center for Creative Leadership (CCL), where he served as Director, Specialized Client Applications, responsible for customized program design and delivery, as well as the Awareness Program for Executive Excellence (APEX), a coaching program for senior executives, in *Fortune 500* corporations.

During 12 years at the Center, Randy was also instrumental in CCL's research and training in executive learning, growth and change. He led design teams for several CCL programs including *The Executive Women's Workshop, Dynamics of Strategy* and *Creating Systems for Executive Development.*

He has written a number of influential articles and is co-author of *Breaking the Glass Ceiling.* He is currently serving a three-year term on the national board of The American Society for Training and Development. He has been a featured speaker at the Conference Board in the United States, Europe and Canada; the Human Resources Planning Society; The American Society for Training & Development and The Australian Society for Training and Development. He is an adjunct Professor at Duke University's Fuqua School, lectures at the Johnson School at Cornell University and is an adjunct instructor at CCL. He holds a PhD from Cornell University.

PHILIP HODGSON: as Client and Programme Director for Action Learning at the UK's Ashridge Management College, Philip's main areas of concern are leadership, implementation of strategy, the management of change and learning organizations. He has been a major contributor to the development of the Strategic Management and Leadership Development Programmes. He is also designing and running a series of long-term self-managed development programs for senior managers.

In recent years his consultancy assignments have been with major financial services, FMCG, computing and chemical organizations, as well as the UK's National Health Service and international scientific research center.

Philip is a member of the Institute of Personnel Development and has a degree in psychology and an MSc in industrial psychology. He has published articles on leadership, new technology and assessment centres, and is the author of *A Practical Guide to Successful Interviewing* and co-author of *Making Change Work, Effective Meetings* and *What Do High Performance Managers Really Do?*

STUART CRAINER: a specialist management writer and commentator, Stuart's articles on the latest management thinking and practice appear in magazines and publications worldwide including: *The Financial Times, The London Times, Directions Magazine* and *Business Life Magazine.*

He is the author of a number of successful books that examine major business issues and global management trends including: *The Financial Times Handbook of Management* (ed), *Making Re-engineering Happen, What Do High Performance Managers Really Do?* (with Eddie Obeng & Philip Hodgson), *Leaders on Leadership, The Real Power of Brands* and *Key Management Ideas.*

"There is no formula or perfect solution. This is the tide of events. We can't turn the tide, but we can ride it."

CHARLES HANDY

Interview with Stuart Crainer, January 1994

"How does one organize an expedition? What equipment is taken, what sources read? What are the little dangers and the large ones? No one has ever written this. This information is not available."

JOHN STEINBECK

From *The Log from the Sea of Cortez*, Heinemann, London, 1941

CONTENTS

PREFACE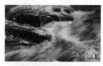

Don't read this book if you can't cope with risk. We have put on paper something that is not completely clear, and our expectation is that it can never be completely clear. We know that people find this uncomfortable, but we are betting that you will find something here that is intriguing enough to draw you in so that you don't mind the risk of discomfort.

The book emerged from a five-year process of dissatisfaction with what was taught in the overlapping areas of management, change, leadership and strategy. Not that we believed there was anything particularly wrong in what was taught, merely that it wasn't enough. We found that the reality of the working lives of the managers we met in our various guises as consultants, researchers and course presenters was not well enough represented by current theories and managerial approaches. Reality and theory appeared disturbingly out of alignment.

> **This book is an antidote to 'tidy' leadership.**

Whenever we talked to people in organizations – no matter where or who they were – we got the impression that the things which mattered, both individually and organizationally, were not as orderly and methodical as the writings on the subject seemed to imply. We felt that the managerial world had got itself into the double bind of writing tidily about management because it is attractive and sells well, and then getting depressed that it's messy but effective leaders couldn't actually live up to the tidy ideals that had been set.

This book is an antidote to "tidy" leadership.

This, we hope, does not mean that it is highly complex or inaccessible. Naturally we have tried to make things clear and simple whenever possible. But, we believe, in the past there has been a huge and irresistible temptation for managers and commentators to oversimplify, to tell it as we would like it to be, not like it is. *The Future of Leadership* sets out to reveal leadership as it is, and as it is truly going to be.

Our predilection for tidiness has spawned an emphasis on trying to do the right thing – the trouble is that, despite our best endeavors, it is easy actually to deliver the wrong thing. The research interview is a good example. There are three reasons why reports from the standard interview may mislead. First, when people talk after the event, in all kinds of ways they tidy up the narrative usually without realizing they are doing so. From being a complex plate of spaghetti, the past is recast as a single strand. The messy reality is sanitized, put in chronological order, and generally spruced up for public consumption.

Second, as a researcher you can frequently get busy managers to give you time to talk about their successes. They are usually delighted to do so. It is much harder to get them to talk about things that haven't worked out so well. Yet the major lessons for them and us may be buried in events, initiatives and shots in the dark which didn't work out. Conventional research usually allows such blemishes and the learning that accompanies them to remain buried.

Third, there is often a sizeable time-lag. An interviewee may be talking about an event that happened two or three years earlier. The research may be three or four years old before the final draft of the book. Add another year for editing and publication, a pause before purchasing the book, and the reader ends up years away from the event itself. And in all likelihood you are hearing only a part of the complete story.

From being a complex plate of spaghetti, the past is recast as a single strand. The messy reality is sanitized, put in chronological order, and generally spruced up for public consumption.

As a result, the classic research technique tells you a lot about the past, but is not good at helping with the future. Of course, we've used interviews in this book, but as illustrations of approaches rather than as examples of how to do it. We have also endeavored to make the examples as up-to-date as possible. This was easier than we thought. When we began to look for uncertainty and ambiguity we found journals and newspapers were full of examples – it was just that they were not reported under the title of uncertainty. When you read them they will be historical, but they are not yet ancient history.

Another risk arises because this is a book about the future. The future hasn't arrived yet, so we can't realistically show you what it looks like. Instead we have built up our content from a series of glimpses, pieces of partial evidence, occasional insights and, yes, even some guesses. Our message is:

When moving down the rapids is it better to look where you are going or to be transfixed by where you have come from?

> let go of your grip on the past as the only way to be taught, and get a better grip on the future as the only way to learn.

Having asked you to look forward, we do not want you to abandon the past. This is not one of those "forget everything you have learned and do it all totally differently" kinds of books. Of course, you should continue to use what has worked in the past, but you also must acknowledge that what was at the leading edge of management thinking five years ago is now no longer at the forefront.

When moving down the rapids is it better to look where you are going or to be transfixed by where you have come from? Nothing stands still, least of all the business world. What worked before is still useful but it is no longer sufficient and will be seriously deficient in the near future. This book offers practical ideas and suggestions on leading in an environment where techniques and equipment have yet to be completely invented.

We are writing for the growing numbers of people who are skeptical about save-your-life competitive formulae and miracle cures. We want to talk to people who have realized that doing nothing is a dangerous option and yet are confused by the wealth of fads and trends in management. They instinctively know that just because something worked over there at that time, it might not be so useful over here now.

If you can't trust someone else telling you what to do, what do you do? Our suggestion is simple. Learn to do it better for yourself and learn to rely on solutions that you have created specifically for your situation.

It isn't easy, risk taking never is. Remember, anything that is easy for you to do is easy for your competitors to copy. And, if it is easy for competitors to do you have to question whether you need to do it. Is it a business necessity or a habit?

Starting from the entrance of ambiguity and uncertainty, we dug under the normal assumptions made about leadership expecting to find a few minor overlooked treasures. Instead we found huge caverns that seemed to be largely unexplored. Yes, it would be safer in the short term to stay on the surface, but we invite you to join us and share the learning by sharing the risk.

Randall P White, Philip Hodgson and Stuart Crainer
May 1996

ACKNOWLEDGMENTS

We have a lot of people to thank and acknowledge for help, challenges, support, ideas and sometimes just time given freely along the way. In an expedition of this kind we often didn't know what we wanted, or how to recognize it when we saw and heard it. In many cases we didn't know how to ask about the things we needed to know. This was, at the very least, confusing for interviewees and helpers alike. It is to the great credit of all those listed below that they showed patience and perseverance in the face of much authorial uncertainty.

So, in no particular order, we'd like to mention: Don Petrie and his colleagues at the Learning Alliance in Calgary, Canada and Shell Canada; Jennifer White of Canadian Occidental; Marie McKee and colleagues at Corning Incorporated, and Nick Miles of Whirlpool, for introducing us to their colleagues and letting us get a little closer to the leading edges of their organizations and their thinking about uncertainty.

Many useful comments also came from Theresa Barnett, Paul Turner and Mike Lidbetter of TSB Bank in the UK; Angela O'Connell and Mike Mulholland then of Barclays Property Services UK; Jerry Kaber then of Fletcher Challenge Ltd., Auckland, New Zealand; Roger Davies of British Airways; Barrie Brown of British Airports Authority; and Eddie Obeng of Pentacle – The Virtual Business School.

In various other projects and consultancy assignments we have had the opportunity to explore the practical impact of managers trying to handle uncertainty. We have valued the support and cooperation of James Duckworth, Mike Fox, Kees van der Waaij, David Smith and Constance Jacobson of Unilever, London and Rotterdam; George Weidmann, Toni Schönenberger and Prabhu Guptara of Union Bank of Switzerland; Ed Smith, Roger Thomas, Gill Goldie-Scott, Gareth Davies and Catherine Macora of Coopers & Lybrand; Bill Blair, Françoise Labro, Madeline Pincott, Helmut Haseroth of Cern Geneva; Sally Taylor of Sears retail group; Jean Floodgate of the Body Shop; Janine Smith and Liz Webber of Harvester UK.

The numerous organizations and individuals who helped test early versions of the Ambiguity Preference Scale: Harvard Pilgrim Health Care; the

Institute of Management Studies; Avon; National Conference of State Legislators; First Data Corporation; Colleen Stenholt and the executives at Northwestern Mutual Life; Steve Forrer; David Burger; Les Woller; Amy Webb; Len Greenhalgh; Betty Ann Bailey and Jane Hodgson.

David DeVries and Kim Kehoe listened patiently to early versions of our ideas and took us seriously when they could equally well have laughed at us.

Many people at the American Society for Training & Development and the Human Resources Planning Society encouraged us with the formulations of our presentations, but a particular mention to Richard Green from Campbell's Soup who encouraged us to test our ideas at the 1995 HRPS international meetings.

At Ashridge Management College, Michael Osbaldeston, Peter Beddowes, Alex Knight and Bill Sheddon were helpful volunteers on whom we tried early question sets. As chief executive, Mike also gave us lots of support during the writing and publishing stages of the book. Laurence Handy invited Randall to cross the Atlantic to talk about his previous work, which helped contribute to the new. Paul Pinnington, Roger Pudney, Jack Hardie, Sara Panter, Erwin Scholtz, Howell Schroeder, Janet Smallwood, John Heptonstall and Malcolm Schofield, as members of the notorious team seven, frequently supported the trialing of some new but not yet proven material when all they really knew was that it represented more risk. Andrew Ettinger and the staff of the Learning Resource Center, helped trace references, check facts and generally achieve the miraculous. Cath Jones did stoic work pulling together various versions of the *Fortune* lists. Keith Milmer, Stefan Wills and Tracey-Lee Wingrove conducted some of the early interviews with care. Tracy Bowdrey Long and the other administration staff of team seven helped bring some calm to joint meetings of the authors and arranged all the things that needed to be arranged but were probably forgotten by one of us.

At the Center for Creative Leadership, Walt Ulmer, the previous president, and David Noer, executive vice-president, gave their time and useful advice. Sally Alexander, Jill Pinto and Lu Noe managed Randall and Philip during their creative meetings in the USA, protected them from interruptions and made everything happen on time.

Paul Griffiths of Oxford Computing Center did sterling work on the statistical analysis with very short timescales; Denis Quaintance was an early interviewee and encourager of the need to investigate uncertainty. Lisa Cheraskin from Eli Lilly and participants in executive development programs at Duke and Cornell Universities have offered advice, examples and encouragement.

Many of the quotes in this book are from people who were and still are struggling with uncertainty in circumstances where they have let us into their confidence and therefore do not wish to be personally identified in the text. Naturally, we respect that confidence and would like to make special thanks to those we can't name here. We treasure their honesty and value their trust.

Kate Salkilld, our editor at Pitman, was a tower of strength and enthusiasm for the project. She and her colleagues in London and the USA have shown that publishing can be fun – even for authors.

Finally, our families – specifically Katie, Jane and Ro – who have helped, commented on, contributed to, made sacrifices for and only occasionally complained about all of this. They have become part of the book as they have inevitably been part of the process of writing it.

To you all, many thanks and happy reading!

PERMISSIONS

Grateful acknowledgment is made to the following individuals, companies and organizations for permission to use extracts from the works detailed:

Peter B Vaill of George Washington University first popularized the image of white water, describing a world of "permanent white water" in which "change is coming in all directions."

Harvard Business Review:

Argyris, C, "Teaching smart people how to learn," May–June 1991 © The President and Fellows of Harvard College 1991.

Drucker, PF, "The new productivity challenge," November–December 1991 © The President and Fellows of Harvard College 1991.

de Geus, AP, "Planning as learning," March–April 1988 © The President and Fellows of Harvard College 1988.

Hamel, G and Prahalad, CK, "Competing for the future," July–August 1994 © The President and Fellows of Harvard College 1994.

Pascale, R, Athos, A and Goss, T, "The reinvention roller coaster," November–December 1993 © The President and Fellows of Harvard College 1993.

Taylor, W, "The logic of global business: an interview with Percy Barnevik," March–April 1991 © The President and Fellows of Harvard College 1991.

INSEAD:

de Vries, Manfred Kets, "Branson's Virgin: the coming of age of a counter-cultural enterprise," © 1995 INSEAD, Fontainebleau, France.

Fortune:

Schendler, B, "Bill Gates and Paul Allen talk," © 1995 Time Inc. All rights reserved.

Jacob, R, "The resurrection of Michael Dell," © 1995 Time Inc. All rights reserved.

INTRODUCTION

The world is changing. Old ways of doing things are being replaced, improved and, sometimes, simply destroyed, cast aside as the world moves on. Products emerge and disappear; brands are promoted and eradicated; legendary names bite the corporate dust. The way we make things is being revolutionized. The way we buy and consume products is undergoing a transformation. The way we manage is being shaken like a cocktail. The list is endless and affects the fundamentals we once took for granted – the way we work, the way we play, the way we live our lives.

Forget about safety. Forget about the reassurance of your company's name in neon. Forget about meandering in mid-stream taking it easy. This is the world of white water where we have to change to survive; where we have to develop to thrive; and, paradoxically, where the very act of change increases the risk that we won't survive.

In the middle of this hubbub of change and turbulence, leadership can appear to be a safe haven offering security. Leadership appears to offer a chance of escape to a world where we know the rules, where we know what is expected of us, where we know what to do and how we will be rewarded. Leadership offers a return to the old world of regular heroes giving you the message straight, inspiring you and showing the way ahead.

Think again. The world is changing and leadership is no exception. There are no islands in the stream. Leadership is not static; it is active and changing constantly. Our notions of what leadership is have to change if we are to prosper and utilize leadership to

> **This is the world of white water where we have to change to survive; where we have to develop to thrive; and, paradoxically, where the very act of change increases the risk that we won't survive.**

its full potential. Unquestionably, the full power of leadership is not being fully exploited. In his book *Predicting Executive Success*, Mel Sorcher estimates that one-third of those chosen for senior executive positions are subsequently seen as disappointments.[1] Anecdotal information gathered in previous research suggests that the number may be as high as 50 per cent.[2] Recent years have seen a succession of high profile corporate leaders bite the dust.

The world is changing and leadership is no exception. There are no islands in the stream. Leadership is not static; it is active and changing constantly.

This does not mean that leadership no longer works, but that our interpretation and application of leadership leaves a great deal to be desired. *The Future of Leadership* sets out to show that the heroes may have gone, but leadership still counts. It does not provide a neat formula of what you can do to immediately turn yourself into a corporate leader. The world – and the world of leadership – is too complex to be explained by platitudinous lists of leadership traits. Instead, it maps out the new world order and what we can do (and increasingly must do) as individuals and organizations to become leaders of the future.

In this age of teamwork, paradoxically, the challenge is an individual one. People increasingly have to take responsibility for developing themselves. They have to put themselves in situations and environments where they develop new skills and perspectives. But, white water leadership is much more. Leadership must embrace the culture of an organization and, dauntingly, of society. Every organization – no matter where it is, what it does or who it employs – must ask itself if it is nurturing and developing a leadership culture.

The challenge is a cultural one. And there is more. The challenge is not only individual and cultural. It is also organizational. In a period of turbulent change, organizations must embrace change rather than carrying on as before. Organizations have to make the moves the right moves at the right time, all of the time.

Skeptics might say: "Yes, the world is changing, but hasn't it always changed? Isn't all this talk of revolution and reinvention designed by consultants and business schools to boost their business? Don't the fundamentals of sound management and effective leadership still remain?"

The skeptics are right – and they are wrong. It is a truism that the world is changing at a faster pace than ever before, but it is nevertheless true. More telephone lines will have been installed in China in the next seven years than during the entire century in North America. Ten years ago a word-processing program had 15,000 lines of computer code and was generated by five people. Now programs have over 500,000 lines of code and are built by teams of fifty. A weekday edition of the *New York Times* contains more information than the average person was likely to come across in a lifetime during seventeenth-century England.[3] Trends like mass customization, fast food, instantaneous document delivery (where express mail has given way to fax which is giving way to the Internet) as well as socio-economic displacement are making change a reality for us all.

An organizational, technological and managerial revolution is under way. There is a constant need for organizations to reinvent themselves. But, this does not mean that everything we know is now redundant or worthless. In their best-selling *Reengineering the Corporation*, Michael Hammer and James Champy suggest organizations equip themselves with a blank piece of paper and start again.[4] All you need is a pen and paper and off you go: revolution by marking pen. After the patchy record of implementing reengineering (one estimate puts the failure rate at 70 per cent), no doubt Champy and Hammer would agree that it is not that simple. There is no blank piece of paper. Instead, executives find themselves in a wind tunnel with sheaves of paper being propelled towards them. They catch one and rush around proclaiming they know the answer. All they have found is part of the jigsaw.

The past cannot be dismissed. Instead, the lessons of the past need to be constantly reevaluated so they have a dynamic effect on the present. The important thing is that we learn from history rather than trying to reenact it.

Leadership is evolving. This involves learning from the past and moving forward. Leaders of the future will build on the skills and attitudes that they have established during previous generations of leadership development.

If you want to gauge how far we have already come, look at the radical changes which leadership has undergone in practice and in theory. Look at the new corporate leaders and compare them with their predecessors. Compare Michael Eisner with Walt Disney. Compare Bill Gates to IBM's Thomas Watson. The change is fundamental. The names are different and so, too, are the attitudes, approaches and aspirations. Leadership moves on.

Here is the heart of the problem and of the challenge. Leadership used to be about certainty.

A generation ago, leaders aspired to military role models. The emphasis was on benign dictatorship, but dictatorship nevertheless. The leader identified a mission and the rest of the organization proceeded in that direction. Climbing up the organization was the route to career success. Today's leaders must carry people with them in a host of different directions; they must transcend the uncertainties and insecurities of the modern business environment. And followers must be prepared to fend for themselves.

Here is the heart of the problem and of the challenge. Leadership used to be about certainty. Throughout history, great leaders always appeared to know what to do. Certainty is addictive and entertaining. In the movies, leaders make it simple – they do what needs doing whether they are John Wayne or Arnold Schwarzenegger. In this world, the leadership task is about how to get people to where they have to be. When the route from A to B was known, leadership was a matter of direction and steady progress.

In the 1990s and beyond, instead of slowmoving flows, leaders find themselves hurtling down rapids. White water leadership is the new corporate necessity. *Huckleberry Finn* has become *Deliverance*. Now, the most strategically important aspects of an organization's future lie in the area of uncertainty. So the first component which a leader has to learn to do differently is to learn to move towards uncertainty rather than away from it.

Change, and the uncertainty and ambiguity which accompany it, was once the preserve of senior management. Only at the highest corporate echelon did managers have to encounter ambiguity about their role, objectives and contribution to the organization. Now uncertainty is the domain of the many rather than the preserve of the few.

Leadership in the future will not only need to be able to cope with the emotional impact of a step-by-step change, but also to help people in the organization rapidly reach a new, more effective way of working. Previous success will be no guarantee of future success. Certainty has given way to uncertainty.

It may sound as if the traditional heroes are dead, only to be replaced by a new breed of corporate superheroes. White water leadership requires new skills and perspectives, but not superhuman ones. Corporate man does not suddenly become superman. Neither does corporate woman suddenly transform into superwoman. To mix the comic strip metaphors, despite the hyperbole, the corporate world is not Gotham City.

The source of white water

The ideas in *The Future of Leadership* have emerged over a number of years of teaching, researching and consulting on both sides of the Atlantic. The fledgling ideas were tested in a series of face-to-face interviews with corporate leaders. As the ideas evolved, more action research clarified them and confirmed that they struck a chord with many of the leaders we shared them with and who were asked to contribute their personal experiences.

The book's central image emerged naturally from the research. Leadership has moved from the control of large ships through more mobile, smaller ships with rigid hulls to the guidance of flexible rubber rafts. The environ-

Learning is the key tool in this process, especially the ability to identify and learn the things that the individual or the organization find hard to learn.

ment has changed from the comfortable enormity of calm seas to tumultuous rapids.

From our research, we have identified five key skills which are essential to white water leadership. They are not a prescription for success. Nor will they cure all known organizational ills. There may be bullet points, but we don't believe they are platitudinous. Indeed, their ramifications – individually, organizationally and culturally – are profound.

The five key skills essential to white water leadership are:

● difficult learning

● maximizing energy

● resonant simplicity

● multiple focus

● mastering inner sense.

Difficult learning

Fear of failure is a major blockage to developing skills for handling uncertainty. Today's corporate leaders have to balance the conflicting needs of offering security and certainty to their staff while, at the same time, promoting more change and innovation than has been seen in the lifetime of the organization and the staff.

Learning is the key tool in this process, especially the ability to identify and learn the things that the individual or the organization find hard to learn. This frequently involves a reorientation to taking risks and making mistakes. How many executives can honestly say they work for organizations in which risk taking is positively encouraged? How many executives admit to their mistakes? How many actively and deliberately learn from them?

Maximizing energy

A common feature of people who handle ambiguity well seems to be an easy access to energy, both in themselves and in others. When data are not clear or certain, there is often a need to adopt an experimental trial and error approach to a large proportion of the workload. This can be very wearing and uses a lot of physical and emotional energy. The masters of uncertainty seem to have energy to spare.

How many executives channel their own and other people's energies effectively?

Resonant simplicity

Although numbers of levels in organizations have been cut and lines of communication shortened, time and time again key messages fail to get through. In periods of change, chaos and complexity, the leader who has the ability to capture the essence of an issue in a way that resonates with the rest of the organization is going to get the message through. How much resonance do you achieve in your organization?

Multiple focus

Modern organizations have many objectives. Some of these will be in conflict, such as the need for long-term investment versus immediate pressure of the stock market. It is often the case that your urgent task is my interruption. Our research suggests that, contrary to classic time management teaching, a lot of senior managers take the view that there is no such thing as an interruption. How focused are you on the short-term? How focused on the long-term? How can the two be balanced effectively to the benefit of the individual and the organization?

Mastering inner sense

In a culture and society which remains data driven, often part of the problem is that limited data are available or that they simply can't be trusted. In these circumstances the only source of data may be what we have called inner sense. How often do you follow your intuitive judgment – and admit to it? How do you encourage others to do the same?

There is nothing earthshattering in these skills. They are achievable, understandable, and incredibly powerful. They do not guarantee success. Nothing can. But we can be sure that:

● the future will be radically different from the past;

● leadership will be essential and new forms of leadership even more vital. The leaders of today will be gone tomorrow; we need to discover tomorrow's leaders;

● the pace of change will continue to increase. Announcing plans to spin-off its data storage and imaging businesses, 3M stated: "We're a 93-year-old company, and we have our own way of doing things. We couldn't keep pace." 3M is not noted for its slowness. Indeed, it is routinely celebrated for its speed of innovation. Fast, but not fast enough. "We used to take four days from getting raw material to putting the product on the truck, and now we take 25 minutes. It's still not good enough."[5] Change seems to feed change;

● the urge to find "one best way" solutions will remain instinctive and alluring.

Make no mistake. In the 1990s and beyond, leadership counts. In one interview, a certain company calculated that it costs about $100 million when a person makes it to senior level and then does not perform well. It is guessed that 30 to 70 per cent of senior level people fail and disappear in 18 months or fewer. At best, it is a 50–50 proposition.[6]

The Future of Leadership examines the skills necessary to ride the corporate rapids. It aims to help managers come to terms with the new uncertainties and sets the leadership agenda for the next millennium. Managers once believed that reading a book might solve their problems. This book creates more problems in a corporate world already beset with problems.

In the new corporate world, executives and their organizations are faced with a plethora of choices every single day. Choice overwhelms. This book may create problems but it presents a simple choice: stay ashore and pretend the world remains the same, or set afloat on an adventure in uncertainty.

Notes and references

1   Sorcher, M, *Predicting Executive Success*, John Wiley, New York, 1985.
2   White, RP and DeVries, D, "Mistakes in the selection of senior executives," Center for Creative Leadership, Greensboro, NC, 1990.
3   Pritchett, P, *The Employee Handbook of New Work Habits for a Radically Changing World*, Pritchett Associates, 1994.
4   Hammer, M, and Champy, J, *Reengineering the Corporation*, HarperBusiness, New York, 1993.
5   Jackson, T, "3M shakes up with spin-off, shutdown and staff cuts," *Financial Times*, November 15, 1995.
6   White, RP, and DeVries, D, "Mistakes in the selection of senior executives," Center for Creative Leadership, Greensboro, NC, 1990.

"The old organizational life which may be comfortable and predictable is disappearing rapidly. The new logic is not like the fads and fashions that have gripped management over the decades. Instead it represents fundamental change in the way organizations will operate. People who develop the skills to be effective in organizations which follow the new logic will thrive. Those who do not will be just as obsolete as poorly skilled production workers in a high-technology manufacturing facility."

EDWARD LAWLER[1]

"There are no routes back to the safe harbor of prediction – no skilled mariners able to find their way across a deterministic ocean. The challenge for us is to see beyond the innumerable fragments to the whole, stepping back far enough to appreciate how things move and change as a coherent entity. We do, after all, live in a fuzzy world, where boundaries have an elusive nature."

MARGARET WHEATLEY[2]

Chapter 1

THE PURSUIT OF CERTAINTY

* Where are we and how did we get here?
* The river is straight and the current is steady.
* We are going downstream.

We have been reared on a diet of certainty. Executives still believe that the future is predictable and knowable. They still believe in solutions to problems when all their experience suggests that there are no instant, all-encompassing solutions to the challenges they now face. They observe the law of the refrigerator – what comes to hand is not necessarily what you want to hand.

THE KING OF CERTAINTY

We talked with a very sharp, intelligent young manager. She knew strategy inside out. Competitive advantage? Core competencies? Strategic intent? She had consumed it all. But it didn't help. She had just been given a new job. She had to reintroduce a product which had completely failed back into the marketplace. Given a promotional budget and marketing support it seemed a straightforward enough task. Flick to page 365 and off you go. But, and it was a very large but indeed, producing the product cost her company $7 – its competitors managed to produce their product for just a few cents.

What help is strategy? Where are the strategy gurus when you need them? In such a situation – and managers increasingly find themselves in parallel situations – there is no obvious path to choose. She had all the choice in the world, because no one knew any better than she what to do next. The myriad of choices resulted in no action at all. She sat and contemplated the mass of data and the fact that there was no obvious way to analyze it. The pressure mounted.

Such situations are now commonplace. Managers are surrounded by data and information, opinions and surefire solutions, time pressures and financial constraints. They consider various four- and nine-box models. They think of the long term and are under unrelenting short-term pressure. They decide whether something is strategic or tactical, a goal or an objective. It is intellectually stimulating and fills flip charts, but it does not solve the problem.

What managers want – and believe they need if they are to keep their jobs – is to make the best decisions possible using the best data available and then to get others to put the solution into practice.

Simple enough. But, what if the data are too extensive for one person, or even an entire department, to wade through? What if the data are incomplete? What if there are 1,001 possible solutions?

Complexity and choice. These are what now concern managers in the real world of making things happen and of solving problems in ways which make money for the business. The trouble is that we are not used to dealing with complexity or choice.

Indeed, management theory developed precisely as a means of eliminating complexity and choice. It seemed as if there was a "science" to management. Frederick Taylor, the man who brought the world "scientific management," should be given an honorary title: King of Certainty.

To the eyes of the late twentieth-century observer scientific management would be considered anything but scientific. Taylor's science was built around minute observation of the best way a task could be undertaken and completed. Having found the best way people could then be made to follow it, to the second, in the prescribed manner.

Taylorism was based on the notion that there was a single "best way" to fulfill a particular job, and that then it was a matter of matching people to the task and supervising, rewarding and punishing them according to their performance. The job of management was to plan and control the work. "Hardly a competent workman can be found who does not devote a considerable amount of time to studying first how slowly he can work and still convince his employer that he is going at a good pace. Under our system a worker is just told what he is to do and how he is to do it. Any improvement he makes upon the orders given to him is fatal to his success," observed Taylor.[3]

In effect, Taylor sought to dehumanize work. A brilliant man, he was deeply skeptical about the human race. In doing so, he laid the ground for the mass production techniques which speedily emerged after his death. "His unforgivable sin was his assertion that there is no such thing as 'skill' in making and moving things. All such work was the same, Taylor asserted. And all could be analyzed step-by-step, as a series of unskilled operations that could then be combined into any kind of job. Anyone willing to learn these operations would be a 'first-class man,' deserving 'first class pay.' He could do the most advanced work and do it to perfection" Peter Drucker has accurately observed.[4]

Frederick Taylor, the man who brought the world "scientific management," should be given an honorary title: King of Certainty.

A more indirect, but equally correct, critique comes from Kurt Vonnegut's novel *Player Piano* (drawn from Vonnegut's experiences working for General Electric): "'If only it weren't for the people, the goddamned people,' said Finnerty, 'always getting tangled up in the machinery. If it weren't for them, earth would be an engineer's paradise.'"[5] In our view, Taylor sought to create such a paradise.

Taylorism was about efficiency, carrying out physical acts in the best possible way. He changed the way baseball pitchers pitch the ball – from underarm to overarm – because it was more efficient. For this we can be thankful, but he sought to do the same to the world of management. The King of Certainty sought to create certainty throughout his realm. The process was simple – analyze what needs to be done and find the best way to do it from the limited choice available. The data were limited, as were the choices. Implementation was straightforward, scientific and obvious.

Taylor died in 1917 but his legacy lives on. Konosuke Matsushita, founder of the Japanese electronics giant which carries his name, has observed that Western firms remain:

> **"built on the Taylor model. Even worse, so are your heads. With your bosses doing the thinking while the workers wield the screwdrivers, you're convinced deep down that this is the way to run a business. . . . We [Japan] are beyond the Taylor model. Business, we know, is now so complex and difficult, the survival of the firm so hazardous in an environment increasingly unpredictable, competitive and fraught with danger, that its continued existence depends on the day-to-day mobilization of every ounce of intelligence."[6]**

The truth of Matsushita's damning observation is only now being fully explored and uncovered – but only by those insightful enough to do so.

The thing is we still want to believe in the King of Certainty. We wish that $a + b = c$, even if we can't quite discover what a and b actually are. We will force figures and statistics into a linear and straightforward equation. (In fact, economists and other social scientists do this all the time with techniques euphemistically labeled "curve smoothing.") We believe if we define the problem, calculate time and resource allocations and who should be involved in solving the problem, then we can miraculously produce the solution. Cut the choice, force the facts and eureka!: the solution. And, when the solution is reached, it is regarded as fixed and unvarying. Executives cannot resist its neatness, its logic, the work behind it, the beauty of its science.

> **Strip many corporate leaders of their ability to control and their nakedness would be there for all to see.**

We can hear you say: "But leaders are different." Unfortunately, leaders are not exempt from the baleful effects of Taylorism. In fact most of the leaders we know have grown up on it. It is the leader's comfort blanket. It results in linear perspectives which relate next year to last year automatically, without question. It has created leaders fixated by the mantra – bigger, faster, better, more. It has created leaders whose only benchmarks are quarterly results and whose touchstones are market analysts. It has produced leaders who are unable or unwilling to press pause on their life or their business.

Stepping back and asking "Why?" is unfashionable and often unwelcome. Blame Taylor. Considering that bigger, faster, better, more, may not be the best way is controversial – even now. What gets measured gets done. What can be controlled is the ultimate arbiter of the activity of far too many leaders. Control is their language. Strip many corporate leaders of their ability to control and their nakedness would be there for all to see. Of course, there are times when control is necessary, but leaders have to judge when the time is right to wrest control rather than uniformly inflicting it.

Control corrupts as surely as power. "For all but the most remarkable of men and women, authoritarian structures are insidiously corrupting. Leaders hang on to power too long, and many prefer to undermine those who might seek to replace them than to develop potential successors," observed academics John Kay and Aubrey Silberton, in an article in the *National Institute Economic Review*.[7] Used to controlling today, corporate leaders begin to believe they can also control tomorrow.

The trouble is that control freaks believe in solutions. Solutions solve problems and our ability to solve problems is how our performance is measured. Executives are not congratulated when they create problems by posing difficult questions or offering alternative approaches. Indeed, in some organizations these are termed "career limiting moves." Ask too many of the wrong sorts of questions and your career with the corporation is limited and then extinguished.

Back in the world of $a + b$, executives are congratulated when a task is completed – or gives the appearance of being completed. They are congratulated when they come up with solutions even if the solutions prove to be short-term or impractical. They come up with solutions to problems which don't exist. Control, and a regular supply of solutions, are the conventional route to career enhancement.

At a reengineering seminar we listened to a consultant talk for over an hour on the background to reengineering. It was accurate, predictable and reasonable, talking of the nature of continuous change and the deficiencies of traditional management structures and management tools and techniques. But the assembled executives were plainly ill-at-ease. The consultant asked: "Am I covering the areas you want to look at?" One plucked up the courage to express dissatisfaction. "What I want are one-liners so I can sell the idea to my people," he said. He believed in solutions. He knew what he wanted to achieve – a lean, flat, process-based organization. If only he had the means of persuading the people he could do it. If only he had the one-liners, the pithy, persuasive phrases which encapsulated it all. Of course, if one-liners worked, Groucho Marx would have been chief executive of General Motors.

The conclusion is as obvious and inevitable as it is confusing and disorienting: we must abandon the expectation of 100 per cent certainty. We must look beyond instant, immediate, persuasive solutions.

We must seek out questions. More questions lead to different approaches and achieving continual difference is the route to competitive advantage.

Is this glib? We think not. Is this another neat solution? No way. In fact, constant questioning – by everyone of everything – leads to a continually messy, somewhat disorganized process. Control freaks don't like the mess. And we all know that leadership – at least the kind of leadership we are prepared to follow – is never messy and always uniform. We know some leaders and their organizations are moving in that direction (if uncertainty can be said to have a direction). We also know that many have not yet moved. They are stuck, desperately seeking out one-liners.

BEYOND THE BEST WAY

The first rule of white water leadership is: there are no instant solutions. There are no short-term quick fixes which bring long-term competitive advantage. There is no single best way.

Contemplating why some companies succeed while others fail, Eli Lilly CEO, Randall Tobias, observes: "The experts have looked for the magic answers – most recently in reengineering – in globalizing – in quality – in leadership and the like. As our own strategy reflects, we, too, believe that each one of those elements is important. But none – by itself – is the answer."[8]

> **The law of the refrigerator is a constant presence and temptation.**

Managers and organizations remain addicted to the quick fix. There is an air of desperation in the way managers cling to new ideas. Fads and fashions are grabbed with gusto and then discarded. They emerge in a fanfare of superlatives only to disappear almost as quickly. Look at Total Quality Management (TQM). Look at reengineering. Organizations and managers obey the law of the refrigerator without apparently realizing it:

**the things that come to hand are not the things
you want to hand.**

The things you most need are not the things you can easily get. And the things most easily observed and measured are the most often studied. Organizations seek to measure leadership skills in broad brush strokes. They talk of communication skills and so on. Seen in this way such skills are platitudinous.

The law of the refrigerator is a constant presence and temptation. Take the learning organization, one of the fads of the early 1990s.

Peter Senge's *The Fifth Discipline* led the way. An international best-seller, it propelled the MIT professor to international renown. By 1995 Senge was receiving a less enthusiastic response. "It's part of the fad cycle," he told the *Financial Times*. "People consume then drop fads and ideas all the time and corporations are no different."[9]

The learning organization was – and is – a good idea. Corporations and managers embraced the concept with enthusiasm. But, when they opened the refrigerator, the learning organization lurked out of reach at the back. Instead of

> **Few reach the back of the refrigerator to explore what's there.**

pushing things to one side, discarding the decaying vegetables, managers took the easier option – take what you can reach. They took the bottle of beer teetering at the front of the shelf and called it the learning organization.

Research at the Massachusetts Institute of Technology suggests that management fads follow a regular life cycle. This starts with academic discovery. The new idea is then formulated into a technique and published in an academic publication. It is then more widely promoted as a means of increasing productivity, reducing costs or whatever is currently exercising managerial minds. Consultants then pick the idea up and treat it as the universal panacea. After practical attempts fail to deliver the promised impressive results, there is realization of how difficult it is to convert the bright idea into sustainable practice. Finally, there follows committed exploitation by a small number of companies. Few reach the back of the refrigerator to explore what's there.

Ironically, blame for this obsession with the latest trend – otherwise known as flavor of the month – can be partly attributed to the professionalization of management. Once management became regarded as a profession, it was assumed that there were a number of skills and ideas which needed to be mastered before someone could proclaim themselves a professional manager. The skills of management were regarded like a bag of golf clubs. When the occasion demanded a particular skill it was extracted from the bag and put to work. New skills could occasionally be added to the managerial bag of tricks when, and if, required.

This mentality persists. Executives are routinely sent on courses to add another skill to their bulging portfolio of accomplishments. "Most ideas on management have been around for a very long time, and the skill of the manager consists in knowing them all and, rather as he might choose the appropriate golf club for a particular situation, choosing the particular ideas which are most appropriate for the position and time in which he finds himself," writes ex-ICI chief, Sir John Harvey-Jones in *Managing to Survive*.[10]

In the bunker we pull out a trusty old sand wedge and aim for the hole. But, what if the sand is quicksand and the hole is mobile? In the managerial era when golf was an appropriate metaphor, we looked for managers who had the clubs and knew which one to play. We wanted managers who knew the course because they had played it countless times before, who would choose the right clubs and execute the shot safely, if not spectacularly. We read Michael Porter (himself a brilliant young golfer) and sought to perform like Tom Kite.

The golfer/manager became known as corporate man, cool under pressure, reliable and ready to spend his or her life with a single organization. Corporate man's characteristics (corporate woman was yet to come) were concisely mapped out by Chester Barnard. "The most important single contribution required of an executive, certainly the most universal qualification, is loyalty [allowing] domination by the organization personality," noted Barnard in *The Functions of the Executive*.[11] Later, in *Organization Man*, William Whyte provided a lengthy analysis of this new creature of the twentieth century.

The death knell for corporate man was sounded by Rosabeth Moss Kanter in her first major book, *Men and Women of the Corporation*.[12] Kanter examined the innermost workings of a bureaucratic organization and, in effect, marked the demise of comfortable corporate America. Among her generally depressing findings was that the central characteristic expected of a manager was "dependability." Too bad we didn't pay attention to her death notice which was first published in 1977.

Unfortunately, managerial life is no longer so straightforward. Dependable at what? Loyal to whom? Listen to Gary Hamel, co-author of *Competing for the Future*:

"It was once the case that unless you were caught with your hand in the till, or publicly slandered your boss, you could count on a job for life in many large companies. Loyalty was valued more than capability, and there was always a musty corner where mediocrity could hide. Entitlement produced a reasonably malleable workforce, and dependency enforced a begrudging kind of loyalty. That was then, this is now."[13]

This is now and today's managerial golf bag is too heavy and cumbersome to carry around. You wouldn't even make it to the first tee. Typically, work by the UK's Management Charter Initiative to identify standard competencies for all middle managers emerged with several hundred. Neurosurgeons get by with fewer. While no such comparable work exists in the USA, most large organizations have identified an average of between seven and ten critical competencies. British Petroleum has nine competencies for its senior managers including leadership and team-building skills. IBM UK has six competencies for senior managers – intellect, tenacity, vision, impact, skills in active management and skills in general management. In the USA, AT&T has 13 and a single Hewlett Packard unit has a checklist of 26 leadership characteristics. Simplifying the complex is never easy, and often impossible, but it can be useful.

> **The fad industry has emerged and the chief beneficiaries are management consultants and business schools.**

The problem is that simplification is not by itself an answer to anything. Yet, the faddishness of managers continues as they seek out new skills and new solutions to perennial problems. They yearn for simplicity rather than simplification. "It has become professionally legitimate in the United States to accept and utilize ideas without an in-depth grasp of their underlying foundation, and without the commitment necessary to sustain them," observes Richard Pascale, who listed more than 30 fads which have emerged in the past 40 years in *Managing on the Edge*.[14]

The fad industry has emerged and the chief beneficiaries are management consultants and business schools. In too many (though not all) cases they are peddling fashions and instant solutions, not core skills for the future. The global management consultancy industry is worth $18 billion and the executive training industry is estimated at $40 billion. In 1993 AT&T, like many other large companies, spent a massive amount on consultants, a total of $347 million, an amount so large it was calculated by one newspaper as being equivalent to paying 1,150 full-time managers.[15]

The search for the secret of management has taken managers and organizations through bewildering loops and has spawned an entirely new vocabulary. Managers have embraced brainstorming as a useful tool, they have explored Douglas MacGregor's Theory X and Theory Y, negotiated Blake and Mouton's Managerial Grid, been driven on by Management by Objectives, discovered strategic management through Igor Ansoff in the late 1960s, been converted by Tom Peters and Robert Waterman's *In Search of Excellence*, and have, no doubt, also tried their hand with quality circles and various forms of Total Quality Management. And yet, there is no single best way to manage – simply a rag-bag of shared experiences, short-lived best practice and high expectations that the ideas will deliver instant results.

It is not that these various ideas are poor concepts. Many do work, but they are not set in tablets of stone. They have to be flexible, and used when needed, rather than as all-encompassing solutions. There are a huge variety of great concepts. But if they are to work they have to be applied at the right time, in the right circumstances by the right people with the right intentions. They have to be adapted, molded, sometimes cajoled into the reality of the situation. And then they must be refined, developed, enhanced, perhaps replaced.

"Management has always been beset by fads and fashions, gurus and demagogues. But never before has there been such a sheer volume of new approaches," says Edward Lawler of the Center for Effective Organizations. "This has led many managers to reach one of two incorrect conclusions: that the new approaches are all hype with no substance, or that a particular program is the answer. The reality is more complex and challenging."[16] And, in the complexity lies the challenge.

FACING A MULTITUDE OF OBJECTIVES

And, as we believe in solutions, we also believe in clear objectives. Leaders take us from A to B. Right? No more. Behind what became known as Management By Objectives (MBO) was the basic premise that $a + b = c$. MBO was one of the big ideas of the late 1950s and 1960s. Its remnants and behaviors remain firmly entrenched in many organizations – notably in performance appraisal systems – although its original aim tends to be misunderstood.

MBO was most notably championed by Peter Drucker in his *Practice of Management.*[17] Drucker argued that all managers should have clearly delineated and communicated objectives which reflected and supported the objectives laid out by senior managers. "MBO is a process in which members of complex organizations, working in conjunction with one another, identify common goals and coordinate their efforts towards achieving them. Emphasis is on the future and change, since an objective or goal . . . is a state or a condition to be achieved at some future time," note Stephen Carroll and Henry Tosi in *Management By Objectives.*[18]

MBO assumes that a goal can be set and then people will be able to work towards it. You find the solution (c) and then seek out the a and the b you need to reach it. Map out the future and it will happen. Under MBO, management is a race over orderly hurdles. If you win the race, your business succeeds. If you knock over a hurdle you can go back and try again. An often cited example of MBO at work is President Kennedy's inspirational announcement that a man on the moon before the end of the 1960s was the USA's objective. It was a bold and visionary statement – just the sort of thing a leader should do (at least in the 1960s). Kennedy set out the objective and NASA delivered. Could the same be done now? Perhaps, given resources and a clear run, it could, but it is unlikely.

MBO led inexorably to the corporate discovery of strategy, the means of moving from analysis to solution. In 1965 Igor Ansoff's *Corporate Strategy* was published. "This book represented a kind of crescendo in the development of strategic planning theory, offering a degree of elaboration seldom attempted since," Henry Mintzberg later observed.[19] Unstintingly serious, analytical and complex, *Corporate Strategy* had a highly significant impact on the business world. It propelled consideration of strategy into a new dimension. "The end product of strategic decisions is deceptively simple; a combination of products and markets is selected for the firm. This combination is arrived at by addition of new product-markets, divestment from some old ones, and expansion of the present position," writes Ansoff.

While the end product was "deceptively simple," the processes and decisions beforehand produced a labyrinth followed only by the most dedicated of managers. Ansoff's sub-title was "An Analytical Approach to Business Policy for Growth and Expansion." The book provided a highly complex "cascade of decisions." Analysis – and in particular "gap analysis" (the gap between where you are now and where you want to be) – was the key to unlocking strategy.

While *Corporate Strategy* was a notable book for its time, it led to organizations repeatedly making strategic plans which were not implemented. As we continue to observe today, the red (or green or blue) book sits on the shelf and collects dust. "Strategic planning was a plausible invention, and received an enthusiastic reception from the business community. But subsequent experience with strategic planning led to mixed results. In a minority of firms, strategic planning restored their profitability and became an established part of the management process. However a substantial majority encountered a phenomenon, which was named 'paralysis by analysis': strategic plans were made but remained unimplemented, and profits/growth continued to stagnate," Ansoff recently wrote.[20]

> **If the future is unknowable then strategy is turned on its head – and, if strategic thinking does not change, then it will be turning in its grave.**

We've all met planners and executives who conceive great strategies safe in the knowledge that they probably won't see the light of day – and if they do the new day's conditions are likely to be radically different anyway. They know it, see it and carry on. Bill Gates recalls an early meeting with two executives from IBM. "When IBM came to us in 1980, we thought they were just talking about buying our BASIC for their new PC project. The two guys who came said, 'We're just the planning guys, and most of the things we plan don't get done, so don't get too excited.'"[21] There were – and still are – many executives whose experiences and attitudes fit the IBM duo.

It seems that along the way the roots of strategy have been forgotten. The word is derived from the Greek *stratos*, meaning army, and *legein*, meaning to lead. In the modern corporation, the army and leader infrequently appear to be in step. It is not simply that the roots of strategy have been lost in the frenzy of reports and plans. MBO, strategic management and planning are based on the assumption and belief that the future is knowable. We believe that this basic premise no longer holds true. Leaders in the field increasingly find themselves having to come to terms with the unknowable rather than the knowable.

If the future is unknowable then strategy is turned on its head – and, if strategic thinking does not change, then it will be turning in its grave. In *The Rise and Fall of Strategic Planning*, Henry Mintzberg argues that "strategy is not the consequence of planning but the opposite: its starting point." Mintzberg exposes the fallacies and failings at the root of planning. These include:

- **processes** – a fascination with elaborate processes creates bureaucracy and strangles innovation;

- **data** – Mintzberg argues that "hard" data, the lifeblood of the traditional strategist, is a source of information; "soft" data, however, provides the wisdom – "Hard information can be no better and is often at times far worse than soft information." In *The Nature of Managerial Work*, Mintzberg similarly observed that managers relied on "soft information" rather than exhaustive written reports and exchange it in short bursts in the corporate corridors;

- **detachment** – Mintzberg refutes the notion of managers creating strategic plans from ivory towers. "Effective strategists are not people who abstract themselves from the daily detail but quite the opposite: they are the ones who *immerse* themselves in it, while being able to abstract the *strategic messages* from it."

25

In the 1990s the legacy of MBO and strategy in all its manifestations are failing managers. Why? Well, clearly we're now talking another language – one characterized by "messages," innovation and intuition. And we now live in a more complex, more unstable and faster moving environment.

Gary Hamel has pithily identified three key barriers to "reinventing strategy":

- **perceptual** – the lack of "genetic variety" in top teams. Too many come from the same industries, companies, disciplines and cultural backgrounds. This blinds them to new opportunities;

- **political** – the most powerful people are usually those whose knowledge is most out-of-date;

- **practical** – it is difficult to reinvent strategy in an ill-defined, still emerging industry (such as digital communications) or subsector (such as electronic publishing) where existing industry boundaries are shifting.[22]

Hamel is right but we believe the real problems and challenges may go even deeper. First, there are no straight lines. The world is not linear (and never was) and is certainly far from straightforward. Linear thinking produces linear solutions which offer a false sense of security. They lead to misleading assumptions that today's predictions are likely to hold good tomorrow.

"Strategy does not just involve *planning*; it also involves *doing*. And sometimes the doing actually comes before the planning. This view of strategy flies in the face of the linear process we all learned in school: plan, then act. While this sequence may be logical, in reality we often act and then use the results of our actions to decide on the next step," say Stephen and Shannon Rye Wall in *The New Strategists*.[23]

The sequence is blurred and made even more confusing by the fact that managers now have a multitude of objectives, each equally compelling, competing for their time, attention and energy. Talking to groups of managers usually reveals that each has, on average, seven key objectives. At an orga-

The race is an endless slalom.

nizational level, this number can be multiplied with individual and corporate objectives involved in a constant battle for attention and dominance. They are often in direct conflict with each other and are not neatly arranged in a straight line. The race is an endless slalom.

FROM ONE DIMENSION TO THREE

Clearly, MBO also had an effect on the way leaders practiced leadership. Old models of leadership were based on the management basics of plan, organize and control. (Leaders identified the destination and ensured that the workers delivered come what may, using fair means or foul.) The roots of this can be traced back to Henri Fayol's work at the beginning of the century.[24] Plan, organize, control practiced leadership in one dimension.

In the 1980s, amid a flurry of work on leadership, this was supplemented by new leadership roles of creating a vision, setting a direction and empowering people. This second dimension brought a new vocabulary, but it was grounded in the same ideas. We're here, we want to be there, let's go, or let's go as a group.

Leadership has evolved – in theory and in practice. It has been supplemented, destroyed and rebuilt, carved anew. One dimension has become two but, in the late 1990s, even two-dimensional leadership is proving insufficient for the needs of organizations and leaders. The future demands much more.

A recent global study of CEOs carried out by consultants Hay McBer observed: "During the first 100 years of industrial capitalism, heads of industry relied more on coercive and pace-setting styles. By the 1960s and 1970s, CEOs often exhibited democratic and authoritative leadership styles. Today it is clear that CEOs must develop coaching and affiliative styles of leadership."[25] Leadership has moved from one dimension to three (see figure 1.1) and all three dimensions are constantly at work.

Think of the sensible progression of MBO. Now try thinking of a different scenario. We don't know where we are; we want to be in a multitude of places; and don't know what to do to start moving. It

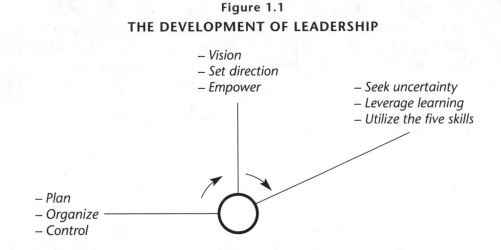

Figure 1.1
THE DEVELOPMENT OF LEADERSHIP

– Vision
– Set direction
– Empower

– Seek uncertainty
– Leverage learning
– Utilize the five skills

– Plan
– Organize
– Control

is a discomfiting thought. It is also a business reality. Think of the possibilities.

Where do you want to be?

There is a remarkable similarity in the ambitions and aspirations of our major corporations. They aim for higher market share, in greater numbers of markets, at higher rates of profitability, in a more global organization, with smaller numbers of employees whose value-added creates return on investment that's second to none.

Too many visions are a jumble of superlatives.

Eli Lilly's mission statement, framed by CEO Randall Tobias, describes this more succinctly than most: "Create and deliver superior health care solutions – by combining pharmaceutical innovation, existing pharmaceutical technology, disease prevention and management and information technologies – to provide customers worldwide with optimal clinical and economic outcomes."[26] Tobias is making this vision happen. The trouble with many other attempts at visionary leadership is that sadly the visions often fail the leadership by falling to some common obstacles.

The first is that the vision is meaningless to the people who are supposed to be energized by it. Too many visions are a jumble of superlatives. The generic vision is "to be the best with the lowest, using the highest, achieving the fastest, being the newest, employing the cleverest, caring the most." So many vision and mission statements appear to have been generated by unthinking software rather than as passionate declarations of what is believable and achievable by the people concerned. As our colleagues, Colin Williams and George Binney, observe "It's not a vision, it's an hallucination."[27]

To be effective, a vision must convey meaning, contain realistic depth and resonate with people. Only then will it help strategies to become implemented and change to take place.

And how do organizations get there?

Similarly, the means of achieving organizational objectives usually include some or all of the following:

- focusing on our core competencies
- launching new products in new markets and old products in new markets and new products in old markets
- cutting expenses, particularly through cutting people
- exporting *in toto* the way we do things
- improving Return on Investment (or some other capital measure that is understandable to everyone and is valued by financial analysts)
- ensuring that quarter-to-quarter our capital performance is the most efficient of anyone in our industry.

The possible routes forward are many. The trouble is organizations want it all and their stockholders want it now. Remember *Alice's Adventures in Wonderland*?

> "Would you tell me, please, which way I ought to go from here?"
> "That depends a good deal on where you want to get to," said the Cat.
> "I don't much care where....." said Alice.
> "Then it doesn't matter which way you go," said the Cat.
>
> (LEWIS CARROLL, 1865)

FORGET THE REVOLUTION

There is no revolution.

Yes, the business world is changing at breakneck, maybe exponential, speed. Yes, technology is radically altering the shape of organizations and the skills required of us all. But just because a revolution is under way does not mean that we are all natural revolutionaries. Forget Che Guevara. Think George Washington. Forget revolution – sometimes we can't even achieve evolution.

Typically, only 10 per cent of the things a manager does make a real difference and move the company forward. A small shift in overall behavior – perhaps two per cent – could have a much larger effect on performance – perhaps 20 per cent.[28]

Indeed, all the research into how managers spend their time suggests that only a small percentage of their working day is actually spent on important tasks which achieve anything. One executive we interviewed differentiated between periods of hyper-activity and ordinary energy output – "In the office not more than a quarter of my time is spent in hyper-activity. The rest of the time I am under very high pressure – sorting things out, responding, attending meetings, speaking. In the end, I am tied down until eight o'clock or whenever it is and I am dead tired, but they are not hyper-activity projects – that's when you're 65 and running up a hill."[29]

> **Forget revolution – sometimes we can't even achieve evolution.**

In work for a previous book, *What Do High Performance Managers Really Do?*, we estimated that conventional managers probably operate to just 40 per cent of their true ability. They spend 10 per cent of their time being really effective by doing what is important and 30 per cent of their time gaining credibility in order to be really effective for that other 10 per cent. The rest of the time they spend doing things that are not important, or don't produce the outcome they want.[30] Such estimates make salutary reading for managers who spend many hours every week at their desks – many more hours than they would actually need to spend if they were working to their full effectiveness.

It is not revolutionary to suggest that managers could spend their time more effectively or productively. Virtually every single piece of research into managerial behavior comes to the same conclusion. But what has been done about it? Think if this happened in any other sphere. If research showed policemen or airline pilots were highly ineffective there would be an outcry. The same goes for any other job and any other profession. If every piece of research showed that doctors wasted large amounts of time and energy, things would change.

Executives the world over carry on much as before. They equate busyness with effectiveness. They become bogged down in the minutiae of the business. And, as anyone who has run anything knows, there is no end to the minutiae. In any business you can work 80 hours a week for years and still not be doing the things you should be doing. Quantity never makes for quality. The temptation is always to do the easy and immediate tasks, the ones you know how to do, rather than the tasks which really need doing to build the business.

Executives like to say "yes" because that's what gets them up the organization. They say yes, and yes again, even when they know they shouldn't, even when they know they are overcommitted, even when they know someone could do the job better. "When you say no, you've lost it. If you've said yes and it doesn't turn out to be very exciting, it doesn't seem to be such a big loss as when you've said no and you've missed it. So you may say yes to some silly things, but that doesn't seem as bad to me as saying no and then regretting the lost opportunity. So I rarely say no to anything," said one CEO we interviewed.

How does he deal with all the things he has agreed to do? "The only way to cope with getting into overload is to extend the number of hours in the day which is why I work in the evenings to do the things I want to do. It's not about achieving balance. It's actually about saying can I find the energy, time, inclination, to make sure that I can say yes many more times? It's totally against this stuff about managing your time, no job should take more than eight hours a day, five days a week and half the paper you get should just be stuck in the wastebasket. All that's nonsense. Now maybe there's a few people who can work like that and maybe they have very organized, rational and highly productive lives in other areas. But, it's not for me."[31]

Along similar lines, the corporate president of a service business argued: "There's no such thing as an interruption in a complex environment. If you're the type who is easily interrupted you won't be successful. Almost everything is relevant. I have never known of a successful leader who doesn't handle trivia and strategy almost interchangeably. You must spend time on who gets a slot in the parking lot and then turn to long-term recruiting."[32]

Is this really what it's all about? While you are so busy dealing with the hassles, worries and pressures of the present, what of tomorrow? The slots in the parking lot may have initials neatly painted, but what about the future of the business? In a daunting damnation of contemporary management, CK Prahalad and Gary Hamel estimate that organizations spend less than three per cent of their time on consideration of the long-term future.[33] How can they when they are already so busy?

Henry Mintzberg's groundbreaking *The Nature of Managerial Work* found that managers were hostages to the moment. Immediate needs and interruptions dominated their working lives. Mintzberg's work was published in 1973. Have things changed? Are managers now more adept at fully utilizing their time? No. They are working harder, doing more of the same things under ever greater stress.

Forget the dream of the leisure age where we work three or four days a week and spend the rest of the time playing golf or painting the house. Work is spreading – no matter what we do, where we work or our place in the organization. According to Harvard's Juliet Schor, in *The Overworked American*, in the 20 years to 1991 the annual work schedule of Americans increased by an average of 163 hours a year – which is equivalent to one month's extra work.[34] Overtime has been labeled the "autoworker's cocaine." In Japan there is even a word for death through overwork – *karoshi*. We have learned to live with the prospect of *karoshi* as surely as a heavy smoker lives with the prospect of lung cancer.

"The pressure of the managerial environment does not encourage the development of reflective planners, the classical literature notwithstanding," wrote Henry Mintzberg in 1973. "The job breeds adaptive information-manipulators who prefer the live, concrete situation. The manager works in an environment of stimulus-response, and he develops in his work a clear preference for live action."[35] Mintzberg's comments hold true over two decades on. "My perception of what constitutes effective management is not so different as it was. But now there is a lot more ineffective management," he now observes.[36]

> **Press pause. Busyness is not effectiveness. But it has created a climate of urgency.**

Busyness – or plain ineffectiveness – is not a localized phenomenon. It is not only the curse of American working lives. In Europe it is notable that in the UK people generally work more hours than anywhere else in the continent. In the UK 45 per cent of male senior managers and 23 per cent of women work over 50 hours a week. When they find a moment they should stop to consider how Germans manage to work far fewer hours while Germany has the highest national income per head in Europe.[37]

Press pause. Busyness is not effectiveness. But it has created a climate of urgency. We expect things to happen now. Everything is urgent, top priority, ASAP. We fax people, e-mail them, send them packages by Federal Express, DHL and the rest. In one celebrated case a major Manhattan-based company sent packages by FedEx from one floor to another. Managers are supposed to be busy. Their work is always urgent and is required to be urgent.

But that does not mean that managers are busy doing the right things or that everything they do should be an urgent matter of life and death. "It's very easy to have everything be urgent and important. But you can't be in that mode for long without burning out," says Richard Snyder who runs Dell's operations in North and South America. Snyder is attempting to change the Dell culture which was aligned to constant urgency. "Everything was here and now and very reactive. Ninety per cent of our business was done in emergency mode," recalls one Dell staffer.[38]

Instead of concentrating on tasks that are urgent and often not important, future leaders must contemplate the important jobs, ones that are often critical to their long-term survival, which are not urgent today, but will be some time. If these are not considered it may soon be too late.

"I always try to get the difference between what is urgent and what is important," said the area manager for a railroad when we spoke to him. "The urgent tasks tend to be reactive things that come down from headquarters or they need the information on this or that. As opposed to the important things, which we have set on our agenda, our key list of things we are going to do for the year. . . . Items do change but we try and stick to the agenda and focus in on it for the whole of the year. We try and minimize the HQ effect that could knock us from our agenda. Obviously we have to go along with it to a certain extent but we try to make sure that HQ doesn't knock us off with their urgent items."[39] The area manager is caught between the devil and the deep blue sea – HQ says jump and do it, so he does it, while remembering that important things are not being done. How many other managers find themselves in similar situations?

> **Instead of concentrating on tasks that are urgent and often not important, future leaders must contemplate the important jobs . . . which are not urgent today, but will be some time.**

As we have already seen, as an adjunct to the myth of urgency, managers feel the need to accept as much work as possible. They can't say no because this implies weakness. "People advance through getting known within the organization by taking on a lot of work, by doing that work effectively. I fell into the trap, as many others do, of actually taking on too much," said a partner in a major accountancy firm we interviewed. "You can't keep all the balls in the air, but you are not prepared to say no. Something drops

Figure 1.2
THE MYTH OF URGENCY

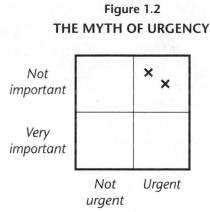

and you realize that you should have said 'Sorry I can't take that on.' Now, being on the other side of the fence, there is nothing worse than if someone says yes to something and I then find they were already 90 per cent committed and should not have taken it on but they felt compelled by ambition and because I asked them to do it."[40]

Figure 1.2 shows that managers spend too much time in the top righthand corner of the quadrant dealing with matters they believe to be urgent but which are, in fact, not important. The balance needs to be shifted so that they spend more time dealing with non-urgent but highly important issues.

The myth of urgency has spread to organizational thinking. In response to an unknown future, organizations have pinned their hopes on moving faster. The existential philosophy is that in order to hit a moving target, you are always nearer by not keeping still. But nearer where?

We are told that speed is the current competitive edge. Leaders who can perform are under constant pressure to achieve more and faster. (Remember the earlier example of the 3M division which has become faster and faster but still can't compete?)

Speed is a business necessity, but there is probably a limit to how far speed can help if the road is under repair or if you're heading down the same or wrong road or, worst of all, if you are caught in corporate gridlock with everyone heading down the same road. Also, if you drive your car at 600 miles an hour rather than 60, then stopping or steering around obstacles becomes considerably harder. Things come at you so much faster you cannot react in time. You either accept the inevitable pile-ups or pull over and think of the skills you need to speed up work and decide in which direction you are going.

Leaders need to pull over and perhaps refer back to *Through the Looking-Glass And What Alice Found There*:

> "Well of course in our country," said Alice, still panting a little, "you'd generally get to somewhere else – if you ran very fast for a long time as we've been doing."
>
> "A slow sort of country!" said the Red Queen. "Now, here, you see, it takes all the running you can do to keep in the same place. If you want to get somewhere else, you must run at least twice as fast as that!"
>
> (LEWIS CARROLL, 1871)

The Red Queen may be the fictional creation of a Victorian eccentric, but she is right: faith in speed alone will get you nowhere. Time-based competition may be the equivalent of trying to drive our organizations faster and faster along the same mental roads. If fast is good, urgency is normal – for individuals and the organization.

Faith in speed alone will get you nowhere.

The common response to this is to suggest that managers and management require a complete overhaul. The preoccupation of management thinkers is with personal and corporate transformation. This all-embracing notion is often idealistic. Dramatic transformation in personal behavior is often seen by others as the route to trauma, rather than transformation. Instead of reinvention and transformation, individuals and organizations should focus on supplementing their leadership skills and style.

Small but significant change is realistic, achievable and will provide a revolution. Traumatic change is uncontrollable. At a personal level if it is dramatic it is probably seen as fake and unsustainable and, at the corporate level, as plain confusing. It is the method of very last resort. Executives cannot – and should not – reinvent themselves, nor can organizations. Overnight solutions belong to yesterday and constitute wishful thinking.

One executive we interviewed was changing the entire branch structure of a 5,000-person financial services organization. "The grand theorists would suggest we could take all the branches out and put the new ones in," he said. "In reality, I know that it's best to work at a manageable pace which the people can cope with. If I rip everything out I lose an enormous amount of goodwill and the goodwill of those managers is crucial to our success. Over a period of time I can plan it . . . move the whole thing forward, bit-by-bit like a jigsaw, rather than through revolutions."[41]

Another CEO made it clear that change through revolution was executive suicide. "I have come to believe that evolution is probably more important than revolution in this organization. It's the sort of organization where if you go out on a limb, some people chop the limb off for the fun of it and other people chop the limb off because they fundamentally disagree with you. And therefore, large risks are not the ways in which the organization is likely to change and develop."[42]

Skeptics might suggest that the entire idea of change without revolution is an escape clause. It is not. These are real managers making change happen. They know the practicalities and the limitations. Don't forget, their jobs and careers are on the line.

We cannot and should not jettison the past in search of the perfect future. We have to learn from the past and adapt it. The trouble is we are often ill-equipped to do so.

BUILD ON THE PAST – DON'T RECREATE IT

The thinking engendered by MBO and traditional views of strategy has had many and varied effects. Critically, MBO relies on knowledge of the past. We have traveled a certain route before in a certain way doing certain things. Let's do it again. Or, let's do it faster, cheaper or with fewer people.

Today's leaders have to learn to rely less on copying what others have done in the past. Much of the research and writing on leadership that has been used to guide leaders has been based on past behavior and not on present and future requirements. Such benchmarking activity is useful, but the best benchmarking can do is bring you up-to-date with where your competitors were yesterday or are today. In addition, there is a question about whether what works for one business in a specific industry will work for another, even in the same industry. Benchmarking should use the past as a touchstone for the future. Too often, its rigidity creates a tombstone for the future. Remember the Peters and Waterman dictum "We're no worse than anyone else"?

> **Benchmarking should use the past as a touchstone for the future. Too often, its rigidity creates a tombstone for the future.**

Organizations have sought to recreate the past and so, too, have individuals. Many senior managers have grown up and developed their current skills based on previous methods of development. They have copied role models; they have watched what others do. They have felt it neither necessary nor appropriate to make what Karl Popper called "extravagant leaps" based on extravagant guesses.[43] In *The Logic of Scientific Discovery*, Popper argued that progress came through extravagant guesses followed by unrestrained criticism. Only the guesses which survived the criticism would be used. This, clearly, is not a comfortable process. It is fraught with risk.

Executives have steered clear of such extravagance. Instead, they have operated in zones of safety and comfort, often supported by comfortable organizations whose Return On Investment or other organizational measures were acceptable at that point in time.

Think of a great athlete. Carl Lewis didn't go out thinking that he was simply trying to match yesterday's standard. He wanted to create his own new standard – and then set out to beat it every time. Carry this through to management – executives have been thinking of matching yesterday's peak performance rather than moving the performance standard forward.

Extrapolating the future from the past continually provides scenarios for the future which are woefully incorrect. Take economic predictions. Immediately after World War II, Phillips and the

The future will not be like the past.

London School of Economics developed a miraculous machine – seven feet tall, it involved a series of perspex tanks, pipes and valves through which water was pumped (courtesy of the windshield wiper motors from a Lancaster bomber). The water symbolized money and the machine was an economic forecaster. Now, economic indicators are examined in seconds by computer software programs. Smaller they may be; perfect predictors of the future they are not. Governments routinely realign economic forecasts only a few months into the carefully mapped out future.

The reason for this is that economic models, however complex, take in a mass of historical data to provide a prediction. When basic premises shift, the models no longer work. For all the pundits, commentators and complex programs and systems, there is no foolproof, all-embracing economic guide. The *Financial Times* recently observed that until there is such a guide "all economic models will be biased towards expecting the future to be like the past, and will often fail to identify the most important changes in economic behavior."[44]

Amid all the vigorous debating about managing change and the post-industrial revolution, one thing can be simply stated: the future will not be like the past.

Yet, it has been assumed that what made a manager effective in the past will make him or her effective in the future. Ironically, this has never been true of movement upward in the organization. The measure of being a good general manager is to acquire new skills and to stop using old skills. But, in the future, even staying in the same job will mean letting go of the past, developing new skills and deploying old skills in new ways. The expert white water rafter views each rapid as a place to enhance the use of the paddle, instinctively recognizes the importance of survival and is constantly aware of Richard Pascale's regular admonition: "Nothing fails like success."

The past is past. You can either build on it or live in it. The catalog of corporate failures and near failures in the last decade proves the dangers of living in the past. Look at the controversy generated when the companies featured in Tom Peters and Robert Waterman's *In Search of Excellence* fell from grace. Magazines ran stories on how wrong the book was, how Peters and Waterman should have known better. "Oops!" ran the *Business Week* cover story exposing the declining fortunes of the excellent corporations. It was a good story – well-paid, so-called experts get it wrong. This overlooked why the

"Nothing fails like success."

fortunes of the companies had deteriorated. They did so perhaps because they kept doing the things which had made them successful in the past in the expectation that they would work in the future. The companies believed in the myth of their own mastery. Peters and Waterman were right. It was the companies which were wrong.

IBM was among the companies featured in *In Search of Excellence*. Indeed, it was the most obvious choice in the entire book. Thomas Watson Sr created IBM from nothing into a single-minded juggernaut which simply steamrollered through its competitors. Strong-willed, determined and very large, IBM appeared unstoppable. It was also undrivable, as easy to handle as a supertanker in a hurricane. IBM needed to find different answers to different situations, but was set on a course which provided it with the same answers time and time again no matter what the question, no matter how much the situation had changed. Remember the idea of PCs? IBM's response was too late and too begrudging – and incredibly costly.

Similarly, after the death of Walt Disney the company lost its direction. It assumed that its previous success would continue. It was years before it began to compete head-on for the adult movie dollar through Touchstone Films. More recently Euro Disney's early years have been at best characterized as a disastrous failure, partly due to Disney's belief that it could simply recreate American magic in a French world. Success here does not guarantee success over there. Success today does not guarantee success tomorrow.

Look elsewhere. Pharmaceutical companies were tempted with complacency, when 70 per cent margins only served to exaggerate and encourage a belief in their timeless infallibility. Automobile manufacturers remained firmly rooted in the 1950s until the 1980s when they discovered their customers had deserted them. Whatever the business, executives and organizations have an ostrich-like habit of burying their heads in the sand.

Once they move the sand or shift their heads, things can change. Corporations like Eli Lilly, IBM and Disney are now moving forward. GM has shaken off the past and can now produce something like the GM

> **Success today does not guarantee success tomorrow.**

Saturn which challenges the conventional orthodoxy of how cars are designed, manufactured and sold. Ask someone who has just bought a Saturn about their experience – it is more like a birthday celebration than buying a car. Did we feel that way 15 years ago when we bought from GM?

The conclusion must be that the old ways of doing things are never sufficient. But what does this mean for corporate leaders and executives?

The activities of management were once summed up in the acronym POSDCORB (Planning, Organizing, Staffing, Directing, Coordinating, Reporting and Budgeting). For the new generation of corporate leaders, planning, organizing and controlling are no longer enough. Yes, they still do them, but this isn't the entire range of activities required to successfully cope with the future. Remember the golf bag.

Nor does experience actually help solve the conundrum. Experience is not the key to effective leadership. Look around at the evidence. Experience counts, but only if the individual makes it count. There are, as the saying goes, too many people with 35 years' experience who have had one year's experience repeated 35 times.

Experience can only be made to count if today's corporate leaders think differently and do so continually. IBM was, after all, full of experienced, highly intelligent, intensively trained managers when it moved too slowly to join the PC revolution. "Competitive advantage is based not on doing what others already do well, but on doing what others cannot do as well," observes John Kay of the London Business School. "We know that this is true for us as individuals. We can see – with greater difficulty – that this is true for firms; that real corporate success is based on distinctive capabilities, not on imitating the successful."[45]

Take Richard Branson's Virgin Group. He took on the big airlines on their most lucrative route, the Atlantic. He started by offering excursion rates with reasonable comfort. Now he's going after the high end of the market and succeeding. Virgin is branching out into financial services and cola. Big risks, but they are made commercially viable and possible because Branson and Virgin appear ready and able to learn from the past, maximizing experience rather than quietly acquiring it without knowing how to make it work for the business.

> **Competitive advantage is based not on doing what others already do well, but on doing what others cannot do as well**

Look at Charles Schwab who went into discount brokerage and took on the big brokerage houses. Schwab's corporation now has a market capitalization of nearly $4 billion. Or Fred Smith, who borrowed money from his father to set up Federal Express and now does more business in a single night than he used to do in a year. People told him it wouldn't work.

Richard Branson and Charles Schwab know that simply thinking differently at the beginning doesn't ensure success. The world is full of business people who have had a brilliantly different idea, but whose businesses have milked the idea dry and then stagnated. You need to keep on thinking differently. Just when you think it is

> **The message must be: continuously upgrade.**

safe to relax you need to come up with something new. Companies need to keep on reinventing, which means that their executives must keep on facing uncertainty and reinventing themselves.

It is not easy – but who has suggested that managing was ever easy? In many ways senior managers are working with mental software that was designed for a previous generation. They are struggling on, adapting, fitting the new environment into the cramped confines of the past. They are laboring with quills when they should be mastering virtual reality. The message must be: continuously upgrade.

Notes and references

1 Lawler, E, "New logic is here to stay," *Financial Times*, January 28, 1994.
2 Wheatley, MJ, *Leadership and the New Science*, Berrett-Koehler, San Francisco, 1992.
3 Taylor, FW, *The Principles of Scientific Management*, Harper & Row, New York, 1913.
4 Drucker, P, "The New Productivity Challenge," *Harvard Business Review*, November–December 1991.
5 Vonnegut, K, *Player Piano*, Paladin, London, 1990 (first published 1952).
6 Quoted in Pascale, R, *Managing on the Edge*, Viking, New York, 1990.
7 Kay, J, and Silberton, A, *National Institute Economic Review*, Winter, 1995.
8 Tobias, RL, "The best days: address to shareholders," Eli Lilly Annual Meeting of Shareholders, April 17, 1995.
9 Quoted in Griffith, V, "Corporate fashion victim," *Financial Times*, April 12, 1995.
10 Harvey-Jones, J, *Managing to Survive*, Heinemann, London, 1992.
11 Barnard, C, *The Functions of the Executive*, Harvard University Press, Cambridge, Mass, 1938.
12 Kanter, RM, *Men and Women of the Corporation*, Basic Books, New York, 1977.
13 Hamel, G, Foreword to *The Financial Times Handbook of Management* (Crainer, S, ed), FT/Pitman, London, 1995.
14 Pascale, R, *Managing on the Edge*, Viking, New York, 1990.
15 Thackray, J, "All aboard the consulting gravy train," *The Observer*, November 6, 1994.

16 Lawler, E, "New logic is here to stay," *Financial Times*, January 28, 1994.
17 Drucker, PF, *Practice of Management*, Harper, New York, 1954.
18 Carroll, S, and Tosi, HL, *Management By Objectives*, Macmillan, New York, 1973.
19 Mintzberg, H, *The Rise and Fall of Strategic Planning*, Prentice Hall, New York, 1994.
20 Ansoff, HI, *Milestones in Management Volume 5*, Schaffer Poeschel, Switzerland, 1994.
21 Schendler, B, "Bill Gates and Paul Allen talk," *Fortune*, October 2, 1995.
22 Quoted in Lorenz, C, "No less than rebirth," *Financial Times*, October 4, 1993.
23 Wall, SJ, and Wall, SR, *The New Strategists*, Free Press, New York, 1995.
24 Fayol, H, *General and Industrial Management*, Pitman, London, 1949.
25 *Global CEOs Study*, Hay McBer, London, 1995.
26 Tobias, RL, "The best days: address to shareholders," Eli Lilly Annual Meeting of Shareholders, April 17, 1995.
27 Williams, C, and Binney, G, *Leaning into the Future*, Nicholas Brealey, London, 1995.
28 Hodgson, P, and Crainer, S, *What Do High Performance Managers Really Do?*, FT/Pitman, London, 1993.
29 Author interview.
30 Hodgson, P, and Crainer, S, *What Do High Performance Managers Really Do?*, FT/Pitman, London, 1993.
31 Author interview.
32 Author interview.
33 Hamel, G, and Prahalad, CK, *Competing for the Future*, Harvard Business School Press, Boston, Mass, 1994.
34 Schor, J, *The Overworked American*, Basic Books, New York, 1991.
35 Mintzberg, H, *The Nature of Managerial Work*, Harper & Row, New York, 1973.
36 Interview with Stuart Crainer, March 1994.
37 *Survey of Working Hours*, Austin Knight, 1995.
38 Jacob, R, "The resurrection of Michael Dell," *Fortune*, September 18, 1995.
39 Author interview.
40 Author interview.
41 Author interview.
42 Author interview.
43 Popper, K, *The Logic of Scientific Discovery*, Hutchinson, London, 1959.
44 "The past is no guide," *Financial Times*, September 29, 1995.
45 Kay, J, "Is there a competitive advantage of nations?," *Siemens Review*, 5/95.

"The world is a messy place. If we want to stay on top of the corporate ladder, we must plunge into the mess. We must learn to work with the mess."

OIL COMPANY CEO[1]

"Geez, it was only 20 years ago that we were sitting there, eating pizza, talking about what we thought a PC would be like, and what we could do."

PAUL ALLEN

CO-FOUNDER OF MICROSOFT[2]

"We came to the conclusion that we would be unable to forecast any significant events out front. You can't forecast the way the world's going to be in five years' time, sometimes two years, two months or next week. Once you accept that you can't forecast events then you design your company so it can take the shocks from unexpected directions and not really cream the company."

MIKE HARPER

WHEN CEO OF CON AGRA[3]

SEEKING OUT UNCERTAINTY

* If the river is straight and the current steady
where are the rapids?

* How can we find them?

* Do we have the skills to ride them?

Leaders once sought to establish certainty. Now, the profusion of choice means there is perpetual and inescapable confusion between objectives and means of achieving them. Future leaders must actively pursue uncertainty. If they do, the possibilities are immense, the excitement greater and the risks substantial.

With uncertainty comes greater numbers of choices. Too often we restrict our choices to the tried and true. Leaders must now manage the tension that arises between options for the predictable and going with the flow. They must live with and encourage looking for new ways to do things while at the same time delivering high performance in the short term. Out of necessity they must become conflict attractors rather than conflict avoiders.

MAKING IT UP AS YOU GO

In medieval times, many areas of the world were completely uncharted territory, *terra incognita*. The mapmakers of the time had a simple solution to the uncertainty which was then an inherent part of their art. The unexplored places were simply left out of their maps or marked by "There be dragons." In the late twentieth century, executive

> ## "If you want to be content you should be a dog."

leaders are in the habit of doing much the same. Given a choice between *terra incognita* and *terra firma* they choose the reassuring ground of what they know every time.

Now they must seek out the unknown. Leaders who have previously relied on a master plan must get used to the feeling well-expressed by the hero of the first *Indiana Jones* film. When asked what his plan was, his answer was simple: "I don't know; I'm making this up as I go." Uncertainty is the new reality.

The family-run Stone Container Corporation of Chicago would appear to have little need to reinvent itself for the future. Its profitability grew fifteen-fold in the 1980s boosting annual sales to $5.5 billion. Yet, speaking at the 1993 meeting of the International Strategic Management Society, the company's president and chief executive, Roger Stone, described how his company is revitalizing itself.

The keys to modern corporate learning and transformation, according to Stone, are: to become even more "customer driven" and quality focused; to stimulate innovation throughout the company; to measure corporate and individual performance on every possible dimension; to "manage backwards from the future, rather than short term"; to simplify structures and processes; and, most importantly, to foster a process of "creative discontent" within the company. Stone concluded: "If you want to be content you should be a dog."[4]

In the canine-free corporate world, uncertainty is part of the job. Listen to this executive, an area manager with a railroad:

49

In the canine-free corporate world, uncertainty is part of the job.

"Logically, I don't know if you need an area manager. I don't add anything apart from if something goes wrong I am the one who will get up before the media and if someone gets killed I am the one that will end up in court. Literally. These are my two responsibilities. I have no specific responsibilities as an overseer, gelling people together or acting as the link between HQ and what is going on down on the ground. So the bit I add is that I collate, filter out all the views from down below and feed them upwards into the process and make sure they happen. Also I collect all the information I can, keep my ears to the ground to hear what is going on, filter it and ensure that it comes out. A bit like the hourglass principle. I am the filter bit in the middle, with the stuff above and the stuff down below, that's all I am."[5]

A decade ago would his job have been so clouded with ambiguity, so uncertain? We think not.

We interviewed a highly experienced project manager describing the workings of a major IT project: "The champion was the project director, but it wasn't quite." She paused as she realized that the working arrangement dealing with tens of millions of dollars was disturbingly vague and imprecise. She gamely carried on: "It was clear-cut because he was working for the organization. He was always the champion within the organization and across the industry, but he had no authority as such."[6] The more she thought about it, the more blurred it became. As she thought it through, complexity took over.

Listen to Andrew Grove, CEO of Intel, with 1994 sales of $11.5 billion, on the new imperatives for corporate leaders:

"You have no choice but to operate in a world shaped by globalization and the information revolution. There are two options: adapt or die. The new environment dictates two rules: first, everything happens faster; second, anything that can be done will be done, if not by you, then by someone else, somewhere. **Let there be no misunderstanding: these changes lead to a less kind, less gentle and less predictable workplace. As managers in such a workplace, you need to develop a higher tolerance for disorder."**[7]

In this new reality we face multiple choices and interpretations. The new reality is characterized by uncertainty – the behavioral response to multiple choices

> **There are two options: adapt or die.**

where there is no obvious way of making a choice. Uncertainty used to be the sole domain of mathematics and science. No more.

For most of us, uncertainty is *terra incognita*, uncharted and unknown. But that doesn't mean that it doesn't exist. As we have seen, managers prefer certainty. They are not alone. Psychologist Adam Phillips, author of *Terrors and Experts*, argues that psychologists have also preferred a course of professional certainty. He contends that psychologists are not masters of a science with a set of knowledge and techniques at their disposal. Instead, their expertise lies in "the truths of uncertainty." Rather than pushing patients towards developing self-knowledge, Phillips says they should be throwing it into doubt. "Too much definition leaves too much out," argues Phillips.[8]

But where does leadership fit in? Surely it is about creating certainty, providing the definition? True. All the textbooks suggest that leaders create certainty. (They are also filled with definitions which leave too much out.) Leaders set clear goals. Everyone knows what they have to do. They are John Waynes. In a perfect world perhaps leaders do create certainty, but not now in our far from perfect world. Forget the reassurance of neat packages; forget comfortable delineation. "I value ambiguity almost above all," says Oscar-winning actress Emma Thompson.[9] Michael Douglas phrases it more colorfully: "I enjoy discord. I

> **For most of us, uncertainty is *terra incognita*, uncharted and unknown. But that doesn't mean that it doesn't exist.**

must say, I enjoy slam dancing. I enjoy putting it up in your face without a clear protagonist or antagonist. I'm attracted to ambivalence because that's what I see around us."[10]

We have moved in one generation from clarity to uncertainty.

Executives and leaders must also seek out and value the ambivalence, ambiguity and uncertainty which threatens to engulf them. Some already make it work. "The HR textbooks tell you to spend a lot of time getting role clarity, but sometimes role ambiguity can be useful. The people who tolerate ambiguity are more likely to be builders – so they tolerate ambiguity on the way to some achievement," said a banking executive. "The highest level of role ambiguity I ever came across was consulting. Am I parent, teacher, mentor or guide?"[11]

We have moved in one generation from clarity to uncertainty. In this uncertain world, leadership is not something you practice only on Mondays and Wednesdays. Certainty may be something you seek out in your spare time, not in your job. Uncertainty is for weekdays. General Colin Powell spends his leisure time with aging Volvos. The attraction is simply that the nuts, bolts and pistons are "not abstract, but concrete, not unknown, but certain," he explains in his autobiography.[12] British actor and comedian Rowan Atkinson, the creator of Mr Bean, is similarly drawn to the reassurance of machinery – on tour he can be found helping the riggers and electricians rather than preparing his emotions for performance. Atkinson is reputedly prouder of his truck driver's license than his myriad of acting awards. Driving a truck, he is in charge. If you can't find certainty during the week, find some on the weekend.

If you don't find uncertainty on Monday: create some.

If you don't find uncertainty on Monday: create some. "If I can't fire people – and I never would want to – how can I instill a sense of crisis? How can I persuade people that if nothing changes, the company will slowly die?" asks Minoru Makihara, president of the Mitsubishi Corporation.[13]

Uncertainty means the end of the road for any notion of one right way. Instead, there are a host of alternatives and possibilities. "In a complex, changing world, most leadership challenges pose dilemmas: damned if you do, damned if you don't . . . The need to keep adapting, shifting, rebalancing is likely to be a lot more useful than knowing the right way to do something," our colleague Leonard Sayles notes.[14] The rightfulness of managers, not to mention the righteousness of some, has disappeared into the corporate ether. And, as we shall see, better wrongfulness than rightfulness.

Right is wrong. But why? Simply and, we believe undeniably, the problem is that while the number of choices facing leaders have increased, the ways of coping with choice have not increased by the same magnitude.

Think about it. Take a straightforward act managers do every day of their working lives: communicating an important issue to a colleague. You now have many more choices about how you go about this once simple act. You can:

- go down the corridor and pay her or him a visit
- send a fax
- send a message on internal electronic mail
- write a note the old-fashioned way and wait for a response
- leave a voice mail message
- set up a voice or video conference
- send a message by external Internet
- go to lunch
- use the corporate network
- use a third party who'll be seeing your colleague
- update a shared computer file through groupware like Lotus Notes.

How well you evaluate the choice is of less importance to us in this example than playing out the sheer number of choices we now have.

Indeed, acknowledging and understanding the range of choices is essential. If you are in a supermarket and have a choice of dozens of wines at similar prices, you either choose the one you had last time or begin to evaluate the choices you face. If you always automatically go with your previous choice the rest of the wine world will remain untasted.

And the profusion of choice now means you're likely to make more than one choice. You feel that choosing the unknown Chilean wine is a little risky, so you also buy a safe Californian which you know you like. In a managerial situation such behavior might eat into your effectiveness – you send a fax *and* arrange a meeting.

Now take this reasoning and apply it to a much more commercially important set of issues – like the survival of a product you are responsible for marketing. What will you do? How do you respond when the choices and possibilities are immense? Managers are surrounded by choice – and those that think they are not cannot be working to their full effectiveness. In modern organizations the tendency is to hide the uncertainty instead of embracing it.

THE UNCERTAINTY GAP

It would be arrogant to insist that uncertainty was a new phenomenon. For all recorded history, "managers" have faced uncertainty, whether they've been building pyramids, organizing armies or manufacturing muskets.[15] Look at figure 2.1 which represents how any future project appears at a distance.

The further away in time from the closure of the project, the more uncertainties can be contemplated. When you know that you have five years to complete a project, then you know that it is impossible to anticipate every detail in every aspect. As time goes on, and decisions have been made and actions taken, fewer and fewer uncertainties remain if the project is running to schedule. This applies whether you are building a highway, opening a new airport or introducing a new IT system. Any military commander planning a battle or campaign will be familiar with the experience of looking into the

Figure 2.1
DISTANT UNCERTAINTY

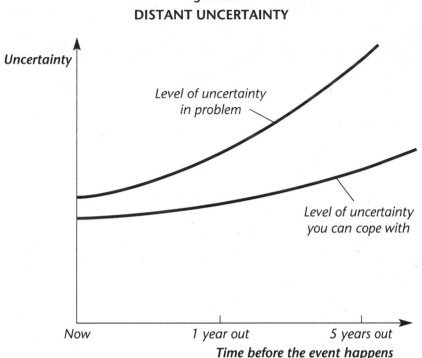

future and recognizing that some things cannot yet be decided, some things have to remain unknown.

In figure 2.2 we represent the remarkable increase in choice which has been offered to managers over the last ten to 20 years. This is not just our view, but is the distillation of what our clients as well as those we interviewed and researched thought about the world. Figure 2.2 plots the amount of choice available for solving any particular problem alongside the manager's capability to make effective use of those choices.

What we are representing is the dramatic increase in choices available to managers which can be applied to a range of situations and problems. The growth in choice associated with a situation far outstrips the capability of managers to cope with that level of choice.

If we combine figures 2.1 and 2.2 we get a representation of the situation that faces most managers today – figure 2.3. In plotting

Figure 2.2
THE PROFUSION OF CHOICE

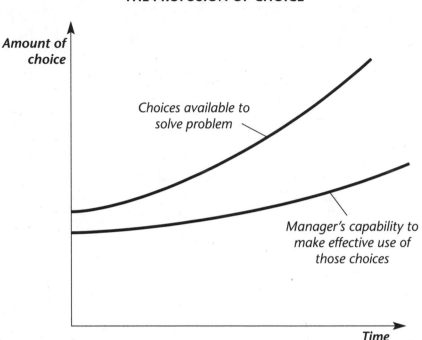

Amount of choice

Choices available to solve problem

Manager's capability to make effective use of those choices

Time

uncertainty against time we have in the upper curve the level of uncertainty represented truly in each problem or situation and, in the lower curve, the capability of a manager to cope with that uncertainty effectively. The gap between the two curves is what we call the uncertainty gap and represents a graphical interpretation of the symptoms which many managers now experience.

The real problem leaders face in reorienting themselves to a new way of working is tolerating (and celebrating) a higher level of uncertainty than their predecessors. At an organizational level, companies have first to admit that the uncertainty gap exists. Then they must pull inside it to maximize its potential.

Listen to the banking executive on the challenge he identifies as facing his organization:

Figure 2.3
THE UNCERTAINTY GAP

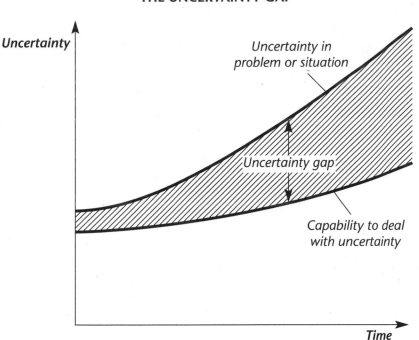

"I think people are confused. They don't think they know what's really going on. I don't think they know what really matters. The executive committee seems to have pulled away from the day-to-day running of the business and we are trying to bridge the gap. We're actually trying to get people to come into that gap, rather than us go back to the way things were which is always a danger. We're trying to get other people to come into the gap, accept responsibility and for us to sort out the ragged edges."[16]

And, in an uncertain world with many, many choices, there are an awful lot of ragged edges.

FROM PROFUSION TO CONFUSION

Choice has increased at every stage of the decision-making process. Managers generally understand and acknowledge that this is the case. It is not simply a matter of having a greater choice of how to communicate, of deciding between e-mail and video conferencing. It is a great deal more.

We accept that we are connected to greater ranges of thinking styles than those we learned growing up. Through technology we are connected to all parts of the globe. Socially we were born and raised in a particular culture, but are now connected to more cultures through work, the ability to travel and the ability to access information instantly. We may not completely understand what it means to be an Amazonian Indian, but at least we now have some perspective on how they live. And we can now better appreciate why the price of coffee or the burning of a piece of rain forest affects them as well as us.

Choice has increased. CNN tells us about a war almost before it has happened and shows it live. We can commiserate with a famous athletics loser, be appalled by crime and marvel at new technological achievements all before breakfast. We accept it all, take it for granted and channel surf seeking out more or trying to avoid more.

> **Choice has increased at every stage of the decision-making process.**

Choice is good, but it is endemic. Think back, say, two generations. As we saw in our discussion about Management by Objectives, at that time managers tended to focus on a single set of objectives. Today, our greater sense of world connectedness, combined with an incessant data stream, means it is far more difficult to aim for any single objective while ignoring contrary objectives, tasks and points of view. And this complexity is heightened by the daily demands and expectations of business. Quarter-to-quarter results drive organizations without mercy. There is nowhere to hide.

Technology has had a huge impact on our lives. The ability to store and retrieve information from databases means that any individual has access to vast amounts of data. The comparatively cheap and ready access that most senior managers have to computer databases (whether they use them or not) means that they can easily tap into historical, financial and market information. It may be that they cannot find the right piece of data when they want it and they may feel submerged in vast quantities of data that prove unnecessary, but the availability of technology means that choice – alternative ways of identifying problems and solving them – is greatly increased.

Choice is good, but these vast amounts of data also carry with them problems of accuracy and appropriateness. Data may be incomplete. Data may be wrong. The data needed may not be there at all. But the database or the network connection may not indicate any of these problems. So, even though the manager has access to greater amounts of data than ever before, there is no guarantee of their accuracy or completeness. This introduces even more uncertainty into the choice system.

Even the most august bodies struggle with the inadequacies and sheer complexity of data. Take productivity. One would have thought that the world's economists would have established a sure-fire means of calculating national productivity. Not so. Between 1990 and 1995 the USA's GDP grew by 3.1 per cent. Well, that's one version – another goes for 2.6 per cent. Depending on your choice of data, productivity increased significantly in the 1980s or remained fairly static. The US Bureau of Economic Analysis has introduced new rules for measurement. These, of course, rewrite economic history at a single stroke. The question is, is it better to go with the new, more sophisticated, more accurate measurement; or to stick with the old methods? Interestingly some economists prefer the old way – after all, it confirms the trends they have drawn attention to and spent a great deal of time and energy making sense of.[17]

Choice is good, but changes in communications technology have also created an increased number of linkages. In the not too distant past, an individual trying to solve a problem may have spoken to a dozen or so colleagues during the course of a week. Now it is possible for that same person to be networked with thousands of people across the globe and across every time zone. This is true whether you are a research scientist, a diplomat or a manager. The increase in the numbers of contacts opens up the number of choices. Who do I spend time with? Who do I ignore? Whose papers should I read? Whose can I safely skip?

The effect of all these shifts in technology and thinking is that senior managers particularly are now routinely acknowledging and dealing with more options and choices than ever before. It is not unusual for a company to design a product in one country, source it from three different countries, build it in one or two more and sell and service it in markets located in still other countries.

The intermediary products which go to make up Ford's Escort model come from 15 countries. These include not only raw materials, but components and entire systems which come from a world-wide network of subcontractors and suppliers. The cars are finally assembled in two plants, one in the UK and one in Germany. Such complexity is no longer any great surprise. DRAMS are made in South East Asia, exported to Mexico for assembly as laptops and PCs and then shipped to markets throughout the world.

It is now so common that it is easy to believe such arrangements are relatively simple. But, in such truly global businesses, every decision is affected, or afflicted, by an array of interlinked issues – tariffs, exchange rates, barriers, support packages, political shifts, language differences. At a personal level there are many more complications. Do we ignore the range of choices at our disposal or seek to integrate them into our thinking and practice? Amid the profusion of choice, there is, in reality, no choice. Some way, somehow, we have to assimilate data, information and knowledge, and convert them into the right decisions for our businesses and our lives. Either we sit back and marvel, or we embrace uncertainty.

The frenetic profusion of alternatives may be something we accept. At home we have the channel changer in our hands. But how do we make sense of it? How do we fit it into our view of the world?

The conventional approach is straightforward. We think in terms of straight lines linking A to B, problem to solution. It is neat and reassuring, but wrong. The pitcher is throwing a curve ball and we are ready for the straight one.

Look back at the uncertainty gap (figure 2.3). The lower curve on the graph represents the growth of techniques to cope with choice. These have been limited because managers still expect to use linear methods to make predictions. Organizations like predictions. Their top managers are expected to make forecasts, budgets and statements to the press and in annual reports about where they will be in one, two or five years. Strategic planning is, despite all the managerial and academic debate, alive and well.

At this point, managers will ask "What about budgets? What about vision? Surely we must have some sense of where we are trying to go?" The problem with the budget is that it is a purely linear device. Similarly, many vision statements are plans disguised by the fatuous reassurance of public relations speak. They give only the possibility of following one foot after the other to a single defined goal.

If the linear approach is leading us nowhere, or somewhere we should have been last year, how should we think? The answer lies in asking better questions and realizing the limits of today's vogueish techniques. As Harvard's Ted Levitt suggests:

> **The pitcher is throwing a curve ball and we are ready for the straight one.**

"You have to expose yourself to your environment and ask questions to develop your sensitivity and sensibility. I see things all the time. I go into factories, offices, stores and look out the window and just see things and ask Why? Why are they doing that? Why are things this way and not that? You ask questions and pretty soon you come up with answers. When you begin to try to answer your own questions, you become much more receptive to reading things which help you to answer questions. Seeing is one thing but perception requires cognitive effort and personal involvement. You bring something to what you see."[18]

Questioning was identified by a number of the leaders we interviewed as an integral part of how they added value to the organization. The manager of a multinational's African operation said:

"I find it difficult to distinguish between the company on one side and me on the other. When I do something, the company is doing it, and I hope what we are doing is adding value at every stage of a project, right from the first meeting. You can add value simply by asking questions – do you think you have adequately looked at this or don't you think it would be good to do this as well. Even if the project doesn't go forward you might have added value to the idea and that follows through. You build. The sponsor of the project may think it is brilliant and will work out, but you subject it to constructive criticism in the hope that you can build a project which is smaller or bigger and certainly sounder than it was when you came in."[19]

In an effort to make sense of uncertainty, it has become popular to make reference to chaos theory and to offer pictures of fractals and images of butterflies. Indeed, the imagery of management writing has undergone a creative renaissance during the last decade. The old images of machines and cogs have been cast aside. Take the view of McKinsey consultants Bleeke and Ernst in *Collaborating to Compete*:

"Global corporations of the future will be rather like amoebas. This single-celled aquatic animal is among the most ancient life-forms on earth. It gets all its nourishment from its environment through its permeable outer walls. These walls define the creature as distinct from its environment, but allow much of what is inside to flow out and much of what is outside to come in. The amoeba is always changing shape, taking and giving with the surroundings, yet it always retains its integrity and identity as a unique creature."[20]

There is more. "Many companies need to reinvent themselves. And reinvention is not changing what is, but creating what isn't. A butterfly is not more caterpillar or a better or improved caterpillar; a butterfly is a different creature. Reinvention entails a series of continuous metamorphoses of this magnitude over time," says Richard Pascale.[21] Great images, but the question must be: do they help?

The mathematical theory of chaos has spawned a lot of images and a lot of butterflies; they are always causing climatic disasters in other countries. The theory is, after all, far removed from the reality of business. Where are the strange attractors? What is phase space to a manager or a leader? But the attraction of chaos imagery and theory is that it encompasses a wider concept of non-linear systems. Executives feel the need for a new way of thinking and latch onto the most fashionable alternative.

In the new reality, the appropriateness of chaos theory cannot be dismissed. At the very least we should be sensitive to the possibilities that the theories and images offer. Most business organizations have some of the properties of a mix of complexity and chaos. Another attraction is the idea that the complexity we see in the world is the result of underlying simplicity and that simple systems should be regarded as creative not static. Murray Gell-Mann of the Santa Fe Institute has a phrase for this. He talks of "surface complexity arising out of deep simplicity." "Complex adaptive systems are pattern seekers, they interact with the environment, 'learn' from the experience and adapt as a result," says Gell-Mann.[22]

Managers in the real world recognize and suffer from the surface complexity all too well – that's what they get bogged down in. So, they need to tap into these deep simplicities which account for and, who knows, might explain much of the complexity. Again, tapping into these simplicities is often a matter of asking questions. From the profusion of colorful chaos-related imagery, two themes emerge quite clearly:

1 Linear models of the world based on Newton's idea that action leads to reaction are insufficient to handle some kinds of circumstances – namely complexity and uncertainty.

2 Many business problems contain elements which are inherently unpredictable. Remember the stock market crash of 1987? Remember the story of corporate folklore that in the 1950s IBM calculated the European market for non-military computers was five? Remember the prediction of Digital's Ken Olsen that we wouldn't see computers on desks? We have already mentioned how economic models fail to detect or predict major changes in the economy. Yet, predictions continue simply because most forecasters choose to ignore the possibility of major shifts in economic

behavior and performance. It is human nature to write off cataclysmic events as momentary glitches in history.

Economic upheaval tends to be dramatic and unexpected. In contrast, corporate equivalents tend to be slower to evolve. Look at GM overlooking the effects of the gas crisis in the 1970s. It went on producing the big cars which it said the market demanded. The Japanese had other ideas.

In September 1992, when the UK was forced to leave the Exchange Rate Mechanism and effectively devalue its currency, forecasters had been unable to predict the timing of this upheaval even when it was imminent. A chance combination of a run on the Italian lira, statements from the Bundesbank and uncertainty about the outcome of the French referendum forced the issue. Individually the events could have been anticipated. In unison, however, they were beyond some of the world's leading minds. If you happened to be a UK mortgage holder whose mortgage spiked by five points in a single evening this example would have stuck in your mind.

Forecasters routinely overlook the random and unpredictable. The very nature of their job dictates that they have to. They extrapolate from their models and often get it wrong. Being right some of the time is okay. Managers do much the same. Different models – same deficiencies.

THE UNKNOWABLE FUTURE

Today's rules will not apply tomorrow – no matter what tomorrow brings.

If the future is unknowable and ridden with uncertainty what do organizations do? "Let chaos reign, then rein in chaos," advocates Intel's Andrew Grove.[23] Usually organizations do nothing of the sort. They fail to recognize that today's triumphs are tomorrow's disasters. And fail to realize that the challenge is to turn today's disasters into tomorrow's triumphs.

Safe today, deadly tomorrow. Large insurance companies pay out for natural disasters and corporate disasters whether they are oil spills, ships sinking or offices burning down. In addition, however, there are a host of emerging issues which they must continually monitor and keep abreast of. "As measuring and detection equipment are continually refined, products and substances previously regarded as harmless will be recognized as hazardous to health. In addition, more and more

**Safe today,
deadly tomorrow.**

refined techniques make it possible to target responsible parties even more precisely and thus result in even more claims for damages," noted Munich Reinsurance's 1995 Annual Report. What is safe and acceptable today is tomorrow's disaster. Asbestos was safe 40 years ago.

In practice, faced with the unknowable and uncertain, organizations follow three options:

- ignore
- contain
- adapt.

Ignore: deny the data or declare it to be irrelevant

There is always tension between past patterns, achievements and future possibilities. Organizations and their managers must learn to embrace and accept those tensions. In practice, unfortunately, they too often ignore the tension and say we will increase what we did last year by 10 per cent. They regard the future as linear, not chaotic. They assume next year will be the same.

Back to MBO – invent the future and it will happen. Organizations avoid confronting uncertainty by creating an apparent long-term world. Indeed, there is mounting pressure for managers to adopt longer term strategies. After all, they are told, the Japanese economic miracle was based round companies which looked forward decades. Fons Trompenaars, author of *Riding the Waves of Culture*,[24] cites the example of when the Japanese were trying to take over the operations of Yosemite National Park in California. The first thing the Japanese submitted was a 250-year business plan. Initially, after they had got up off the floor, the thoughts of the American managers turned to an horrific (or reassuring, depending on your point of view) statistic – 250 years is 1,000 quarterly reports. "Americans tend to think about the improvement of the next quarter, while the Japanese do not ignore the short term but tend to place it in the context of the long-term future. That is as close as managers can get to reconciling different time frames," says Trompenaars.[25]

> **In reality, the corporate capacity for self-delusion is enormous.**

How can executives look to the future when they are worrying about how they can get through this month? How can they look far ahead when even the immediate future is uncertain? Yet, that is what they are expected to do. They must consolidate and declare ambitious growth objects. They must focus on local markets as well as internal cooperation. They must improve their individual effectiveness while becoming great team players. They must continue being active while increasing the amount of time spent in reflecting.

These pressures are enormous and paradoxical. In the Western world we have tended to shy away from paradox, and yet the leaders of tomorrow will need to be fluent in handling paradoxes – to move from situations which provide either/or alternatives to ones with both/and solutions.

In reality, the corporate capacity for self-delusion is enormous – witness the oil price rises of the 1970s when the oil companies sought to carry on with business as normal. Or General Motors. Or IBM. The list is long. "In the case of General Motors, the inability of top management to grasp early on the importance of Japanese competition, the consumer demand for better quality, and the shift of consumer interest to safety and economy are given as 'reasons' for the GM problem," Harry Levinson astutely observes in a 1994 article:

> **"IBM has been criticized for its rigid attachment to mainframe computers and for its emphasis on sales and financial matters, rather than on frontier technology. The latter criticism was also made of GM. Perhaps that criticism is an oversimplification, but it certainly appears that IBM's problems are related significant-**

ly to the denial of its own data, just as GM for years denied the reality of the increasing success of its Japanese competitors."[26]

In a risk averse environment, the emphasis is on protecting assets, market share and the organization as a whole rather than remaining open to learning. To do anything else is taking a risk. Most companies concentrate on protection in the present rather than preparation for the future. They protect their assets and protect their ability to learn, grow and change. Too often, protection concentrates on resources and assets. In doing so, organizations constrain the development of these aspects of their business. They believe they have too much to lose and, once you have something to lose, fear takes over. As companies grow, protective instincts tend to expand at a similar rate.

Generally, protection takes a negative form. It tends to mean you are constantly behaving as if the wagons are circled. You are fending off attacks and are not in an expansive learning mode. (However, protection can be positive. Disney has reshaped its view from negative protection to positive protection.)

Assuming the future will turn out like the past provides disappointment after disappointment. Executives are trained to ignore these. Look at annual reports. Have you ever read a corporate annual report which offers a bleak perspective of the future? Despite the fact that companies are impermanent legal manifestations liable to be taken over, hit the rocks or become subsumed into another elusive entity, senior executives rarely admit this is the case. Next year is looking good. We have mapped it out. It will be the same as last year – only better. The year after may be even better and, in five or 10 years, we may well achieve our widely acclaimed corporate goals.

How many times have you read that a drop in profits was caused by unprecedented market conditions? As long ago as 1972, Abraham Brilloff observed:

"Note how corporate managements search for ways to rationalize losses as extraordinary or at least nonrecurring, thereby avoiding their negative effect on the bottom line. As a corollary, the same managements seek to attribute the pluses to the current operating cycle – thereby sweetening the message to shareholders."[27]

And Brilloff's observation was made at a time when corporations were less well-versed in the intricacies of communicating unpalatable messages in positive ways.

If the future doesn't turn out to be the same as the past, executives quickly – and skillfully – claim that this could not have been anticipated or prepared for. But what if it could? Preparing for the unknowable is not as impossible as the phraseology suggests. But, first, you need to learn what worked and didn't work in the past and be willing to do things differently in the future.

Contain: acknowledge the data, but decide to do nothing

The second response to the unknowable future is to contain: organizational stupor; we know about that, but let's wait and see.

In China gambling is illegal. Yet every Thursday evening and Sunday afternoon massive crowds watch and bet on horse-racing, courtesy of the Guangzhou Jockey Club. They are not gambling. Instead, they are participating in a "horse-racing intelligence competition."[28] In the modern corporation, managers can gamble blindly assuming tomorrow's result will be the same as yesterday's or engage in an intelligence competition. Often, they carry on like the Chinese authorities, content to let things be if they are controlled and contained.

Adapt: acknowledge the data and act

The organizations which adapt tend to take action which falls into four categories. Internally they prepare and protect. Externally they seek out patterns and possibilities. Patterns come from analysis of past data; possibilities are derived by taking past patterns and imposing them on future data. Patterns are not used to make predictions. Instead they are used as a testing ground to help prepare for the widest possible range of futures. You are then in the position to make what decisions you can – not necessarily the right ones – to achieve the best possible fit between the organization and its environment.

Recent corporate history proves that no matter who we are or what we do, we need to be ready for upheavals. If IBM had been in prepare mode in the early 1980s rather than protect mode it may have been more responsive. While it was preoccupied with protecting what it had, Apple was preparing for the future (although even Apple now seems to have stopped).

To prepare, we must become more cognizant of the limitations of our methods of prediction. There is a difference between having a paddle and forcing your way down the river and taking a paddle and feeling your way down the river. You can't control the future but you can control your ability to be creatively adaptive to the challenges it produces.

> **As we have seen, we are attracted to patterns which fit our world view. We seek out trends and statistics which support us and overlook the rest.**

Understanding what has been, making sense of data and recognizing underlying patterns are central to preparing for the uncertain future. What could the patterns tell us? As we have seen, we are attracted to patterns which fit our world view. We seek out trends and statistics which support us and overlook the rest. Looking simply at the patterns of the past or a restricted range of patterns is no longer useful.

If we are to adapt we have to be sensitive to faint signals in the internal and external environments. We must ask – what if? We must shake off linear logic and seek out the intangible, the underlying and the irrational: the fuzzy logic.

Working together, fund managers Pareto Partners (responsible for $12 billion of investments) and defense group GM Hughes Electronics, have come up with an Artificial Intelligence investment system. The system follows rational logic but also includes "fuzzy" logic including "sort of" and "somewhat" responses. "We don't want to constrain it with lots of limits and rules, because

> **Leaders, too, must seek out and create their own fuzzy logic.**

69

those are inefficient ways of controlling risk," says Pareto's research director, Ron Leisching. The system is now investing $250 million and has "significantly outperformed" other indices.[29]

This is an important step as it recognizes that the human mind is built around possibilities as much as certainties. Previously Artificial Intelligence has only been able to follow rational logic; by moving into the world of possibilities and uncertainty, its potential is greatly expanded. Leaders, too, must seek out and create their own fuzzy logic.

THRIVING ON CONFLICT

What's stopping us seeking out uncertainty?
We refuse to manage or deal with the conflict which uncertainty inevitably produces.

"Where there is much desire to learn, there of necessity will be much arguing, much writing, many opinions; for opinion in good men is but knowledge in the making," wrote the English poet John Milton. With a huge range of choices at our disposal and a limited armory of means of delivery, disagreement is inevitable – and vital.

"Why is there no conflict at this meeting? Something's wrong when there's no conflict," Disney's Michael Eisner said at a conference of his top managers.[30] In the white water world of uncertainty, agreeing to disagree is crucial.

In managing the tensions between doing what the past tells them will yield sustainable (real and acceptable) performance and taking a risk to achieve exceptionally high performance, white water leaders seek out contention and disagreement. They take yes for an answer and then ask why?

Seeking out uncertainty goes against the grain. We are as attracted to certainty as presidential candidates are to press conferences. It is, at least in the short-term, the surest route to acceptable performance. Think about it.

How many meetings have you been to where agreement is total and difficult issues are shunted to the end of the agenda when everyone is looking at the clock? The average executive must spend thousands of hours in rubber-stamp meetings where discord has been ironed out beforehand or is simply side-lined. Indeed, in the UK it is estimated that four million man hours are spent every day in meetings.[31] These meetings are

White water leaders seek out contention and disagreement.

like ceremonial signings of peace agreements. They are stage managed, but once you are out of the door, the agreement counts for nothing as all the unresolved issues bubble to the surface. One pharmaceutical company we know of has meetings to get ready for meetings. You remember all those treaties Presidents signed with Russian leader Leonid Brezhnev? We all knew it meant nothing – the real issues were carefully tiptoed around – but it made us feel a bit more secure.

How many times have you been the only one in the room to voice disagreement? It can feel lonely. Indeed, in most organizations you are meant to feel lonely if you disagree. The only way forward is to leave or keep quiet. Most choose the latter option. And, even when they leave the real truth of the disagreement rarely surfaces. The boss of UK telecoms company, Mercury, left the company suddenly in September 1995. He cited "personal reasons." What emerged was that he disagreed with the main board policy and felt that to join the board would have been inconsistent with his views. He didn't feel as if he could disagree. But, what is the point of a board of directors? Surely it is to gather diverse opinions and then make an informed decision on behalf of the business.

What happens to people who disagree in your company? As we have seen they usually look elsewhere. They should be promoted or at least congratulated for having the courage to disagree. Look at Ross Perot's thorny relationship with GM after he delivered a golden egg in the shape of EDS. Perot disagreed with how GM was run and came up with ideas to change things. Perot and GM parted company and some of his ideas were later implemented. Wouldn't it have been preferable if Perot's entrepreneurial and individualistic perspective had been harnessed rather than discarded?

71

In his research, Richard Pascale "stumbled" upon a law of cybernetics known as the Law of Requisite Variety. The law states that for any organism to adapt to its external environment, it must incorporate "variety." If you reduce variety internally you are less able to deal with it when it comes at you externally. "But how does variety show up in a social system?" asked Pascale:

> **"It shows up as deviance from the norm – in other words, as conflict. The problem is that most companies are conflict averse. For many it is associated with wounded egos, harmed relationships and turf wars. Contention is often mistaken as an indicator of mismanagement. The trick is to learn to disagree without being disagreeable and channel this contention as a means of self-questioning and keeping an organization on its toes."[32]**

In practice, Pascale believes 50 per cent of the time when contention arises it is smoothed over and avoided. Another 30 per cent of the time it leads to non-productive fighting and no resolution. Only in 20 per cent of the cases is contention truly confronted and resolved. "It's ironic," observes Pascale. "A threat that everyone perceives but no one talks about is far more debilitating than a threat that is clearly revealed and resources mobilized to address it. Companies, like people, tend to be as sick as their secrets," says Pascale – who prescribes revealing the "undiscussables" and that "breakdowns" be regarded as a source of learning.[33] Other commentators, such as INSEAD's Manfred Kets de Vries, suggest similar phenomena.

In his 1993 book, *Knowledge for Action*, Harvard's Chris Argyris examines the behavior of one of his consultancy assignments, itself a consultancy group.[34] The assignment arose when seven successful consultants decided to establish their own company. They hoped that it would be free from the Machiavellian political wrangles they had encountered in other organizations. In practice, their dreams were disappointed. Indeed, by the time Argyris was called in, internal wrangling consumed too many of its productive energies.

The anonymous consultants featured in *Knowledge for Action* were, in fact, falling prey to what Argyris calls defensive routines. Faced with a personally threatening problem, the executives were adept at covering it up or bypassing it entirely. Board meetings, therefore, concentrated on trivial topics – there was always one person keen to avoid discussion of an important issue. Outside the boardroom the big issues were discussed and blame apportioned so that divisions built up relentlessly between the original founders. This approach affected the behavior of the rest of the organization – others consciously kept information to a minimum so that executives weren't forced to face up to something new.

> **Thriving on conflict is easier said than done.**

The fact that Argyris' client is a group of management consultants helps convey the importance of his message. If highly trained, intelligent executives fall into such traps, what chance have ordinary mortals? For a start, mere mortals have to face up to potential and real problems. They must distrust consensus and embrace contention.

Thriving on conflict is easier said than done. We all like people who agree with us. We like people who have the same perspectives, fears and passions. That is why when managers recruit people they tend to recruit like-minded individuals. Conflict is instinctively buried.

"I think a lot of people learn to control their reactions to it [uncertainty] and that can appear to be tolerance because they manage to keep the stress it induces in them under control," observed the banking executive we interviewed. "They would sooner not have it, but they can cope with it. And then there are a number of people who fall apart at the big open space. They fall apart because you say: 'Please define this' and they're not used to thinking that way. Or they feel it personally threatening because, I think, a lot of people define themselves by what they do. If that isn't very clear then I think they feel unclear about themselves. Living, tolerating and thriving on uncertainty is not common. People escape with the belief that there is a right answer."[35]

The past has taught us that a narrow band of acceptable behavior is essential. Otherwise we are invaded by uncontrollable renegades and mavericks. Now we need to nurture a much broader band of acceptable behavior. As Don Hambrick noted in a 1987 article, leaders need to surround themselves with people who counter their weaknesses and supplement their strengths.[36]

Nowhere is the issue of confronting contention more apparent than in our attitudes and responses to cultural diversity. Ask once again: what's stopping us seeking out uncertainty? And another answer emerges:

We have yet to come to terms with the implications of managing cultural diversity.

Choice requires that managers understand and manage contention. Also, they must manage and understand the cultural nuances which often fuel contention and disagreement.

General Colin Powell's memoirs were a runaway bestseller in the USA where they were entitled *My American Journey*. In the UK the book was also successful, under the title *A Soldier's Tale*. In France, Powell's life story was sold as *L'Enfant Du Bronx* [Child of the Bronx]. Similarly, Charles Handy's book *The Empty Raincoat* is known as *The Age of Paradox* in the USA. What does this tell us? Are Europeans more ill at ease with the concept of paradox than Americans? Are Americans unable to appreciate the image of the empty raincoat? Perhaps. But, what this publishing phenomenon displays is that our expectations, perceptions and ways of thinking differ fundamentally from culture to culture.

Exasperated and perplexed, managers might say: "We're all the same, aren't we?" But, a manager from Pueblo, Colorado, does not think in the same way as one from Malaga, Spain, or Tokyo, Japan. The managers may share certain techniques, attitudes and approaches, but there are significant cultural differences in their behavior and perspectives.

"The international manager needs to go beyond awareness of cultural differences. He or she needs to respect these differences and take advantage of diversity through reconciling cross-cultural dilemmas. The international manager reconciles cultural dilemmas," says Fons Trompenaars.[37]

Culture can be distilled down to understanding what is tolerable and intolerable behavior in a particular environment. As acceptable and unacceptable behavior is constantly being redefined only a great deal of awareness of a particular culture will allow you to understand it and manage within it successfully.

Yet, the business world can be surprisingly out of touch. Look at the examples. American multinationals which have European operations still routinely put American managers in charge. Why? There are plenty of highly skilled managers in Spain or Italy or the UK. They do so because they wish to export their corporate culture. They want a division in southern Italy to be managed in the same way as one in Georgia. They want cultural certainty. It doesn't work.

Culture cannot be exported wholesale. It can be exported but has to be redefined to fit local circumstances. Look at the trials and failures encountered by Apple in Japan. Ahead of the pack, Apple identified Japan as a potentially important market at the end of the 1970s. In 1980 it went into partnership with a Japanese company – rather curiously its chosen partner was Toray, a textile company. It didn't work and subsequent partnerships failed. Also, the company's US marketing was transported and translated wholesale into Japanese. That didn't work either. Managers came and went. It wasn't until CEO John Scully invested time and energy in Japan that Apple's activities there began to take shape. It now has a Japanese manager – a mark of cultural respect and sensitivity (not to mention business sense) which might have saved the company a great deal of time and money if it had been done in the first place.

In an environment beset by uncertainty and change the challenge for organizations is to create corporate cultures which can thrive on uncertainty. Though this has a straightforward ring to it, it is highly complex. Corporate cultures are an amalgam of individual values, aspirations and personalities, which, in turn, are strongly influenced by national cultures.

"Basic to understanding other cultures is the awareness that culture is a series of rules and methods that a society has evolved to deal with the recurring problems it faces. They have become so basic that, like breathing, we no longer

> **Culture cannot be exported wholesale.**

In an environment beset by uncertainty and change, the challenge for organizations is to create corporate cultures which can thrive on uncertainty. Though this has a straightforward ring to it, it is highly complex.

think about how we approach or resolve them," says Fons Trompenaars. "Every country and every organization faces dilemmas in relationships with people; dilemmas in relationship to time; and dilemmas in relations between people and the natural environment. Culture is the way in which people resolve dilemmas emerging from universal problems."

In *Multicultural Management*, Farid Elashmawi and Philip Harris write:

"Transcultural managers or cross-culturally sensitive managers can:

- **readily adapt their mindsets (which include the way they perceive and accept people and environments)**
- **be familiar with varying systems of human relations and systems**
- **flexibly interact with people of differing cultures, disciplines and genders**
- **be positive about 'unusual' circumstances and transitional experiences**
- **integrate other members belonging to minority races, cultures, genders, disciplines, skills into their workgroups**
- **identify and seize transnational opportunities."**[38]

And, if all of this is true, it's clear why it is so difficult to manage across cultures. Many of the skills involved in working transnationally are also about managing uncertainty.

BEYOND THE PRESSURE TO PERFORM

What's stopping us seeking out uncertainty? The pressure to make things happen now, to achieve measurable results.

Choice is expanding but our means of dealing with the choice is developing far more slowly. The final component of the uncertainty gap is the gap itself, the gulf between the choices and the tools and techniques we possess. The gap is growing.

This growth is fueled by the premise that growth and performance improvement are an underlying backdrop to everything a manager does.

Dramatically improved performance usually demands dramatic shifts in methods and styles. Evidence from the scientific, sporting and dramatic arenas suggest that the people who break these barriers tend not to be the easiest people to control and manage. They have usually achieved their much higher performance by rejecting, or at least dramatically modifying, the methods and techniques that were the norm.

In 1952 when Capt. Charles "Chuck" Yeager broke the sound barrier in the Bell X–1 he and his colleagues talked about pushing back the envelope of performance.[39] This is what the innovators who achieve major performance breakthroughs also achieve. They push against the envelope of organizational and management expectations. Generally managers are not keen on or trained to do this. They tend to be appointed not just to manage the next, but to be guardians of the existing.

Chuck Yeager discovered that on going through the 654 miles an hour barrier (Mach One) the controls reversed. Pushing the stick brought the plane up. This was obviously very startling, but it is a useful analogy for what happens to people and organizations when they try to push back the envelope and break the equivalent of the sound barrier.

The trouble is we tend to rely on single individuals to break performance barriers. Can we risk our futures on so few individuals? We believe that organizations have to take such a risk – but they can mitigate the risk of putting their faith in a single individual by creating risk-taking cultures which embrace the possibilities and the potential rather than ignoring them or containing them.

Look at figure 2.4, the Sigmoid Curve. Its message is simple. **When the going is good, move on, look elsewhere, do something new, seek out difference.** It is a message which is gaining credence.

Figure 2.4
THE SIGMOID CURVE

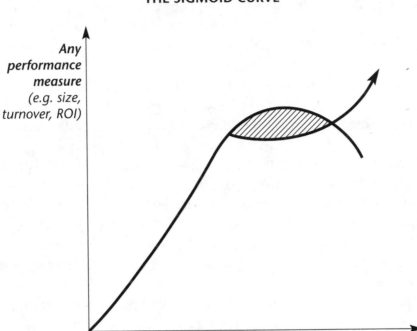

In the mid-1980s Goodyear Tire and Rubber had what it labeled a "perfection strategy." The company argued that as soon as performance began to plateau you had to find other sources of change. Good wasn't good enough. Whether Goodyear's interpretation worked or not, it was an excellent idea. Sir James Goldsmith put an offer in and the company's quest for "perfection" came to an end. From the quest to improve it moved to protection.

Airlines, for example, Scandinavian Airline System (SAS) and British Airways (BA), radically reorganized their operations and considerably improved market share and profitability. Yet, a few years later, customers had got used to the improved levels of service, and wanted more. The dramatic learning curve that all the SAS and BA staff had gone though during the first revolution had been overtaken by the learning and hence the expectation curve their customers had traveled on. It was again time to stand at the foot of another apparently vertical learning rock face.

Pressure for growth means that managerial and organizational sound barriers continually need to be broken. Yet you, and the world, expect successful companies to continue to grow their success. Organizations and leaders must produce results now and in the future. Leaders can't take themselves off to a health farm or an Arizona ranch and return as reinvented creatures with new ideas, approaches and aspirations. They must stay there while the job is being done.

> **The catch-22 is that organizations and people need to maintain what they currently do, for short- and medium-term results. At the same time the organization must recognize and encourage the threatening and seek to achieve the impossible.**

As we have seen, there are countless examples dredged up by the movement against *In Search of Excellence* to show that only a few years after being identified as excellent, many of those companies had fallen from grace. Similarly, there was an almost 100 per cent turnover between editions of *One Hundred Best Companies to Work for in America*.[40] Presumably they carried on doing what had made them excellent in the first place rather than pushing back their envelopes. By getting it right they were also sowing the seeds for getting it wrong.

"Success is a lousy teacher – it seduces smart people into thinking they can't lose. I'm not good on self-congratulation. It has no value. The more successful I am the more vulnerable I feel. I can't tell you the number of business plans that have been formulated on 'Hey, we're gonna beat Microsoft' – thousands. When you do something well, people expect even better next time round," says Bill Gates.[41]

The catch-22 is that organizations and people need to maintain what they currently do, for short- and medium-term results. At the same time the organization must recognize and encourage the threatening and seek to achieve the impossible. Only then will the company be able to do something completely different to break through the next barrier of exceptionally high performance. Paradoxically, the successes of today will produce both the source for tomorrow's successes and, if no change occurs in the organization, failure.

Golfer Nick Faldo has been one of the best in the world for the last decade. Yet, at one time, he was written off as someone who had initially promised a great deal but hadn't quite delivered. Faldo could have chosen to ignore the doubters and point to his reassuringly high earnings. But, discontented with being merely successful, Faldo took himself off to coach David Leadbetter. He transformed his technique and became the top-ranked golfer in the world.

Talking of what it takes to get to the top, Faldo has said: "It requires more than having a good technique. It's about character as well. I don't know that you can put your finger on exactly what it takes to climb up to that level. And I don't know that you can easily see it from the outside." Commenting on another golfer who had failed to fulfill early promise, Faldo observed: "He is practicing to maintain his game rather than practicing to improve it."[42] While transforming his performance, Faldo carried on playing. As the long-term transition began, he still delivered results in the short-term. Executives have to seek to do the same.

Figure 2.5
THE ESCALATOR OF CHANGE

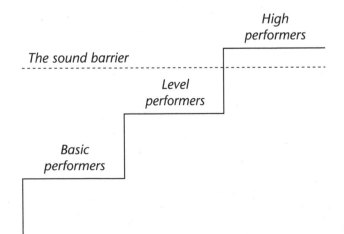

Look at the escalator of change (figure 2.5). We climb one hazardously mobile step on the escalator and then must move onto the next, and the next – and so on. In this permanently transient world there are three broad levels of performance available:

● the basics

● the level performers

● the high performers.

The basics

These represent the basic requirements all competitors need to know to be able to enter the market. If you aren't able to do this, then you can't even join the game, much as baseball players must be able to hit, run and catch to be of any value to the team. The basics demand having the requisite skills and knowledge to overcome barriers to entry.

The level performers

The second level is what the better players are doing. We can include here the individual idiosyncrasies of each person or organization – the personality or cultural package that makes them recognizable as what or who they are. They are using material or ideas that are partly invented on their premises, but it is likely that the ideas and mental models are not completely unique to that company or individual. Something like them exists and is used elsewhere by competitors.

Even the brightest and best ideas are liable soon to emerge elsewhere. As Karl Jung, among others, pointed out, an idea will emerge in several different places about the same time even though the people concerned don't talk about it. He called it synchronicity. With teams of bright, intelligent, hard-working executives scouring the globe for best practice, the chances of you finding that $e=mc^2$ before the others is not encouraging – the chance of you discovering it and your competitors doing nothing is non-existent.

The high performers

The third level is the one that at the time people will call the astoundingly high performance level – its base is the sound barrier which needs to be broken to reach the new level. When anyone breaks this kind of barrier, they will also create a loud bang that echoes through the rest of their industry or field of operation. By going through that barrier they will probably cause the reframing of the market or the technology or at least the thinking patterns by which that work goes on.

The effect may not be instantaneous. In politics the appointment of Gorbachev as the premier of the USSR heralded a new era which emerged over a period of five or so years.

In business Steven Jobs and the creation of Apple achieved a similar effect. When Steven Jobs generated his Apple II, which was sufficiently accessible to people who were not electronic or computer enthusiasts, the envelope for computing was pushed further back, whether they realized it or not, and the security of mainframe manufacturers started to come into doubt. Unusually, Jobs managed to pull off this remarkable achievement twice – the Apple Mac was also revolutionary.

The decay of high performance

Recognition and awards come after the fact because it takes time to recognize the nature of the changes which have been achieved.

Once a barrier has been broken the performance that achieved it must now fall into the second category of achievable performance. Exceptional performance decays into routine or acceptable performance.

These kinds of examples of pushing back the barriers of performance are both highly creative and highly destructive. They are the turning-points at which performance improvement of not three per cent but 300 per cent will occur. They are the reason for whole shifts in markets.

When the electrostatic plate was finally able to make a reproducible image and the Xerox process was born the printing industry could never stay the same. It tried its damnedest and switched to ignore and contain mode, but who can stop progress? When the Apple Mac was

Figure 2.6
THE DECAY OF HIGH PERFORMANCE

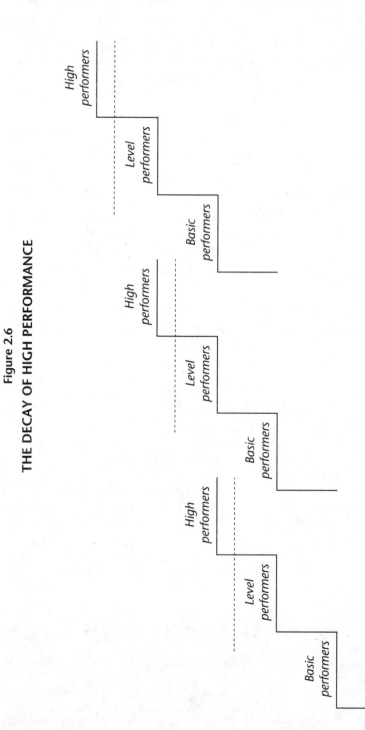

introduced the rest of the PC industry shuddered. It has taken years but they have now retooled, upgraded and are now squeezing Apple to the core. Too often, as in the printing industry, there is a fight to stay the same and predictable changes actually take years to process through the industry. Change percolates through rather than explodes through for a wide variety of reasons.

> **Time and time again it is the believers who come out on top.**

The problem for any leader who wants to work at what the scientists studying complexity at the Santa Fe Institute describe as "the edge of chaos" is that it has proved largely impossible to forecast when, where and how breakthroughs in performance will occur. Who anticipated Gorbachev's revolution? Who believed Jobs and Apple could transform the computer world? Time and time again it is the believers who come out on top. They do so because they adapt and because they accept uncertainty as a fact rather than a frightening specter on the horizon.

Notes and references

1 Quoted in Zohar, D, "Mess, wonderful mess," *Independent on Sunday*, November 12, 1995.
2 Schendler, B, "Bill Gates and Paul Allen talk," *Fortune*, October 2, 1995.
3 Quoted in Kotter, J, *Leadership*, video.
4 Lorenz, C, "Quantum leaps in a dangerous game," *Financial Times*, September 22, 1993.
5 Author interview.
6 Author interview.
7 Grove, AS, "A high-tech CEO updates his views on managing and careers," *Fortune*, September 18, 1995.
8 Phillips, A, *Terrors and Experts*, Faber & Faber, London, 1995.
9 Parker, I, "Beyond the cringe," *Independent on Sunday*, September 3, 1995.
10 Quoted in Anthony, A, "Singular white male," *The Observer*, November 26, 1995.
11 Author interview.
12 Powell, C (with Persico, J), *My American Journey*, Random House, New York, 1995.
13 Quoted in Dawkins, W, "When no cheers greet a recovery," *Financial Times*, December 1, 1995.
14 Sayles, L, Center for Creative Leadership Conference, Greensboro, NC, "New demands for leadership: responding to turbulence," January 6, 1994.

15 For a review of the theoretical literature see Milliken, FJ, "Three types of perceived uncertainty about the environment: state, effect and response," *Academy of Management Review*, vol. 12, no. 1, 1987.

16 Author interview.

17 "Productivity and the Hubble constant," *The Economist*, October 14, 1995.

18 Interview with Stuart Crainer, 1989.

19 Author interview.

20 Bleeke, J, and Ernst, D (eds), *Collaborating to Compete*, John Wiley, New York, 1993.

21 Pascale, R, Athos, A, and Goss, T, "The reinvention roller coaster," *Harvard Business Review*, November–December 1993.

22 Lewin, R, *Complexity*, JM Dent, London, 1993.

23 Grove, AS, "A high-tech CEO updates his views on managing and careers," *Fortune*, September 18, 1995.

24 Trompenaars, F, *Riding the Waves of Culture*, Nicholas Brealey, London, 1993.

25 Trompenaars, F, "Cultural factors of international management," *Financial Times Handbook of Management* (Crainer, S, ed), FT/Pitman, London, 1995.

26 Levinson, H, "Why the behemoths fell," *American Psychologist*, vol. 49, no. 5, May 1994.

27 Brilloff, A, *Unaccountable Accounting*, Harper & Row, New York, 1972.

28 "China's uncertain odds," *The Economist*, September 2, 1995.

29 "The model fund manager," *The Economist*, September 9, 1995.

30 Quoted in Huey, J, "Eisner explains everything," *Fortune*, April 1995.

31 Hodgson, P, and Hodgson, J, *Effective Meetings*, Century Business, London, 1992.

32 Quoted in Crainer, S (ed), *Financial Times Handbook of Management*, FT/Pitman, London, 1995.

33 Quoted in Crainer, S (ed), *Financial Times Handbook of Management*, FT/Pitman, London, 1995.

34 Argyris, C, *Knowledge for Action*, Jossey-Bass, San Francisco, 1993.

35 Author interview.

36 Hambrick, D, "The top management team: key to strategic success," *California Management Review*, Fall, 1987.

37 Trompenaars, F, "Cultural factors of international management," *The Financial Times Handbook of Management* (Crainer, S, ed), FT/Pitman, London, 1995.

38 Elashmawi, F and Harris, P, *Multicultural Management*, Gulf Publishing, Houston, Texas, 1993.

39 Greenwood, JT (ed), *Milestones in Aviation*, McMillan Publishing, New York, 1989, published for the Smithsonian Institution: National Air and Space Museum.

40 See Levering, R and Moskowitz, M, *One Hundred Best Companies to Work for in America*, Plume, New York, 1994.

41 Quoted in White, L, "Net prophet," *Sunday Times*, November 12, 1995.

42 Quoted in *Independent on Sunday*, August 8, 1993.

"Any company that aspires to succeed in the tougher business environment of the 1990s must first resolve a basic dilemma: success in the marketplace increasingly depends on learning, yet most people don't know how to learn. What's more, those members of the organization who many assume to be the best at learning are, in fact, not very good at it. Because many professionals are almost always successful at what they do, they rarely experience failure. And because they have rarely failed, they have never learned how to learn from failure."

CHRIS ARGYRIS
HARVARD BUSINESS SCHOOL[1]

"My job is to put the best people on the biggest opportunities and the best allocation of dollars in the right place."

JACK WELCH
CEO, GENERAL ELECTRIC[2]

THE NEW LEADERSHIP FUNDAMENTALS

* How can we embrace a culture which survives and thrives on uncertainty?

* What kind of people do we need?

* What do they need to do?

In the future white water leaders will identify productive areas of uncertainty and confusion and lead the organization into those areas in order to gain competitive (or other kinds of) advantage.

They will do so with role models that always contain some radical elements which emphasize the importance of utilizing and leveraging learning, personally and organizationally.

ROLE MODELS

The newest role of leaders is unnerving. It is like walking towards gunfire rather than seeking shelter. Leaders can no longer turn to convenient role models in search of inspiration. Yesterday's role models – whether corporate, military or political – provide lessons valuable for yesterday's leadership. In the past, most successful leaders only needed to be good at copying what a few "pathfinder" leaders had done. Innovating, thinking deeply about why they did things, and actively looking for ways to improve by learning and challenging were often unnecessary and unrewarded behaviors. It was certainly not what leaders were for.

Now, the nearest and most appropriate role models for future leaders come from unusual and universal sources, rather than the idiosyncrasies of a few pathfinders.

But, first, what can the new fundamentals of leadership be distilled down to? What does the future leader actually do and hope to achieve?

We believe that the leader's role is to identify productive areas of uncertainty and confusion and to lead the organization into those areas in order to gain competitive (or other kinds of) advantage.

We have identified two groups of people which offer some of the attitudes, approaches and perspectives white water leaders now require. We spent time seeking out the people who seem best equipped to cope in an uncertain world and make uncertainty work. We also identified the specific attitudes and skills used by successful corporate leaders. Our conclusions are far removed from the usual military and sporting role models beloved by leaders the world over. To our surprise, two groups emerged as particularly adept at handling uncertainty:

> **The newest role of leaders is unnerving. It is like walking towards gunfire rather than seeking shelter.**

- children

- experienced travelers.

But, why and, perhaps more importantly, how?

Unleashing the child

In *Repacking Your Bags*, by Richard Leider and David Shapiro, Leider tells how he, Richard 'Rocky' Kimball and another friend are on safari in the heart of Tanzania:

> "A vacation, according to the dictionary, is a 'respite from something.' This, on the other hand, is a journey into something – what Rocky calls 'The Land of I Don't Knows.' It's a rare opportunity to venture down untrodden paths, to get out from under the safety net of interpreted experience. It's an opportunity that I've really been hungering for.
>
> "Rocky says that when he crosses from the 'Land of I Know' into the 'Land of I Don't Know' that he has to attain a beginner's mind, to be non-judgmental, and to go into situations admitting that he knows nothing at all. He tries to see the people around him as neither strange nor foreign, but simply as people – his own people."[3]

In the world of white water where uncertainty reigns, we all have to escape the safety net of interpreted experience. We must move beyond. We must attain a beginner's mind and come to terms with the "foreignness" of people and situations. We have to unleash childlikeness on the challenges we now face.

The leader as child? The child as leader? It flies in the face of all traditional concepts of leadership roles and role models. Leaders, by convention, are supermen and superwomen, larger than life, strong, indomitable and all-knowing. But think about how much uncertainty children face just in the process of growing up – discovering the world around them, their strengths and weaknesses, and infinitely more.

The skills and perspectives of supermen and superwomen are ill-matched against uncertainty. Childlikeness makes business sense. Work can equal play without the bottom line being forgotten. Microsoft, for example, has proved particularly adept at harnessing the learning capabilities and energy we find in children. It may now be a huge corporation but it retains the atmosphere and the behaviors of a precocious upstart. It outwitted the field through its naïve smartness and seems determined to hang on to it. Typically, its corporate headquarters at Redmond, near Seattle, is nick-named "the campus." Consciously or unconsciously, Microsoft seeks to utilize the freewheeling, flexible, stay-up-all-night, ideas-driven atmos-phere of a college campus. The dividing lines between work and play are blurred to the point of not existing. With 16,000 employees the average age is an astonishing 31 years and its programmers are even younger – most are under 25 years old. A Microsoft employee observed in a recent article that the company "offers us the life we had in school, except we get paid to do our work. And, unlike school, we get to do the really cool stuff."[4] Microsoft is school without the homework, the uniform, or the externally imposed discipline.

> **We have to unleash childlikeness on the challenges we now face.**

"Who wants to be part of the establishment. Jeez, they're there to be overthrown, that's how the world works. You're young and estab-lish a new way of looking at things," commented Bill Gates in 1995 – when he was already a billionaire and should, by conventional wis-dom, be getting used to being part of the establishment.[5]

Of course, there is a downside. Microsoft is poor at meeting its own self-imposed deadlines – Windows 95 was more than nine months late. And we are yet to discover what happens when the pro-grammers get older. Will they suddenly become solid corporate citi-zens who come down hard on the freeflowing ideas factory or will they be too burned out to care?

In another example, we heard of a computing company which took the unusual initiative of opening a city center cybercafe. Local kids and Internet afficionados moved in and spent their time surfing while sipping an espresso. The company then asked a few of the most confident and proficient to come into the company and spend time with its senior managers showing them how to use the company's own products. Sometimes the geeks can teach the suits a great deal.

Many other companies have tried to create Microsoft's campus mentality with employees involved in a creative free for all. Most have moved away from the concept by the time they grow to a significant size – believing that a traditional approach is then more appropriate. The child is unleashed and then shepherded away to a quiet corner for a lesson in how to behave in a big corporation.

Interestingly, moviemakers are attracted to the idea of letting a childlike mind loose in the grown-up world of business or anywhere else bedeviled by orthodoxy. The film *Being There* featured Peter Sellers as an innocent gardener whose homespun wisdom won him political acclaim. Tom Hanks in *Big* was a corporate executive with a childlike passion for toys. The message was humorous, but underneath there is a more important point. We realize that children can see things as they really are. They can strip away the jargon, the complexity we have loaded onto something, and get to its heart. They ask awkward questions and are not saddled with preconceptions. They live with uncertainty all the time, but are able to cope, grow, develop and learn.

Childlikeness is not childishness – though occasionally a tantrum may be preferable to ignoring a problem. Discussing their working relationship together, David Bowie says of producer and guru figure Brian Eno: "Brian has always worked intuitively . . . creating a situation of childlikeness in the studio, which sounds glib, but it's not, it's really important, a sense of play. Brian creates an area where you aren't afraid."[6]

There is an element of this childlikeness in many successful artists and sports stars. At his peak, John McEnroe retained all of his childlike qualities. He was constantly willing to try something new, to change the tempo and his entire game was built around the speed, flexibility and intuitive judgment of his touch with the racquet on the ball. McEnroe's downside was that his childlikeness sometimes became childishness.

Practically, what lessons can children teach us? Children can handle, cope with and grow from uncertainty for a number of reasons.

Creativity

Children are naturally and instinctively creative. Contrast this with organizations which naturally and instinctively distrust creativity. In the traditional company, creative elements are cordoned off. It is risky to do the new and different. The nerds and geeks inhabit a world of their own, set apart from the mainstream. Difficult to manage, organizations choose not to manage them. The stereotype suggests that though they may have bright ideas, they have no grasp of commercial reality. Compartmentalized they can be controlled and the pernicious effects of their off-beat creativity won't infiltrate the rest of the organization.

"Creative people are often narcissistic. You need to support them. There were a large number of skeptics and it was my job to keep the skeptics at a distance –

> **That's putting whipped cream on garbage.**

both internally and on the board. A manager has to keep the wolves at the door," said one CEO we interviewed betraying the mentality of the corporate bunker.[7]

Look at what's happened with IT departments. We all know about the ridiculously huge power of technology. Corporations know about it. Executives know about it – some even use it. Yet, evidence suggests that though corporations bankroll investment in IT it has generally failed to reap significant benefits in corporate effectiveness and performance. The geeks and nerds remain outside the corporate noose of control or understanding.

As a result, corporations are now desperately trying to extract the most from their investment in IT. According to research in the USA, organizations are set to invest a massive $40 billion in reengineering their information systems in 1997. Acerbically, William Wheeler of Coopers & Lybrand, told *Fortune* magazine: "That's putting whipped cream on garbage."[8]

Managers often have only a limited understanding of what IT can do for their organization. They have a broad sympathy with investing in high technology, but have a restricted view of its practical power and business advantage. For example, a survey by

Henley Management College of more than 200 chief executives, directors and other senior managers found that many top managers just did not understand the strategic importance of IT.[9]

If asked, it is likely that a great many managers would identify the benefits of IT in simple cost terms. IT reduces an organization's staff count, therefore it saves money. (The same goes for reengineering.) As Harvard's Shoshana Zuboff points out in her book, *In the Age of the Smart Machine*, companies have regarded IT as a means of reducing staff numbers through the automation of their jobs.[10] The trouble is that the jobs which have been automated out of existence are often those which involve direct contact with customers. Zuboff argues that instead of automating tasks, IT's job should be to "informate" people – an ungainly, but apposite word combining inform and educate. By regarding IT as a numbers and cost-cutting mechanism organizations are failing to optimize its full potential which goes far beyond cost reduction.

> **Without creative people, the organization will grind to a halt.**

IT has proved next to impossible to manage. Why? One of the reasons must be that many of those in IT functions are stereotypical techno-lovers. Techno-phobe executives find it hard to deal with them and communicate with them, regarding their management as close to impossible. The IT experts remain largely marginalized and their creativity often has little impact, or far less impact than it should, if the organization is to reap the full IT benefits.

Once upon a time, organizations could – and did – sideline their creatives and get on with the real business of running the company. Not now. Creativity has to be part of everyone's job. Cordoning off a vital source of creativity – and potential competitive advantage – is no longer an alternative. Instead, creativity has to be instilled into the lifeblood of the organization. Without creative people, the organization will grind to a halt.

Absorbing stimuli

Children move easily from one activity to another. One minute they are happily contemplating a jigsaw, the next they are painting. They take in different stimuli effortlessly. They move on quickly without letting go of what they have just learned.

As we have seen, executives also jump from one job to another, phone call to video conference, sales call to board meeting. The trouble is that while they are adept at taking in stimuli, they are poor at learning from it so that it can be used at a later date. They go through a wide range of experiences and emotions every day of the week and then go home to start afresh on the next day. They are continually letting go of what they have just learned and experienced.

Accepting no right way

Children do not know there is a right way to do anything. This is a positive advantage – for children, and for corporations (though not necessarily for parents). They seek out different methods, however unusual or different. They are not handicapped by the way things have always been done, the way something should be done or the way used by a particular individual.

Children not only think differently. Allied to this is their innocence – they think the best of people; executives perpetually fear the worst. "Most people can do something better than the current role they are in," said one of the executives we interviewed, but such views are often not widely held or translated into practice.

Think what you would do if you were charged with introducing a new brand of car into the country. Your budget is large (but minuscule compared to Ford's or GM's) and your target is to capture a mere 1 per cent of the car market. The downside is that you are competing against the automotive giants. Probably you would spend heavily on advertising and set up dealerships. You would highlight some differentiation in your product and target a particular area. Start with the West Coast, say California, and then move on.

But if you accept no right way and start asking questions you may do things very differently indeed. Taiwanese company Daewoo launched itself in the UK in 1995. Its cars are based on old GM designs. Its approach has got around this apparent handicap. It has taken the dealers out of the equation. It has no network of franchisees each taking their commission. Instead you can go into a chain of bicycle and automotive parts stores and buy a Daewoo. The store chain doesn't even take a commission – it benefits from the extra customers. Daewoo's display has two or three cars and three staff. In addition, there are interactive multimedia stations and a child activity center. Who said cars have to be sold in the way they always have been sold? It is different and it works. Daewoo sold 12,000 cars in the first eight months – 0.9 per cent of the UK market and is well ahead on its target of 1 per cent by 1997.

If we accept there is no single right way, we have to try out new ways. In a corporate context, seeking out new approaches can take on apparently bizarre forms. British writer David Whyte has established a novel niche market. His book, *The Heart Aroused: Poetry and the Preservation of the Soul in Corporate America*, is a surprise bestseller.[11] Whyte is employed by multinationals such as AT&T, Boeing and Arthur Andersen to enhance creativity and simply to awaken executives to other sources of ideas and value. He reads poetry to them. Some fall asleep, some are inspired. Indeed, Whyte is such an inspiration that one high-ranking AT&T executive left the company having been awakened to the meaninglessness of his job.

British Airways has its own corporate jester. His job is to ask questions, to appear unannounced at meetings and stir up debate. "A big company is a bit like a medieval court where the king can do no wrong. No one questions the king or the senior courtiers. But if you are not careful this can lead you down into the abyss," explains the current corporate jester, Paul Birch. "Any highly successful business – such as BA – is in danger of over-confidence. Success is probably the most dangerous time. You carry on doing things you know have made you successful while the world changes around you."[12] Being described by others as the corporate jester is probably the ultimate career-limiting perception. But deliberately setting up a process to challenge and stir things up might just work.

Learning

There is a famous observation that it is the mouse which teaches the kitten how to catch mice and not the mother cat.[13] As the mice become tougher to catch, so the kitten learns how to catch tougher mice. The point is that children, or kittens, progressively learn by playing and play by learning. The lessons for corporations is that when learning is play it is highly effective – look at Microsoft. When learning is work it is ineffective – look at all the executives "forced" to go on training courses. The learning which sticks has a joy of discovery, playfulness. Many executives have been to brainstorming seminars where an atmosphere of deliberate playfulness often stimulates high levels of executive learning for an hour or so. Corporations of the future are going to need to find ways to extend that hour to cover the entire working day.

Adaptability

"For me the difficult part is when you come to that sense of realizing that it isn't going to work. You are putting all this effort in and you come to the point when you realize you're wasting your time, bashing your head against a brick wall. The other thing is overcoming frustration. I want to see it happen and I want results and people expect to see it happen quickly and I knew that if we didn't get results I wouldn't be long there. Learning to cope with the frustration I found difficult. That was a learning point for me. Being big enough to say take your time it will come, don't get frustrated, don't get exasperated and don't get burned out. There have been times in the last two years when I have felt as if I am on a slippery slope to mental and physical exhaustion," said one executive we interviewed who was embroiled in a program of radical change.

Children are good at dealing with the unknown and unexpected. If something unusual occurs they attempt to make sense of it, to understand. Somewhere along the line we have lost this precious curiosity. "When you're a kid and you're learning it's okay because a lot of things are confusing and you persevere with it," says Bill Gates.[14] Children persist at learning in a way which is difficult to achieve in an organization full of truculent and ambitious adults ready to make you seem a fool if you've failed or come up with a crazy idea. After all, getting it wrong may cost you your job.

Leaders as travelers

True leaders are also like experienced travelers. Travelers are romantic figures. We are attracted to the idea of the quest, struggling against the odds, overcoming the might of nature. *In Search of Excellence* was a great title because it suggested a quest – in fact, a more proper description of the book would be "Here is our current view of excellence."

We like the idea of the quest so much that we send managers on outdoor training exercises. We want to turn them into explorers and adventurers, often without thinking why.

Of course, the managers of the late 1990s are travelers, skipping from one airport to another, time zone to time zone. They travel, but are they true travelers? Too often they are mere passengers. And, in the new reality who wants passengers?

As you become more adventurous it is notable that excitement and uncertainty increases. Check on our scale in figure 3.1 where you think your preference for uncertainty puts you.

The **couch potato** settles for the unexciting security of remaining stationary on the couch with a pizza and the channel changer. Next up the scale comes the **spectator** – some excitement, but a great deal of certainty and no direct involvement in the action; the **passenger** is part of the journey although not contributing to choices made about direction and speed. Moving up the scale towards maximum excitement and maximum uncertainty the **traveler** becomes the **explorer** who can become the **adventurer**. It is noticeable that as excitement and uncertainty increase so, for the most part, does involvement.

> **True leaders are also like experienced travelers.**

But, what is it that experienced travelers do which we are seeking to emulate?

Figure 3.1
THE ADVENTURER SCALE

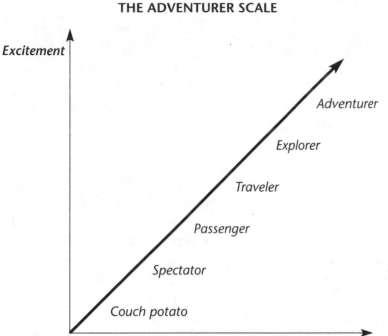

Focus on the quest

Experienced travelers combine focus on their particular quest with a pragmatic realization that there are a multitude of ways of getting there. They take the obscure byways and are entertained and educated by diversions, without losing sight of why they are there in the first place. They combine focus on given objectives with a flexibility to explore the unexpected byways. Competitive advantage comes from going off the beaten track and moving to an area of uncertainty.

"I am good at organizational jigsaws. I am always building the plan and I can see a long time ahead and I don't care what it takes to develop the right people, I think I am working towards that plan," said one executive. "Evolution is not revolutionary. Because of that I am always building. I don't care what level, whether it is the cleaner or whoever, it is a question of talent. I like to think that I'm juggling it to fit the grand picture. I suppose the weakness is that people might accuse me of being slow to react to new situations because I am a thinker. I sit back and think of the problem, all its permutations and weigh them up mentally. I have an idea and bounce it off several people."[15]

Competitive advantage comes from going off the beaten track and moving to an area of uncertainty.

This pragmatic interpretation of the quest has important implications for corporate missions. Instead of being fixed and unvarying "solutions," white water leaders regard missions as continually evolving. "You can subtly switch the message," said one executive we interviewed. "The mission we had previously was to become a world class service organization. You know of the emphasis on service in the organization. Now with the current mission we are still providing world class service but effectively the whole organization is providing world class support to our customers of which we are part. It is a subtle choice of words but they enable you in a credible way to add on all the other things. I have changed how we are organized so it is linked to a new concept of what we are trying to do. I don't think you can do anything other than keep showing a message, keep talking about it with people, finding out what it is they worry about in this new situation."[16]

Take risks to learn and achieve

In order to reach their destination, especially one they have never traveled to before, the best travelers take risks to learn and achieve.

White water leaders regard missions as continually evolving.

They are open to experience – their own and that of others – and can adapt to unforeseen circumstances.

Planes, trains and automobiles are often delayed and sometimes take you where you don't want to go. Experienced travelers shrug their shoulders and change their behavior and expectations to meet the new demands of the situation. Remember the movie, *Planes, Trains and Automobiles* with John Candy and Steve Martin? The perennially unsuccessful and apparently clueless John Candy character was a far better traveler than the suave and sophisticated character played by Steve Martin.

Understand and play the system

They are like fish in water.[17] Some people move through the system effortlessly – others get gridlocked and struggle with the constraints and distractions. Travelers take it for granted that they can, and do, move through the organization easily and swiftly. Achieving agreement from people and getting clearance for projects are minor hindrances rather than weighty obstacles to reaching their goals.

> **Difference, then, needs to be encouraged and understood.**

This is often an unconscious skill. Travelers do it so well they often don't realize what they are doing. It is akin to a hurdler reaching his or her peak – automatically they take the right number of strides between hurdles. They don't need to think or alter their stride pattern. It is natural and effective.

By talking to people, approaching allies in the right way at the right time, knowing how the system works, travelers are able to work around a great deal of delaying bureaucracy and corporate politics to concentrate on action. They seem at ease in the corporate waters and, additionally, are acutely aware of which environment – which waters – they operate most effectively in.

Respect cultural differences and perspectives

Travelers are sensitive to cultural differences and perspectives. They realize that if we were all the same – clones of each other – the world would be a boring uncreative place. But difference also produces difficulty because we do not all think, act and react the same way to the same stimuli. Difference, then, needs to be encouraged and understood.

Thrive on discovery

Experienced travelers are prepared to go where others haven't gone before. They seek out challenges. "Some people have asked me why I am doing this. It's the excitement that goes with change. I can already feel the juices of adventure building up," said Bill Cockburn on his appointment as chief executive of the UK retailing chain WH Smith.[18] After 34 years with the UK's Post Office, Cockburn still relished the chance to explore new territory.

Are you seeking out the big surprises?

Or listen to Nobel laureate Seamus Heaney on writing poetry: "Unless a poem surprises you a little bit, some little gate is opened by the words within themselves, then the poem could be perfectly okay, but it won't hold you forever. There has to be a little surprise, a big surprise is even better, but a little surprise will do. It is to do with the unforeseen being recognized as completely true."[19] Are you seeking out the big surprises?

Use a combination of hard factual data and inner sense

Travelers use maps, compass, timetables, but also have an inner sense of where to go, what to do and how to behave. When all other sources of information fail, they trust their instinct to know what to do.

Enrich perspectives through experiences

They learn through each and every experience. No matter how many times experienced travelers have followed a particular route, they are always on the look out for the new or unexpected.

Captain Scott O'Grady came to world attention in 1995 when for a week in June he was missing in Bosnia. Listen to O'Grady on the joy of flying: "Flying is what I do and I hadn't been up for two weeks. I'd logged about 800 hours in F-16s, and the plane still thrilled me as much as it had the first time four years before. The most experienced F-16 pilots learn something new each time out."[20]

Feel comfortable traveling alone or in groups

Experienced travelers support each other, offer ideas and suggestions, but have the confidence to travel alone if need be. They make good companions, but are not afraid of their own company.

Maximize opportunities

With a few hours to kill after missing a connecting flight they do something, rather than hanging around cursing their misfortune. They regard lost time as a gift rather than a waste. They make the most of learning opportunities at every turn, no matter where they are and what they are doing.

Remain constantly on the move

Travelers are restless. CK Prahalad makes a telling comparison between CNN and CBS. CNN has very little bureaucracy, makes most of its big decisions on the run, and spends less in 24 hours than CBS spends in one hour for apparently equivalent news coverage. The people at CNN are powerful because they keep moving, they don't use fixed authority, they appear to invent it each time afresh. It is very tiring, and people do get burned out, but it is also tremendously competitive to other TV news systems.

The conclusion? Managers should always be seeking an upgrade to experienced traveler class.

LEVERAGING ORGANIZATIONAL LEARNING

Children and experienced travelers share a number of things in common. Both are adaptable and flexible. Most importantly, however, they are constantly learning. For them, everything is an opportunity for learning whether it is a new country, a different paintbrush or meeting new people.

If we are to move towards uncertainty, leveraging learning is a corporate and personal imperative no matter what your business, no matter what your aspirations, no matter what your status or skills. Learning is the driving force behind future leaders and the organizations of the future. And learning is the gateway to the other skills of white water leadership.

"The rate at which organizations learn may become the only sustainable source of competitive advantage," says Ray Stata of Analog Devices.[21] The company with a culture geared to and driven by learning may (remember there are no certainties) have a headstart in the hyper-competitive future. The importance of learning more about how, why and when can no longer be understated or put to one side.

In a 1988 article, Arie de Geus, a former planning director at Shell, showed that one-third of *Fortune 500* industrial companies listed in 1970 had disappeared by 1983. The average corporate survival rate for large companies in the early 1980s was only about half as long as the life of a human being. A look at *Fortune* or virtually any other listing provides speedy evidence of the turbulence at work. Last year's loss-makers included Time Warner, Tyson Foods, Comcast Corporation, Worldcom and Salomon. It is an international phenomenon. Typically, 43 companies ranked in the UK's top 500 listing left the list in 1995, possibly never to reappear.

However, a few organizations were identified by de Geus which had survived for 75 years or more. De Geus suggested that the key to their longevity was their ability to conduct "experiments in the margin." They were always looking for new business opportunities which continually challenged the organization to grow and learn.[22]

Corning Glass has been similarly dynamic – it has continually taken in and nurtured start-ups so that they can later be spun off as separate companies.[23] This ability to grow (although not necessarily in size) and to learn has become the backbone of any organization wishing to survive and prosper in changing and turbulent markets.

We would hazard a confident guess that what links the declining fortunes of these disparate groups boils down to a breakdown of learning. They were either too busy learning about yesterday to begin learning about tomorrow, or regarded learning as something you do at school, not in a modern corporation.

> **The learning organization encapsulates a whole series of complex and messy processes into a single easy-sounding phrase.**

Skeptics will argue that the interest in improving learning is similar to the interest in improving quality which was very attractive five years earlier. Sadly, there is mounting evidence that more than half of all quality initiatives fail within two years.[24] Will the learning organization prove similarly disappointing? Part of the problem is that the faddish popularity of the term "learning organization" gives the impression that you can install a learning organization as easily as you can install a new piece of equipment. As a latest fad, the learning organization disappoints because it doesn't come in turnkey form. The learning organization is not an end state – a product. In reality the learning organization is not a product, but a process. In fact, the learning organization encapsulates a whole series of complex and messy processes into a single easy-sounding phrase.

This messiness means that useful definitions of the learning organization are elusive. In *The Learning Company*, Mike Pedler, John Burgoyne and Tom Boydell say it is "an organization that facilitates the learning of all its members and continuously transforms itself."[25] A CEO we worked with summed up this need: "I don't just want my managers to do a few things differently now; I want them continually to be different in the future."[26]

Continual experimentation and adaptation to a changing set of circumstances is not a new idea. As we have seen, the decline and failure of many household names and famous industries across the world demonstrates that because you were once very good doesn't mean you will always be good. The rapid rise, and fall, of companies has shown that one good idea will get you going, but a succession of good ideas is needed to keep you in business. This applies to organizations and to each and every individual within them. Learning is the only sustainable source of such inspiration.

Not only that. Learning dynamically bridges the divide between the organization and the individual. The various definitions struggle to reconcile the learning of individuals and the concept of organizational learning. The best known champion of the concept and practice of the learning organization is Peter Senge from the Massachusetts Institute of Technology (MIT). In his book *The Fifth Discipline* (and the subsequent *Fifth Discipline Fieldbook*[27]), Senge suggests that there are five components of a learning organization.

> **The rapid rise, and fall, of companies has shown that one good idea will get you going, but a succession of good ideas is needed to keep you in business.**

1 **Systems thinking** – using the concept of systems archetypes, managers can spot repetitive patterns, such as the way certain kinds of problems persist, or the way systems have their own built-in limits to growth.

2 **Personal mastery** – this idea is grounded in the familiar competencies and skills associated with management, but also includes spiritual growth – opening oneself up to a progressively deeper reality – and living life from a creative rather than a reactive viewpoint. This discipline involves two underlying movements – continually learning how to see current reality more clearly – and the ensuing gap between vision and reality produces the creative tension from which learning arises.

3 **Mental models** – this essentially deals with the organization's driving and fundamental values and principles. Senge alerts managers to the power of patterns of thinking at the organizational level and the importance of non-defensive inquiry into the nature of these patterns.

4 **Shared vision** – Senge stresses the importance of co-creation and argues that shared vision can only be built on personal vision. He claims that shared vision is present when the task that follows from the vision is no longer seen by the team members as separate from the self.

5 **Team learning** – the discipline of team learning involves two practices: dialog and discussion. The former is characterized by its exploratory nature, the latter by the opposite process of narrowing down the field to the best alternative for the decisions that need to be made. The two are mutually complementary, but the benefits of combining them only come from having previously separated them. Most teams lack the ability to distinguish between the two and to move consciously between them.[28]

There is a perennial danger of allowing the concept to overtake the reality. Academic definitions cannot be instantly applied in the real world. As a result, managers need to promote learning so that it gradually emerges as a key part of an organization's culture. Being convinced of the merits of the learning organization is not usually a matter of dramatic conversion.

Former chairman of car maker Rover, Sir Graham Day, describes the evolution of his realization:

> "During the mid-1980s a number of us, particularly in manufacturing business, somewhat belatedly became aware that our international competitiveness was being negatively impacted by the static knowledge and skills of our people at all levels. It was a small but critical step to translate this understanding into programs to lift knowledge and skills on a continuing basis. . . . Rover's need to establish what we now term a learning organization came from the imperative to secure the

company's survival. Now it contributes to Rover's increasing competitiveness and value as a business."[29]

Ironically, it is fear of failure – or actual failure – which often kickstarts enthusiasm for learning. Alternatively, it may be a change of chief executive, an obvious challenge in the marketplace, or a new opportunity posed by technology. UK software company Logica hit difficulties at the beginning of the 1990s. A new chairman was brought in who set about fundamental changes, rooting out people "who couldn't learn to think in different ways."[30]

> **While learning can now be shown to be a significant component of getting ahead, continuous learning appears to be an even more significant part of staying ahead.**

Learning to think in different ways works – whether it is inspired by a corporate jester, a poet or a new CEO. Most people appear to like learning and find difference attractive and stimulating. It makes them feel better, and it encourages them to come to work, and to work better at work. The difficulty in sustaining this style of organization is found when it has been imposed from above rather as a passing fad or fashion. In this case then, like fashion, the learning organization will last until the next fad comes along.

While learning can now be shown to be a significant component of getting ahead, continuous learning appears to be an even more significant part of staying ahead. But that is often a complex process. As Paul Turner, director of personnel for credit and operations at TSB (a UK bank recently merged with Lloyds) says:

> **"Models of a learning organization are worthless, unless you are prepared to understand the intricacies and complexity of that organization. Changing our culture from that of a traditional bank has meant an acceptance that we can all change. It has been a challenge to simplify the processes and also recognize that implementation requires more sophistication than was needed in the past."**[31]

Tackling the entire organization as a single unit may appear very daunting. Theresa Barnett, deputy principal of the TSB Bank's staff college, says: "You don't have to convert the whole company in one go, you can develop smaller cells of learning activity and then link those cells together." Of course, just because you have split up the organization into a series of smaller learning units does not mean that the workload is any less or that the challenge to adapt to a new way of thinking is reduced. "To ask department A and department B to learn from each other is a big leap, but once they have developed their learning abilities in cells, then it is easier to link these interactively together. But it takes a lot of work to connect across a complexity of learning departments – especially in a large organization," says Barnett.[32]

The mechanics of creation are complex, but creating the learning organization is not a dereliction of corporate duty. The onus is not simply passed down to the employee. Instead, it is an expansion of responsibility and of trust that includes everyone in the organization. Managing these two elements, critically, requires leadership and highly sophisticated leaders.

Organizationally, leveraging learning requires, at a minimum, two critical activities:

● encouraging learning on and from the job

● creating careers built round learning.

Encouraging learning on and from the job

If an organization is to become truly committed to learning it must first ensure that people are put in positions where they can – and do – learn from their jobs. Not just occasionally, but continually.

We have worked with effective executives to find out how they have learned, grown and changed. Many of them told us that the experiences which taught them the most were on the job, with the good and bad bosses they had had, with the hardships they had endured. Course work, while important, was only a small part of their success.[33]

People learn on the job. Experience is important – but has to be proactively learned from rather than simply and superficially experi-

If an organization is to become truly committed to learning it must first ensure that people are put in positions where they can – and do – learn from their jobs. Not just occasionally, but continually.

enced. We have to be explorers, not spectators. Managerial potential used to be considered as the ability to "get on" or get along in the organization, the ability to lubricate the wheels of corporate culture. It was about power and politics as much as anything else. Organizations are now beginning to see that potential is as much the ability to learn, grow and change, while performance is a separate dimension.

To compete effectively, organizations have begun consciously to use job assignments to develop two groups of managers. One group, currently the recipient of most developmental opportunities, is the high potential managers, those likely to become future leaders of the organization. The second group, the organization's solid citizens, comprises the bulk of managerial talent in large organizations. But as organizations become flatter and these technical/functional managers plateau at earlier ages, organizations need to use on-the-job development to keep them challenged as well. Using job assignments strategically to match the developmental needs of the individual and the business will have positive benefits for the organization.

The idea that one learns from experience is neither novel nor a revelation.[34] In the past several years organizations have started looking at the types of experiences available for developing future leaders. This is an outgrowth of a rediscovery that experience is an invaluable, if not the best, teacher of leadership.

There is a need to understand the types of experiences from which people tend to learn; to understand the types of learning that result from various experiences, targeting specific experiences as developmental opportunities and in turn practicing good stewardship of those opportunities; and to help candidates learn from developmental experiences with coaching both prior to and after the experience.

In the *Lessons of Experience* and *Glass Ceiling* research, job assignments – fixing broken businesses, moving from line to staff jobs, starting new businesses, being on a special project or task force, or managing large scale and scope – were most often mentioned as triggers for learning, growth and change.

Executives reported significant learning experiences stemming from hardships and learning from other people, both the revered and the hated, mostly bosses in their past. But when closely scrutinized, the greatest point of developmental leverage involves the assignments an organization has to offer.

It was found that there are different challenges involved in each assignment type. Fixing a business had different leadership challenges from starting a business. And so, different types of assignments were found to teach different lessons. For example, starting a new business tends to teach standing alone, being in charge, discovering what one really wants to do, getting cooperation from people one has no control over and understanding what makes other people tick. Special projects and task force assignments, on the other hand, teach very different lessons of comfort with uncertainty, knowing how to work with executives and how they think, and negotiation skills.

As the developmental potential of the job increases (for example, it has many elements that are new or there are unfamiliar skills to be applied) the risk to the business (the risk of failure resulting in lost time, money, productivity, etc.) likewise increases. Since most businesses operate in a risk-averse or at best in a balanced risk-taking stance, many potential developmental assignments go to candidates who can already do what is required to get the job done. For example, if there are major problems at one of the company's plants someone will be sent who has fixed things before. This practice often results in an organization developing a cadre of single-experience leaders – leaders who know how to fix things but not how to run a smoothly operating business. When there are no longer those situations facing the organization, the single-experience leader becomes obsolete, a loss for the organization as well as the individual.

A more complete determination of the developmental potential of an assignment then rests with evaluating the abilities and track record of the candidate against the types of learning likely from that assignment. In other words, the developmental potential of the job changes given the candidate for the job. Obviously for a candidate who can already do the job there is little or no potential for further development. And for someone who cannot, the developmental potential and concomitant risk to the business is very high. So organizations have to provide support for development via coaching, counseling and mentoring. There are some important caveats to using assignments for development:

- individuals who are chosen for a developmental assignment ought to be told why they are getting the assignment. Furthermore, some support system ought to be put in place;

- developmental moves won't fix every weakness nor will they build leadership in everyone;

- most organizations don't have enough big assignments to develop all the leaders they'll need in the future. But there are ways to develop people that don't involve sending them to start an operation in Warsaw, Poland, or to shut down a factory in Tanzania. Developing them in place by providing additional (and often targeted) responsibilities can provide development.[35]

Every assignment is potentially developmental for someone. But a critical step in the process is to involve the target of development – the individual – in the process.

Creating careers built around learning

Look at how our careers develop. In the first place, we watch the corporate video or attend an induction program to know the basics of what is expected of us: the corporate values and behavior. Then, we go up through the first level of performance and are taught the essential things to survive and prosper in that business – perhaps it is selling, perhaps it is computing, perhaps it is accounting. Whatever it is we are given the basic rules. Master marketing and you will progress.

Then, if we are very good, we move into a second layer where we can start to adapt some of the things we have been taught to local circumstances. But, if we come up against something we really don't know, our best way of dealing with it is to go and ask someone who does know to help us enhance our knowledge.

During this process, the developing executive is highly conscious of his or her vulnerability. As we have seen, learning involves taking a risk and taking risks makes us vulnerable. People are afraid to make themselves more vulnerable, to expose themselves to potential loss of face, loss of

> **Executives master the business equivalent of the slam dunk and keep doing it.**

opportunity or simply loss. As a result, the executives develop what has been accurately labeled a myth of mastery. By steering clear of trouble spots, situations which make them vulnerable, executives begin to believe that they are invincible. In their own minds they are, in Tom Wolfe's phrase, "Masters of the Universe."

In turn, this provides a formula for executive progression. The people who reach the top are high performers who don't make mistakes. They get it right, but sacrifice things to get it right. They are often better at a particular skill than the people who work for them. They are perfectionists with high IQs who don't tolerate dips in performance. They are also superstitious – believing that if they do what they've always done, things will come right.

As an adjunct to the myth of mastery, executives are often promoted because they are good technically, not because they are good with people. Technical skills – whether they are marketing, finance or technology – are measurable and there for all to see. Executives master the business equivalent of the slam dunk and keep doing it.

Contrast this with managing people, which despite the best efforts of academics, remains steadfastly immeasurable. And, if it can't be measured it tends to be neglected or overlooked. Again and again, talking to CEOs it becomes clear that managing people is the source of their greatest frustration and often their greatest area of ignorance. Ask them to think of a major failure and they often select a people-related one. "I have had three or four subordinates that I should have fired much earlier in the game than I did," recalled the President of one corporation. "I was trying to fix and be fair. In a couple of cases, I did fire and in a couple they lingered and I never got rid of them. I think I was being too humane and focused on individual needs to the detriment of the organization. One I fired too quickly – that was probably unfair. I also covered for a drunk."[36]

People may be a company's greatest asset but the ability to manage, motivate or simply get on with them is often not regarded as important in an executive's career development. Managers who know a corporation's financial systems in intricate detail progress up the hierarchy. So, too, do executives who know the tools and techniques of marketing or who understand the production process.

After they are promoted it becomes clear that they are ill-prepared for their new job. Their flaws are there for all to see. They may be insensitive or aloof, but as these characteristics have never been truly tested at the lower level they never became apparent until now when it is probably too late to do very much about them.

Given the standard career progression it is little wonder that senior executives are highly proficient until it comes to dealing with people. Think of how the standard executive career unfolds (and, even when careers are more insecure than ever before, this pattern still generally holds true). There are three leaps in the development of most people's careers. Their first supervisory experience teaches them that it's more than just the technical aspects of the job – people are a problem.

Then, at mid-levels in most people's careers, they are faced with the first leadership paradox. Suddenly, technical mastery of a given area isn't enough because the people who work for you will know more about a particular area than you do. Learning to direct and motivate people who often do not want you to be their leader becomes a necessary skill. You also need to learn to be a creative problem solver, sorting the strategic from the tactical and the urgent from the non-urgent.

The toughest transition is to become a generalist, a general manager. John Kotter, in *The General Managers*, suggests that it takes 20 years to become one.[37] At this level, you are supposed to be strategic and able to deal with ambiguity. Here there are no right or wrong answers but only good, better, and best answers. It is also at this level that one has the potential to understand higher order people skills like: I can't do this job well by myself, I need the team to get it done.[38] And so, the skills that propel executives up the ladder are not the leadership skills and perspectives needed for making it to the top (see Figure 3.1). Higher order people skills, strategic skills and the skills necessary to deal with uncertainty are needed. Not unimportant in this process is the notion that you are exposed to these skills every day – on the job. So the trick is to be open to learning on a daily basis. For individuals this involves taking risks and not being afraid of getting things wrong. For organizations this involves selecting individuals who are learners and making the most of the experiences available for learning.

Figure 3.1
LEADERSHIP LEAPS[39]

General manager
- be strategic
- deal with ambiguity
- "I can't do this job all by myself – I need help from the team"

Managing managers (mid-level)
- give up technical mastery
- direct and motivate
- creative problem-solving

First supervisory experience
- people are a problem

LEVERAGING PERSONAL LEARNING

Learners are special because they use experience to grow and change. Those organizations that can find the learners will have the competitive advantage in the marketplace. In the final analysis, those organizations can put people in over their heads and as they master certain skills they become high performers. They can be stretched again and again by providing other challenging assignments. Each time they become learners again. As they master one assignment they become high performers, then learners, then high performers, and so on. This does not make the glass half empty but wide open – in the true learning organization, everyone can, and should, be a learner.

Yet, nowhere is the divide between the needs and aspirations of the company and those of its employees more blurred than in discussing learning. Leveraging learning requires the constant addition and evaluation of new organizational and individual skills. People tend to have no real comprehension of the type of commitment it requires to build such an organization. The classic leadership roles of making key decisions and setting direction are inappropriate, as they reinforce attention onto short-term events and, when there is a crisis, place their faith in the leader's charisma.

The learning organization needs leaders who will act as teachers, designers and stewards. There are different skills to be deployed too: challenging mental models, building shared visions, and encouraging more people to think about the entire system rather than just their part of it.

> **In the true learning organization, everyone can, and should, be a learner.**

In *The Learning Company*,[40] Pedler and his co-authors identify a series of characteristics which they argue are significant in creating the learning environment. They include:

- encouraging a much wider debate on strategy and policy formation;

- creating an environment where tensions are welcomed as they can precede creative solutions to problems that were previously seen as "win–lose" resolutions of difficulties;

- "informating" (as Shoshana Zubofff suggested earlier), that is, using information technology to inform and empower the many rather than the few;

- exchanging information – getting closer to internal and external customers and suppliers;

- using the people who meet external customers to bring back useful information about needs and opportunities;

- collaborating rather than competing and making internal and external best practice comparisons;

- encouraging self-development opportunities for everyone in the organization. Individuals are encouraged to take responsibility for their own learning and development.

New skills and perspectives require new leaders – or old leaders who are brave and resilient enough to make the break. "In the simplest sense, a learning organization is a group of people who are continually enhancing their capability to create their future," says Peter Senge. "The traditional meaning of the word *learning* is much deeper than just *taking information in*. It is about changing individuals so that they produce results they care about, accomplish things that are important to them."[41]

Leveraging learning provides a multitude of individual challenges. Leaders must:

- learn how to describe learning

- break the sense of entitlement

- overcome fear

- surrender control.

Describing learning

If learning is so important, why is it often regarded as ephemeral, lacking the hard edge of commercial reality? Partly because managers are seldom very good at describing learning. For an organism that has developed and survived primarily because it is able to learn more effectively than its rival animals on the planet, humans are surprisingly resilient to recognizing they have learned or nurturing the ability to talk about it.

If executives cannot express their needs, aspirations and current state in terms of learning, how can they develop? Most executives are rendered inarticulate at the very mention of learning. Get them on the latest business plan, the launch of a new product and they can be as fluent as you could wish. Ask them what they learned and they dry up. And that is asking them to analyze the past. When you then ask what they are going to learn in the future most have even more difficulty. But ask them about what problems they are having and approaches they might take, suddenly you have applied learning.

Over several years we have been running year-long programs based on the concept of action learning in which managers have to take responsibility for their own learning (as well as working on projects, giving each other feedback, attending classes and auditing their own skills). At the start of the program, the participants are asked to draw up a learning plan for themselves. From time to time during the year they review their learning plans. They often have difficulty in writing their plans in the first place and some way through the year they frequently realize that what they wrote in January was not what they really needed to learn at all. We believe this lack of skill at recognizing, describing and monitoring our own learning is another of those instincts that we unfortunately acquired at an early age.

> **If learning is so important, why is it often regarded as ephemeral, lacking the hard edge of commercial reality?**

Think what you ask your children when they return home from school. In one form or another, you ask: "What did you learn today?" Inevitably, they continue munching on their cheeseburger and say "Oh, not much." After a while the parent is discouraged from asking about the learning. And so, instead of the celebration of learning that our modern organizations require, learning becomes an issue that is put out of mind, ignored until a teacher's report, an exam or some other standardized test is on the horizon.

So why doesn't the child tell its parents what it has learned? Any child would describe the intricate details of a new toy. Part of the problem is that compared with describing a toy – which has size, shape, color, purpose and offers the opportunity for comparisons with friends – learning is much harder to describe. At schools, once children have gotten beyond the stage of simple acquisition of facts (capital cities, etc.) learning does not appear to occur in a continuous stream. Perhaps the learning curve is too smooth – it needs to be more jagged. The child may go for weeks before something becomes clear – a concept in math, variations on how to construct a sentence, how to catch a ball down low.

The participants in our self-managed development programs thought they knew what they wanted to learn, but as the result of learning on the program and with the passage of time, they came to realize that they had learned something extra. Because they had not understood enough about their own learning techniques, they were unable to describe what that would be at the start of the program. They didn't know that they didn't know, so they couldn't predict what they might know.

In both cases the learning came slower and was harder to describe than the working mechanism of a toy. We only really feel that the learning light bulb has been switched on when pieces of data and skill which were previously disparate are now chunked together in a way that makes sense.

The message must be that managers of the future will need to be at least as fluent about learning as they are about their financial planning systems and should value learning above all.

Breaking the sense of entitlement

There have been thousands of books on what it takes to succeed in business. Many more will appear this year. Some are riveting reading, all the more compulsive because they encourage and sustain an idealistic view of what life is like at the top. If we read the books and the magazine profiles, we imagine CEOs looking out over their corporate domain apparently secure in the

> **They didn't know that they didn't know, so they couldn't predict what they might know.**

knowledge of their personal strengths and corporate power. They are highly adept at playing to their strengths and sidestepping or delegating their weaknesses. They excel at looking good at least partly because looking bad is not on their agenda. "There is no such thing as a leader without a big dose of self-confidence," commented one corporate president. "Most problems I thought I could solve. It was only a matter of time."[42]

Partly thanks to media stereotyping and brash confidence, to many executives the chief executive's office (not the job) is the promised land. Here, you can gaze into the distance thinking what you've achieved. Things happen around you, effortlessly. This is real power. And real power is what we are interested in.

The reality is different. Chief executives are not as secure as their appearance may suggest. Take a random sample. During a single winter week, *Fortune* reported that several "CEO 'retirements' offered stark evidence of the seismic shift occurring in the governance of American corporations."[43]

"The more successful one becomes, the higher one's occupational self-esteem. The higher one rises in an organization, the more self-confidence one is likely to develop about one's proficiency and one's roles. Concomitantly, the higher one rises, the less supervision one is likely to have. The combination of these factors frequently gives rise to . . . overconfidence and a sense of entitlement. That, in turn, leads to denial of those realities that threaten the inflated self-image and to contempt for other individuals and organizations. It also leads to less tolerance for deviations from the already successful model," observes psychologist Harry Levinson.[44]

The world of scientific research is full of examples of intolerance of "deviations from the already successful model." US inventor, Stanley Meyer, has produced a water fuel cell – a device that offers the possibility of using water as a fuel to power car motors and other combustion engines. Meyer has now managed to get his device patented around the world, but still experiences a great deal of difficulty in being accepted by mainstream scientists. It is a familiar story. Commenting on the response to Meyer's work, Paul Czysc, Professor of Aeronautics at St Louis University, says: "The reluctance to look foolish inhibits a lot of people from looking at things. They are looked at as a pariah. You touch it and it creates an image of you that you don't want your colleagues to see."[45]

As Dr Frank Close, head of physics at the prestigious Rutherford Laboratory in the UK, says of dramatic new inventions:

> **"At one extreme you might have things that are guaranteed to work but are not very interesting and at the other extreme you have the real long shot which turns out to be revolutionary. . . . Having made some choices you have to ask yourself, how do you go about doing this? Do I have to apply for funds, and who would I be competing with, and what will affect the chance that this will be supported?"**[46]

Sometimes there is a feeling that as CEO the pressure is to some extent reduced – or at least different in nature, less pressing. CEOs are above the pressured daily grind. Take one CEO we interviewed:

> **"When I was determined on developing a career within an organization, then I might have shied away from doing things that might have jeopardized my ability to achieve the leadership position which I quite clearly and openly set out to do a number of years ago. When you get into that position and you've done it for a period of time, unless you're desperately committed to doing it for the rest of your life, which I think fewer and fewer people are, then what's to worry about? I got to where I want to go in this organization and so if I do something that gets me kicked out then it gets me kicked out from a job that I always wanted to do, not kicked out from somewhere getting towards it, which I would have always regretted. So there's a combination of that having gotten to where I want to get, it actually feels less risky."**[47]

Later in our interview, the same CEO reflected:

> **"There is an awful lot of loneliness and insecurity underneath in many senior people which is covered by apparent confidence, the wearing of a costume, competitive and bullish, if not arrogant, behavior. There are actually a lot of people in senior positions who feel exposed. Maybe the behavior we see is a consequence of the way they feel inside, but rarely is it expressed."**[48]

Their insecurity is largely justified. In many cases the average time in the top job is declining. As Don Hambrick and Greg Fukotoni pointed out in 1991, since 1960 some 19 per cent of CEOs in *Fortune 500* served less than three years.[49] With turnover at a variety of large organizations – AmEx, Kellogg's, Westinghouse, GM – we think the pattern of shorter CEO tenure will continue.

The fact is that as their careers develop, people's strengths often become their greatest weaknesses. What gets CEOs to the top is not necessarily what they need to succeed at the top. We are only as good as our last development and if our last development was some years ago then we aren't very good.

Equally, the skills you have now may not be the most useful ones a few years down the line. Someone who starts his or her own business and makes it highly successful may not be the right person to lead it when the company employs hundreds and talks in millions of dollars not thousands. In fact, it is said that the toughest transition is from entrepreneur to business owner or chief executive. There are many instances of entrepreneurs who are good at start-ups but less skilled at leading a larger business. Look at Steven Jobs. Of course, there are others who manage the transition. Bill Gates isn't doing badly. "I tell people here that there are two possibilities – success and failure – but it's the possibility of both that creates the best results. Risk taking is fun when you succeed . . . but I don't know as much about the other side of the equation as I should," says Gates – he knows that failure provides learning, if you allow it; but is so frightened of failure that it drives him to success.[50]

Michael Jordan is a great basketball player but he may not be the greatest coach (and he certainly wasn't a great baseball player). In tennis it is notable that the most sought after coaches weren't actually the greatest of players. Tom Gullickson, a journeyman pro, coached Pete Sampras. The leading golf coach is David Leadbetter, a man without a major title

> **We are only as good as our last development and if our last development was some years ago then we aren't very good.**

to his name, but he can coach. Who hears of the coaches for the three tenors or anyone, for that matter, who is world class? Who is Whitney Houston's voice coach? Why do we accept that coaching in some fields is perfectly normal, but quite unusual in another area? Who is your leadership coach?

Who is your leadership coach?

Why do some people grow with their businesses while others fail to do so? The answer lies in the word grow. Michael Jordan may spend his time practicing his slam dunks, but if eventually he wants to move into coaching he needs to assimilate a completely different set of skills. Those who succeed, who make the leap from a single unit to a mega corporation, are people who learn and develop new skills as the business develops – like the CEO of Owens and Minor, G Gilmer Minor III, who has fashioned himself as "coach." By acquiring the new skills the business now demands they grow and so, too, does the business. Personal growth equals learning and, under the new fundamentals of corporate life, learning equals leadership – organizationally and individually.

Overcoming fear

The major obstacle to individual and organizational learning is fear. And, as the cliché goes, the only thing we should fear is fear itself. Risk-averse cultures breed risk-averse leaders and vice versa. Individuals can and must break the mold.

Executives are uncomfortable with ambiguity and uncertainty because, we suspect, they appreciate at some level that ambiguity involves a kind of learning that they find uncomfortable. There is a real possibility that they could learn something that would be a major development if they were able to get to grips with the opportunity. If they were able to let go, they could take on something new, embrace something unpracticed. But it does involve a risk. The risks are: loss of face, perhaps admitting to themselves (as a perfectionist this is always difficult) that they might not be as good as they would like to appear.

We know of one CEO of a major US corporation who during his senior executive forum handed out awards for Best Failures. Jaws dropped at the very thought. This represented a major cultural shift in that only a year before failures – especially big or public ones – were to be hidden not celebrated. As we write, managers in this company are still in a state of shock and wondering whether this support for doing it differently will remain. In fact, this is one of the first steps to bringing learning out of the corporate closet, to shake things up by taking definitive steps. Shake things up and nothing stays the same. "We run like mad and then we change directions," says MCI Communications CEO Bert Roberts.[51]

> **Risk-averse cultures breed risk-averse leaders and vice versa. Individuals can and must break the mold.**

"Most of the things I have learnt were not learned formally but through accidents and failure. I learned from small catastrophes," admits Charles Handy, author of *The Age of Unreason*.[52] Handy is not alone. Most of us learn in such a haphazard and occasionally unhappy way. If there were awards for Best Failures we would have a large number to choose from.

Indeed, one UK newspaper ran a weekly column entitled "My Biggest Mistake." It was riveting reading as manager after manager confessed to some appalling misjudgment. It was notable that all the mistakes were made in prehistoric times – the executives couldn't admit to recent errors of judgment – and that their vital lessons stayed with the executives. In many cases they haunted them. A mistake made was a lesson learned and remembered.

We could all write similar articles. Perhaps we should, regularly. Yet, though we are often shaken by our failures, too often we are not stirred from our habitual behavior. We don't want to stand out by getting it wrong. We merge with the crowd. Fear of failure is a fundamental instinct, an instinct which organizations only serve to magnify.

In organizations, fear of failure becomes a survival instinct. We go into organizations and we learn and are taught by the organization how to operate. If you start a job on the checkout counter of a retail chain, you will spend a day watching videos (it's cheap and doesn't waste valuable managerial time) about the way the corporation works, its values and ways of doing things. Good idea, but it is prescriptive. It won't tell us about what happens when things go wrong – except if they go too wrong you will be fired. Another retail chain has a better idea. It throws staff in at the deep end by giving them a day at the counter to see how they deal with real customers. Then it can make a decision about whether someone is really right for the job.

We're running scared. Accidents and failures are sucked out of the system. But this does not make the system any more effective. Fear of failure is the major blockage to developing skills for handling uncertainty. But if we are to maximize learning we have to reorient ourselves to taking risks and making, perhaps creating, mistakes. Listen to Jack Welch:

> **In organizations, fear of failure becomes a survival instinct.**

"**Boundaryless behavior is a way of life here. People really do take ideas from A to B. And if you take an idea and share it, you are rewarded. In the old culture, if you had an idea you'd keep it. Sharing it with someone else would have been stupid, because the bureaucracy would have made him the hero, not you.**"[53]

Work at Decision Research, a company based in Eugene, Oregon, studying risk management strategies, suggests that people are more likely to accept risks that they perceive as voluntarily undertaken, controllable, understandable and equally distributed. And, conversely, people are less willing to take on risks which they don't understand and which are unfairly distributed.[54]

Share, understand and confront – then risks, even if they fail, can become learning. Take Disney's initially disastrous venture into Europe. Given the size of its losses, it was undoubtedly tempting for Disney executives to sweep the matter under the corporate carpet and attempt as much as possible to forget about it. Instead,

Disney executives recall its lessons every day. "Euro Disney gave us all a good glass of cold water to the face," admits Disney's Michael Eisner. "There's not a meeting goes by that somebody doesn't say, 'Ah, Euro Disney, Euro Disney. Can we afford to do this?' Okay, I've heard it. I can say we've learned. But I really do feel – about business and about life – that everybody has to make mistakes, it's okay. I have never wavered from the belief that I'm glad we did Euro Disney and that it is a monument to the creativity of our company. But there is a reality of life known as economics, which always comes into the equation no matter how many pyramids you want to climb."[55]

Eisner has discovered there are an awful lot of corporate pyramids. With the acrimonious departure of former studio chairman Jeffrey Katzenberg, Disney faced another crisis. Says Eisner: "It tested whether or not we were a company that could deal in failure as well as success. It tested our management. It tested our board. It tested our major shareholders. And, of course, it tested me."[56]

Eisner has learned the value of failure. "We had a generation of executives who had never been around failure. We had this momentum that never seemed to end. We were climbing this ladder that seemed to have no top. Even I got kind of used to it and comfortable with it," he now admits, realizing that it is one thing having an infinite ladder quite another when the rungs come to an abrupt halt.[57]

Share, understand and confront – then risks, even if they fail, can become learning.

Or listen to the CEO of an insurance company who explained to us how he handled failure:

"If we have a failure I wouldn't say we drag it on for weeks but we try and analyze why we failed, what we did wrong, what could have been improved and, if I can try to find out the reasons why we failed, just to learn. I think some people will simply shrug their shoulders if something goes wrong. If someone says 'I don't give a damn' I've got to say that was an important piece of business

we've got to pick this up. Others may become depressed and you've got to pull them out of it and say we might have messed that one up but we are going to get back into them and we've got a lot of other things going on at the same time."[58]

The same CEO recalled a particular example of how failure had taught him a valuable lesson. He recommended the promotion of someone to the board. The board rejected the candidate and the CEO was left feeling highly embarrassed and mystified. The chairman explained that his failure had been not to talk to the board members individually and personally beforehand. "I honestly hadn't even thought of it," says the CEO. "I knew the person far better than they did and thought they should accept what I was saying. I don't know whether it was partly because they really did disagree with what I was doing, but I think it was also to teach me a lesson, to say don't take it for granted that you can just steamroller something through. In the end it worked out but it stuck in my mind for a long time. I learned a lesson and I wasn't going to operate in that way again."[59]

> **Fear of failure has to give way to respect for failure and learning from failure.**

Fear of failure has to give way to respect for failure and learning from failure. Executives need to toughen up. They are going to be tested and tested again in ways they never previously contemplated. This takes humility and bravura. When Tom Peters was lambasted by the media for the speedy decline in fortunes of companies in *In Search of Excellence* he could have produced a sequel lamely justifying his original ideas. He did not. He moved on and proclaimed "Excellence RIP!" The past is dead, not forgotten. So, what's next?

Move on and then on again. This is what actress Dame Judi Dench said of rehearsals in a recent interview:

"Rehearsals are a time when you are allowed to make mistakes and to try and make choices to move your wings and to fly a little bit in certain directions. It's a very curious thing that sometimes you know

that there is a laugh in a line, your instinct is entirely what tells you there is a laugh and sometimes you can't get it. In a play in the theater you can't get it and quite suddenly one night you will get it."[60]

Fail and fail again, and then you might achieve something unexpected. Stick to your lines and you'll never get the laughs. Along your way you are going to make a fool of yourself – think of how Judi Dench feels when she gets it wrong – and wrong again – in front of an audience solely made up of actors, actresses and the producer, people who are desperate for her to get it right.

Building from failure tests **executive resilience**. Our work with derailed executives found, not surprisingly, that all executives make mistakes (obvious enough, but not something we read a great deal about). At senior levels these mistakes could be costly, capital intensive ones. The crucial thing was that when the successful executives made mistakes they acknowledged and accepted them. The derailed, however, rejected them, often blaming others.

> **Resilient executives learn from experiences, both good and bad. When life gives you lemons, you make lemonade.**

When an executive acts, two capacities are utilized: the technical capacity to do the work (the necessary knowledge, skills and abilities) and thinking about how to do it. The latter demands an overview, a structure of concepts that is used to evaluate experiences and guide actions.

The resilient executive takes in experiences, particularly failures, and incorporates them into a structure of concepts that is used to evaluate future experience and guide future actions. Resilient executives learn from experiences, both good and bad. When life gives you lemons, you make lemonade.

Think about what happens if the traditional control-oriented executive faces a deluge of lemons. Lemonade? Not a chance. They calculate the pros and cons, past experiences, the opinion of others. They hold meetings to discuss the risks. They add it up and make sense of it, and then add it up again. Then, and only then, you might just get a glass of lemonade.

Fear and risk are inextricably linked (see figure 3.2). The inescapable fact is that as experimentation increases, so mistakes will increase and, in the short-term, performance is likely to suffer. If the pressure to perform is on, it can require strong nerves to weather that initial dip in performance. And, since it takes time and practice to overcome the dip and improve performance, who has time? We have to do the same things in the same ways or risk lower performance.

How do you cope with risk? The obvious answer is to start slowly, and in a limited way, create the learning. That is certainly feasible, but another feature comes into play, which is that once people have started down this route, they find their view

> **If you do what you always did, you'll get what you always got.**

changes of what is and what isn't a risk. Things that used to take weeks, waiting for approvals, can now be done in hours or minutes. Take the international pharmaceutical companies – Glaxo, Merck, Eli Lilly and others. They are moving from drug development time frames of 5,000 days to 2,500 days. And they're not planning to do this; they are doing it now.

If you can suddenly learn to move at that sort of speed, you can afford to make some mistakes, because you are now achieving much that was previously beyond you. Doubters should remember the dictum from psycho-cybernetics that if you do what you always did, you'll get what you always got.

Figure 3.2
THE RISK DIP[61]

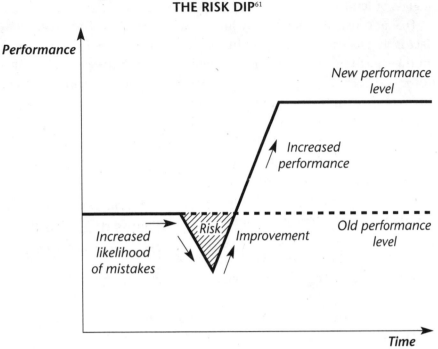

Surrendering control

If we are to embrace risk taking, personally and organizationally, the first (sometimes the only) step is to surrender our belief in control. "There is no such thing as sustaining market leadership; it must be regenerated again and again," say Gary Hamel and CK Prahalad. They suggest that managers don't address these questions "because they won't admit, to themselves or to their employees, that they are less than fully in control of their company's future."[62]

To make learning work the future leader needs to loosen his or her grip on the need to control. Forget Taylor. "Learning has replaced control as the fundamental job of management," wrote Shoshana Zuboff of Harvard Business School in her 1982 book, *In the Age of the Smart Machine.*[63] Yet, over a decade later, a short trip around many organizations will demonstrate that the need to feel in control is still very much alive. The desire for control has been nurtured by years of steady progression – like a family car down a highway. It is difficult to let go of the steering wheel – especially if you think you are the only one who knows how to drive.[64]

Future leaders must hand over control to the people who are doing the learning. Like children, if people are to learn, then they have to be able to experiment. If they are going to experiment, they need to have the flexibility and authority to "try it a different way." Many managers find this shift in their own jobs dis-

If we are to embrace risk taking, personally and organizationally, the first (sometimes the only) step is to surrender our belief in control.

concerting. The manager has to change from certainty to uncertainty. They are suddenly inhabiting a place where the right thing to say is "I don't know but try it anyway, I'll support you if it goes wrong." Unfortunately, apportioning blame remains endemic and automatic.

Leaders need to listen. Leaders need to ask good questions. While many managers are adept at asking good questions they just don't listen. Simply dictating adds no learning value. For a person who wants power, the

Surrendering control need not mean out of control.

facilitating stance seems a poor substitute. But where the transition has worked, direct but static power has been traded for dynamic influence. And time and time again, managers have found that you can achieve more with less if you go by the second route.

Surrendering traditional methods of control is not the route to instant corporate mayhem. Indeed, strategic thinker Ralph Stacey suggests it may be more of a matter of developing new perspectives on the meaning of control. As Stacey points out: "The activity of learning in a group is a form of control that managers do not normally recognize as such. It is a self-organizing, self-policing form of control in which the group itself discovers intention and exercises control."[65]

Surrendering control need not mean out of control. Leaders find themselves in inflatables heading down white water rapids. They need to develop an ability to read the water ahead, to use the water flow, never pushing against the current, and always being prepared to learn a new technique if the existing ones aren't helping to negotiate the rapids.

It is hard for managers to learn to let go, but it is possible. Mike Walsh, chief executive of Union Pacific, made enormous changes to the effectiveness and morale of his huge and widely dispersed organization. He said: "My biggest challenge is to be worthy of the staff, and the staff in this and most other companies are capable of a great deal more responsibility than most managers have a clue."[66] Walsh was committed to profound change, "pushing the needle all the way over," to use his terminology. He called a series of 100 town hall meetings directly reaching one-third of Union Pacific's 30,000 employees. His aim was to share his revolutionary plans. He found a sense of frustration: "People knew what to do, but weren't allowed to do it," he recalls.

One of the key issues was simplification. The old way of reporting track problems went through as many as 14 separate hands between customer and the track inspector to get something done about the problem. The new system has only the customer and the inspector with the superintendent available to resolve disputes. The result is that what used to take months is now down to days or even hours.

Control is the last vestige of Taylor's management driven by certainty. Our colleague Colin Williams accurately notes that executives routinely ask: "Is everything under control?" The obvious assumption is that things should be under control and if they are not someone is going to pay dearly for the oversight.[67]

"Some executives can't cope with changing anything. When new ideas are implemented the old theory of control is left intact. This is a source of continual disappointment, but my disappointment is tempered with a sense of understanding," says Harvard's Chris Argyris. "I am not angry, but just think let's face reality. Disappointment is an opportunity for leverage for change."[68] Argyris is, plainly, a real traveler.

Learning demands trust

132

The corollary of leaders surrendering control is that learning demands trust. "The micro-division of labor has fostered a basic distrust of human beings. People weren't allowed to put the whole puzzle together. Instead they were given small parts because companies feared what people would do if they knew and saw the whole puzzle," observes Charles Handy.[69] And, if you see the whole puzzle, spread out in front of you, invariably it is a mess.

In most organizations in which learning has been successfully introduced, people have learned to trust each other. It is a sad fact, but in the past the Western world seems to have been especially good at creating organizations that ran without the need for trust. Chris Argyris states that there has been a mismatch between people and organizations. To fit people into organizational structures, they have been limited rather than developed, constrained and contained. People have, in turn, failed to develop themselves or accept responsibility for their actions. "Responsibility is not a one-way process. We are personally responsible for our behavior but, unfortunately, many companies change their parking space and not people's sense of responsibility," he says. It is easier to change the structure than the culture – the latter remains inaccessible at the back of the refrigerator.

> **The learning organization is fueled by trust, but how many managers are good at creating and extending trust?**

The price of that omission is a belief that learning has to be institutionalized to be taken seriously. The learning organization is fueled by trust, but how many managers are good at creating and extending trust at all levels (not just their own) in the organization? And it doesn't stop there. The really effective organizations bring suppliers and buyers into their workplace in order to involve them in the total process of design and delivery. For example, supplier conferences at Whirlpool helped turn the company around. The 777 was designed and implemented by Boeing and its partner/suppliers.

Control can be – and is being – surrendered. Every week groups of executives from leading multinationals visit a once unheard of company based in the outskirts of Sao Paulo, Brazil. The location is not the attraction – a nondescript industrial complex. Nor is the company's technology exciting or its products – pumps and cooling units – the most thrilling in the world. The difference lies in the revolutionary way the company is run.

When Ricardo Semler took over Semco from his father he spent the first day firing 60 per cent of the company's top management. Almost without thinking he had set in motion a revolution from which the rest of the business world is now anxious to learn. Today, Semco is a unique success story. It has managed to buck Brazilian commercial chaos, hyper-inflation and recession to increase productivity nearly seven-fold and profits five-fold.

Walking through the door, visiting executives immediately notice that there is no receptionist. Everyone at Semco is expected to meet their own visitors. There are no secretaries, nor are there any personal assistants. Managers do their own photocopying, send their own faxes and make their own coffee. Semco has no dress code so some people wear jackets and ties, others jeans. (Other companies, such as Body Shop as well as a variety of US companies with casual Mondays or casual Fridays, are adapting a similar, less demanding approach to corporate dress.) But the Semco revolution goes far beyond this. "A few years ago, when we wanted to relocate a factory, we closed down for a day and everyone piled into buses to inspect three possible sites," recalls Ricardo Semler. "Their choice hardly thrilled the managers, since it was next to a company that was frequently on strike. But we moved in anyway."[70]

Semco takes workplace democracy to previously unimagined frontiers. Everyone at the company has access to the books; managers set their own salaries; shopfloor workers set their own productivity targets and schedules; workers make decisions once the preserve of managers; even the distribution of the profit-sharing scheme is determined by employees.

"We've taken a company that was moribund and made it thrive, chiefly by refusing to squander our greatest resource, our people," says Semler. He does not regard the transformation of Semco as a lesson to be emulated by other companies. Instead, he believes it simply points to the need for companies and organizations to reinvent themselves for the 1990s. "There are some companies which are prepared to change the way they work. They realize that nothing can be based on what used to be, that there is a better way. But, 99 per cent of companies are not ready, caught in an industrial Jurassic Park."

The plea for businesses to become more democratic and humane is a familiar one. The trouble, Semler candidly admits, is that listening to people, accepting their decisions and inculcating people with the need for democracy is far from easy. "The era of using people as production tools is coming to an end," he argues. "Participation is infinitely more complex to practice than conventional unilateralism, but it is something which companies can no longer ignore or pay lip-service to."

There is still a substantial amount of skepticism about Semco's approach and achievement which Semler has recorded in an international bestseller entitled *Maverick!* The mistake people make, says Semler, is assuming that Semco is some kind of role model. "This is just one more version of how companies can organize themselves and succeed. Democracy alone will not solve all business problems. In fact, as we constantly see nothing prevents autocratic companies from making money."

It is little wonder that traditionalists among the management fraternity find Semler's message unpalatable. Managers are constantly appraised by Semco workers rather than a coterie of fellow executives, and they have to become used to the idea of accepting that their decisions are not sacrosanct. Semler seems to be adept at biting his tongue when decisions don't go his way and admits, "There are a lot of people at Semco whose styles I don't actually like. I wouldn't have recruited them but quite clearly they do their jobs effectively – otherwise people wouldn't support them."

As part of Semco's revolution, to a large extent Semler has become redundant. The chief executive's job rotates between five people. Diminished power is clearly not something which fills him with sadness – instead, it is

> **Democracy alone will not solve all business problems. In fact, as we constantly see nothing prevents autocratic companies from making money.**

confirmation that the Semco approach works. "I haven't hired or fired anyone for eight years or signed a company check. From an operational side I am no longer necessary, though I still draw a salary because there are many other ways of contributing to the company's success," he says. Indeed, Semler believes that what many consider the core activity of management – decision-making – should not be their function at all. "It's only when bosses give up decision-making and let their employees govern themselves that the possibility exists for a business jointly managed by workers and executives. That is true participative management."

Semler's book is a massive bestseller in South America and, interestingly, it has also found a receptive audience in Japan – so much so that Semler's advance was the largest ever paid for a business book in Japan. More than 6,500 readers have written to him to find out more. But the skeptics remain, and Semler admits that it is too early to make cut and dried judgments about Semco's apparent revolution. "Really the work is only 30 per cent completed," he estimates. "In the long term success will come when the system forgets me and becomes self-perpetuating."

The message from Semco and a growing number of other companies is that learning is not the preserve of the few, but a necessity for all. The route to a successful future in a less and less predictable world depends on the ability of everyone in the organization. Remember the Westinghouse advertisement of the 1950s which proclaimed "People are our most important product." Finally, organizations are beginning to realize that people are their greatest asset. They need to mobilize their full skills and aptitudes continually, to recreate and rediscover from the existing organization a new organization best suited to the future.

Learning is not elitist. The need to learn and develop skills is not confined to the top of the organization, or even to its management. Perhaps we should stop talking of management development and simply talk of developing people. Most people feel underused or

Learning is not elitist.

wrongly used at work, and would love to do it differently. They'd love to be consulted, if only someone would ask. Recognizing that need, both publicly and privately, is often one of the key steps to moving along the road to becoming a learning organization.

Head down the road and you learn along the way. "When we started, we did not have a specific plan, there was nothing to refer to and it has been a learning process in itself. With hindsight, much has seemed painfully obvious, a lot of what we have done is about unlocking what is natural in people anyway. However, the process is painful, since people are not encouraged to view work as an environment in which they learn and develop," say Angela O'Connell and Mike Mulholland, then of Barclays Property Holdings.[71]

Elevating learning to the top of the agenda demands a shift in attitudes and behavior. Chris Argyris' pleasure in the growing interest in the role of learning is combined with fears that it might be shortlived. "I am pleased that organizational learning is in vogue but I worry that if we are not careful it will become another fad," he says. "I have little difficulty in talking about organizational learning to chief executives but, as you go down the hierarchy, it is regarded as being a bit dreamy."[72]

Breaking through the dreaminess requires action, commitment, investment, honesty and, yes, a willingness to take risks. Electricity generator Scottish Power emphasizes employability as a key part of its overall incentives package. "We have to face up to the facts of business life: in the future we will employ less people due to greater efficiency," says its director of corporate resources, Mike Kinski. "In this environment, working is about acquiring new skills, becoming more mobile and flexible."[73] Scottish Power now has 21 open learning centers offering its 8,000 employees – and their families – the opportunity to develop the skills they believe are necessary, from MBAs to learning another language. Three years into the initiative, one-third of employees are studying new skills and the aim is to raise this figure to 50 per cent. "Increasingly these sorts of programs will become regarded as part of the rewards package," says Kinski.

In other words, learning is being integrated into the lifeblood of the organization. It is the gateway to competitive advantage. It is also the gateway to the other skills required by organizations set on surviving and prospering in uncertain times.

Notes and references

1 Argyris, C, "Teaching smart people how to learn," *Harvard Business Review*, May–June 1991.

2 Quoted in Van Clieaf, MS, "Executive resource and succession planning," *American Journal of Management Development*, vol. 1, no. 2, 1995.
3 Leider, RJ and Shapiro, DA, *Repacking Your Bags*, Berrett-Koehler, San Francisco, 1995.
4 Quoted in Arthur, C, "All geek to me," *Independent on Sunday*, October 15, 1995.
5 Quoted in White, L, "Net prophet," *Sunday Times*, November 12, 1995.
6 de Lisle, T, "Immaculate conceptions," *Independent on Sunday*, September 10, 1995.
7 Author interview.
8 Quoted in Carr, D, *et al.*, *Breakpoint*, Coopers & Lybrand, Arlington, Virginia, 1992.
9 The Future Work Forum, Henley Management College, 1992.
10 Zuboff, S, *In the Age of the Smart Machine*, Basic Books, New York, 1988.
11 Whyte, D, *The Heart Aroused: Poetry and the Preservation of the Soul in Corporate America*, Doubleday, New York, 1994.
12 Quoted in Guha, K, "BA's court jester," *Financial Times*, October 11, 1995.
13 Observed by the early cybernetician W Ross Ashby and more recently developed by Christopher Bartlett.
14 Quoted in White, L, "Net prophet," *Sunday Times*, November 12, 1995.
15 Author interview.
16 Author interview.
17 Hodgson, P and Crainer, S, *What Do High Performance Managers Really Do?*, FT/Pitman, London, 1993.
18 Olins, R, "Can postman deliver at WH Smith?," *Sunday Times*, November 5, 1995.
19 Quoted in Greig, G, "At the height of his powers," *Sunday Times*, October 8, 1995.
20 O'Grady, S, "F-16 down! My story of survival," *Sunday Times*, November 5, 1995.
21 *Sloan Management Review*, Spring 1989.
22 de Geus, AP, "Planning as learning," *Harvard Business Review*, March–April 1988.
23 For a good description of Corning and its innovative product development process see "Corning Glass: the battle to talk with light" in Magaziner, I and Patinkin, M, *The Silent War*, Random House, New York, 1989 (pp 264–99).
24 Williams, C and Binney, G, *Making Quality Work*, Economist Intelligence Unit, London, 1992.
25 Pedler, M, Burgoyne, J and Boydell, T, *The Learning Company, A Strategy for Sustainable Development*, McGraw-Hill, Maidenhead, 1991.
26 Author interview.
27 Senge, P, Roberts, C, Ross, RB, Smith, BJ and Kleiner, A, *The Fifth Discipline Fieldbook*, Nicholas Brealey, London, 1994.

28 Senge, P, *The Fifth Discipline: The Art and Practice of the Learning Organization*, Doubleday, New York, 1990.

29 Day, G, Preface to *Implementing the Learning Organization*, Thurbin, PJ, FT/Pitman, London, 1994.

30 Taylor, P, "Disciplined Logica returns to favour," *Financial Times*, September 13, 1995.

31 Interview with Philip Hodgson.

32 Interview with Philip Hodgson.

33 White, RP, "Job as classroom: using assignment to leverage development," in Montross, DH and Shinkman, CJ, *Career Development: Theory and Practice*, Charles C Thomas, Springfield, Illinois, 1992.

34 See, for example, McCall, MW, Jr, Lombardo, MM and Morrison, AM, *The Lessons of Experience: How Successful Executives Develop on the Job*, Lexington Books, Lexington, Mass, 1988; and Morrison, AM, White, RP and Van Velsor, E, *Breaking the Glass Ceiling: Can Women Reach the Top of America's Largest Corporations?* (revised edition), Addison Wesley, Reading, MA, 1992, 1994.

35 See, for example, Lombardo, MM and Eichinger, RW, *Eighty-eight Assignments for Development in Place: Enhancing the Development Challenge of Existing Jobs*, Center for Creative Leadership (Tech Rpt 136), Greensboro, 1989; and Eichinger, RW and Lombardo, MM, *Twenty-two Ways to Develop Leadership in Staff Managers*, Center for Creative Leadership (Tech Rpt 144), Greensboro, 1990.

36 Author interview.

37 Kotter, J, *The General Managers*, Free Press, New York, 1982.

38 White, RP, "Choosing leaders, not experts," *Changing European Human Resource Practices*, The Conference Board, Rpt No 1003, 1992.

39 White, RP, "Choosing leaders, not experts," *Changing European Human Resource Practices*, The Conference Board, Rpt No 1003, 1992.

40 Pedler, M, Burgoyne, J and Boydell, T, *The Learning Company*, McGraw-Hill, Maidenhead, 1991.

41 Quoted in Napuk, K, "Live and learn," *Scottish Business Insider*, January 1994.

42 Author interview.

43 "A week of woe for the CEO," *Fortune*, February 22, 1993.

44 Levinson, H, "Why the Behemoths fell: psychological roots of corporate failure," *American Psychologist*, vol. 41, no. 5, May 1994.

45 Quoted in *Equinox*, Channel Four, UK broadcast TV, December 1995.

46 Quoted in *Equinox*, Channel Four, UK broadcast TV, December 1995.

47 Author interview.

48 Author interview.

49 Hambrick, D and Fukotoni, GDS, "The seasons of a CEO's tenure," *Academy of Management Review*, vol. 16, no. 4, 1991.

50 Quoted in White, L, "Net prophet," *Sunday Times*, November 12, 1995.

51 Quoted in Sprout, A, "MCI: can it become the communications comp-

any of the next century?," *Fortune*, October 2, 1995.

52 Interview with Stuart Crainer, January 1994.

53 Quoted in Jackson, T and Gowers, A, "Big enough to make mistakes," *Financial Times*, December 21, 1995.

54 Kleiner, K, "Beware experts carrying stigmas," *New Scientist*, October 21, 1995.

55 Quoted in Huey, J, "Eisner explains everything," *Fortune*, April 17, 1995.

56 Quoted in Huey, J, "Eisner explains everything," *Fortune*, April 17, 1995.

57 Quoted in Huey, J, "Eisner explains everything," *Fortune*, April 17, 1995.

58 Author interview.

59 Author interview.

60 Interview on *South Bank Show*, London Weekend Television, November 1995.

61 Bunker, K and Webb, A, *Learning How to Learn from Experience*, Center for Creative Leadership, Tech Rpt 154, Greensboro, NC, 1992.

62 Hamel, G and Prahalad, CK, "Competing for the future," *Harvard Business Review*, July–August 1994.

63 Zuboff, S, *In the Age of the Smart Machine*, Basic Books, New York, 1988.

64 In a variety of leadership programs conducted at the Center for Creative Leadership, an instrument (FIRO-B, developed by Will Schutz) measuring three dimensions of behavior, including control, is administered. In those groups with the highest level executives, it is not unusual for the modal response on the control dimension to indicate high need to control and low need to be controlled by others.

65 Stacey, R, "Strategy as order emerging from chaos," *Long Range Planning*, vol. 26, 1993.

66 Peters, T, *Speed is Life: Get Fast or Go Broke*, Work Book for video, Excel, 1991.

67 Williams, C and Binney, G, *Leaning into the Future*, Nicholas Brealey, London, 1995.

68 Interview with Stuart Crainer, May 1994.

69 Interview with Stuart Crainer, January 1994.

70 Crainer, S, "Escape from industry's Jurassic Park," *The Times*, October 14, 1993.

71 Interview with Philip Hodgson.

72 Interview with Stuart Crainer, May 1994.

73 Interview with Stuart Crainer, September 1995.

"The soft stuff is always harder
than the hard stuff."
ROGER ENRICO
VICE-CHAIRMAN, PEPSICO[1]

"I am convinced that
nothing we do is more
important than hiring
and developing people.
At the end of the day
you bet on people,
not on strategies."
LARRY BOSSIDY
ALLIED SIGNAL CEO[2]

FIVE SKILLS FOR WHITE WATER LEADERSHIP

✳ What do I need to know, learn and do to live with the rapids?

Making white water leadership work involves five critical skills. They are not taught by education and training institutions and are largely ignored by both theorists and practitioners. They are not – and could not be – exhaustive, but we are convinced they provide the backbone of what future leaders must do and be able to do if they are to lead with and towards, not against, uncertainty.

The skills and the patterns of thought now required tend not to be talked about. We don't attempt to teach them – perhaps because for many they are unteachable. But more worryingly we don't encourage people to learn about them either. Yet we believe that these five skills are quite as much the bedrock of real practical hard-headed management and leadership as spreadsheets, budgets and board meetings. It is simply that we have all grown up in a world that prefers to ignore them, like so much at the back of the refrigerator.

Learning is the key skill. It is what we term an **enabler**. We have identified three enablers:

● **difficult learning**

● **maximizing energy**

● **mastering inner sense.**

These are applied through two **channels**:

● **resonant simplicity**

● **multiple focus.**

Each of these key skills will be described in detail, as well as how they can work together. Much of the supporting material is derived from our interviews with senior executives in the USA and Europe. (See figure 4.1.)

Figure 4.1
THE FIVE SKILLS OF WHITE WATER LEADERSHIP

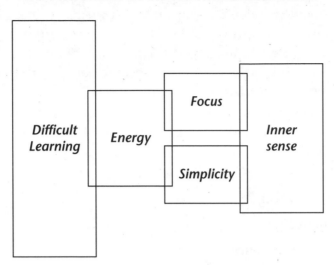

1 DIFFICULT LEARNING

Learning is the gateway and overcoming fear of failure is the key. If learning is to work for individuals and organizations, we have to forsake the temptation of easy learning for the perpetual challenge of difficult learning.

Difficult learning means deliberately seeking out areas of maximum business benefit and developing the capabilities within yourself, your people and your organization to meet the challenge. Difficult learning demands creativity not complacency.

We all know that customers are becoming smarter and more demanding. We spoke to one disgruntled customer recently – a director of a major business that recognizes the need continually to change in order to stay at the front of its market. His complaint was that a favored supplier was not prepared to adapt fast enough to his company's changing circumstances and, as a result, was not going to get the new business. The director, struggling for the right words to describe the situation, used phrases that we have heard increasingly in recent times: "It's not just what they do, it's what they are. They don't seem to have the ability to regenerate to be of value to us. They don't seem to be able to learn the hard lessons necessary to keep up with our changing requirements."[3]

Hard lessons require difficult learning. By refusing to face difficult learning, the supplier was falling behind, failing to develop the relationship. Stagnating relationships end in divorce. Executives may shrug their shoulders. They all complain about intransigent or uncooperative suppliers at some time or another. How can they find the time and energy for difficult learning when they have to balance the conflicting needs of offering security and certainty to their staff while, at the same time, promoting more change and innovation than has been seen in the lifetime of the organization and the staff?

Yet, they must find the time, energy and faith. Changing perceptions challenge habitual and accepted behavior; they demand difficult learning. Developing and different aspirations demand difficult learning. Learning is the key tool in handling uncertainty.

> **Difficult learning demands creativity not complacency.**

And the ability to identify and learn the things that the individual or the organization find hard to learn is the most precious of all.

Difficult learning has to be sought out. It is not delivered or packaged. By all means go ahead and learn more about markets you are already in. But what about the markets you know are there but don't know how to explore? If knowledge is power, unusual, hard won and possibly unique knowledge is even more powerful. The trouble is we instinctively avoid this kind of learning. This automatic reflex can be traced back to early days. Ironically, it is at school where the disappearance of our ability to tackle difficult learning begins. In the classroom children put their hands up if they know the answer to the question posed by the teacher. If they know the answer they are rewarded by the teacher's attention and praise. But what happens to the others who don't put their hands up because they don't know the answer? They keep their heads down, try not to catch the teacher's eye, look round to see if their friends know the answer and whether they will tell them. Of course, the children who are destined to be good poker players put up their hands even if they don't know the answer. (This is something corporate poker players are often highly adept at.)

This situation is replayed thousands of times in most children's school lives. Indeed, we estimate this one lesson is reinforced thousands of times during our school days. The message is simple – and one we remember: if we know the answer we tell everyone and gain approval. If we don't know the answer we keep quiet and don't broadcast our lack of knowledge. We recognize early on that advertising our lack of knowledge is not a good idea.

This brings us back to control and measurement. Schools and examination systems find it easier to test knowledge and reward it. They can discourage our enthusiasm to find things out (though, of course, some don't). It is far easier to reward what is known than to reward an intention to explore and to discover what is unknown. Exploration leads to classroom chaos. It is uncontrollable and immeasurable. The kids have all got their hands up because they all don't know or don't know enough.

Move from a school to a modern organization. As chief executive you wish to create a learning organization. What do you need to do? How should you behave to form an effective learning organization? Part of the answer is that you want all your staff to reverse the instincts acquired at school. If someone doesn't know something essential to the business, keeping their head down and not acknowledging the lack of knowledge may prove to be an expensive mistake.

If you are truly going to create a learning organization then it would have been better if all the employees had learned a different lesson at school. Every time they came across something they didn't know they should have been able to jump up and down waving their hands in the air and when the teacher asked them they would shout: "I don't know the capital of France but I want to find out!"

The transition from school life to the organizational life of the future needs to carry with it a clearer explanation that the rules are different. At school there is a great deal of knowledge. There is a great deal which the teacher knows and which the students do not. In organizations wishing to be at the leading edge, no one can teach you, you have to find things out for yourself. Discovery is the only way. Yet, at organizational level, this can be seen as a weakness.

If we really don't know the figures, if we don't understand the market, if we don't know a particular customer or if we don't know what to do, we feel highly uncomfortable, perhaps fearful. Clearly, in any business situation, lack of knowledge is a significant problem. But lack of intent to find out and remedy the situation is a much bigger problem. In how many meetings do people boast of their skills and achievements and get rewarded for what they know and can do? In how many meetings do people talk about

> **In effective learning organizations, people are praised for identifying what they don't know and what they have yet to find out.**

their failings and deficiencies? How many executives reveal what they can't do and know little about?

Until recently many effective leaders were recognized for their ability because they knew more than others and could do more than others. Their knowledge resulted in superior application of the same knowledge. The future leaders will be expert in what they don't know and what their companies don't know. They will focus their attention on what the company does not know, but needs to learn about fast, in order to achieve its overall objectives. Lack of knowledge will become the hinge point of top managerial decisions and intent to find out will become the most valuable currency.

In effective learning organizations, people are praised for identifying what they don't know and what they have yet to find out. (This praise has to be based on the assumption that they will then do something about it.)

We have speculated that the learning organization will only be truly valued (by, for example, stock market analysts) when it is normal for company annual reports to contain not only the list of company successes for the year, but also a section on company failures to show how much difficult learning the company has invested in.

Instead of easy answers, let's think about difficult questions. Intel chief Andrew Grove advocates constantly asking yourself three key questions.

1 **Am I adding real value or merely passing information along? How do you add more value? By continually looking for ways to make things truly better in your organization. In principle, every hour of your day should be spent increasing the output or the value of the output of the people for whom you're responsible.**

2 **Continually ask, am I plugged into what's happening around me? Inside the company? The industry? Are you a node connected to a network of plugged-in people or are you floating by yourself?**

3 **Are you trying new ideas, new techniques, and new technologies? – and I mean personally. Don't just read about them.**[4]

This demands a radical change in perspective. We are conditioned, in the Western world at least, to expect that learning delivers the right answers. "I hate ambiguity. I like to get everything clear and sorted out. I can see that some of the data doesn't match and no simple solution will match the needs of the situation. I wish I knew more about this subject. I really don't know what to do, and I don't want to make a mistake. Do you run a course on this kind of thing?" a senior manager said to us with an air of desperation.[5]

Rightness and learning are traditionally linked by a straight line of correlation. The more learning I have, the more likely I am to be right. Unfortunately, learning more of anything, especially if it is easy learning, may not be the solution. As we have observed, all the books on strategy might not help when you are in a unique situation which demands an immediate response. The fact is that, though we may champion learning, in reality we are usually championing easy learning. Difficult learning takes time to master, inevitably involves failure but, in the long term, yields competitive advantage.

We believe that by identifying the most profitable areas of difficult learning, organizations can maximize the value of learning. The relationship between difficult learning and value to the organization is illustrated in figure 4.2.

Clearly any organization must aim to be in the High Value side of the square. Some of this will be achieved from learning which is low in difficulty. The trouble is that if learning is low in difficulty competitors can also do it or copy it quickly. A financial services organization launched a financial product new to the market. Within 72 hours its rivals had a

Figure 4.2
COMPETITIVE ADVANTAGE FROM DIFFICULT LEARNING

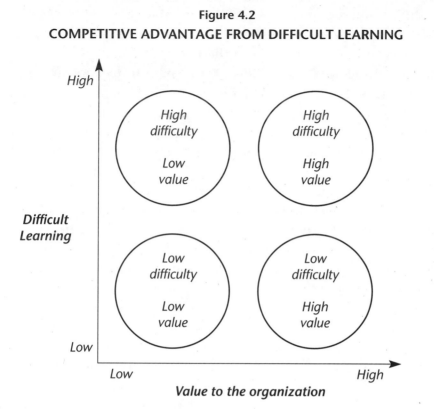

Value to the organization

competitive product available.[6] The only remaining route, therefore, is through continually identifying and pursuing difficult learning.

Low Difficulty/High Value

The things that are easy to learn (low difficulty) and have a high value tend to turn into commodities. They become fads. This does not stop them being useful, but they provide little in the way of sustainable competitive advantage. Your competitors can also learn them and will inevitably do so.

Between 1980 and 1990 chemical giant Union Carbide earned an average of eight per cent net on capital employed – below the industry average of over 10 per cent. At the beginning of the 1990s, Union Carbide's profits were falling, its reputation in tatters after the Bhopal disaster. Its finances were saddled with debt and it faced a hostile bid from a smaller rival. "Over those ten years we had plenty of soft numbers to make us feel comfortable, like winning more chemical engineering awards than anyone else. The other side of the coin was that we weren't up to the rest of the industry in doing everyday things, like accounting. Our strength in technology was a crutch," says the company chief executive and chairman, William Joyce.[7] Low Difficulty/High Value had begun to deliver Low Value.

Instead of resting on the soft numbers, Union Carbide set about changing itself. Armed with technological models it calculated that its return on capital should be around 15 per cent. It then calculated that its targets required annual cost savings of $200 million. As the savings were instigated, the company reassessed the figure and calculated it could make savings of $575 million by 1994. A further saving of $450 million was later added. From employing 1,200 people in 1990, the company accounting function now has a meager 480. Return on capital is rising steadily but significantly.

Corporate anorexia is the easy option.

Union Carbide has undertaken a form of reengineering. This has clearly proved beneficial. Low Difficulty/Low Value has moved to Higher Difficulty/ Higher Value. But there is a major difference between reengineering in its various guises and reinvention. We suspect that Union Carbide remains addicted to the Low Difficulty area and has yet to address the source of potential competitive advantage: High Difficulty.

In fact, cutting costs remains Low Difficulty/High Value and probably always will. It is perpetually tempting, although the value may be short lived. Announce job cuts and you can be sure that your stock price will go up. Some executives have built their careers on being cost-cutters – Jack Grundhofer of Wells Fargo, then First Bank System, did not earn his nickname "The Ripper" because of his commitment to developing the learning organization.

Between 1987 and 1991 over 85 per cent of *Fortune 1000* companies reduced the size of their white-collar staffs. And they do it again and again – the best predictor of whether a company will cut numbers next year is whether it did it this year. The end result is what

Gary Hamel labels "corporate anorexia" – slimmer organizations which are not necessarily any fitter. Hamel argues that corporate anorexia is the easy option. Cutting jobs or selling parts of the business are far easier than increasing total income which requires imaginative identification and targeting of the opportunities.

Hamel says that the fascination with cutting costs has produced managers addicted to the lowest common denominator who can "downsize, declutter, de-layer and divest better than any managers in the world."[8] Cutting costs is an easy answer and its repercussions are not fully understood. Indeed, it does not automatically make business sense. A survey by the Wyatt Company found that less than half of the respondents using restructuring as a means of cost reduction met their cost reduction targets, and a mere 22 per cent actually increased productivity to their satisfaction.[9] That's a lot of pain for not much gain.

> **Too often cuts and more cuts leave the old ways of thinking and leading intact.**

On the human side there is "survivor syndrome" – a now eponymous term made popular by David Noer of the Center for Creative Leadership.[10] Research by Deborah Dougherty and Edward Bowan covering 12 large US companies concluded that downsizing tends to change the product development process. It breaks the networks of informal relationships essential to promoting innovation.[11] Too often cuts and more cuts leave the old ways of thinking and leading intact. Fewer people doing more of the same. "Not only have the organizations become too physically strained and emotionally exhausted to maintain the momentum of improvement, but employees' day to day behavior has reverted to old, familiar patterns," observe Sumantra Ghoshal and Christopher Bartlett in a 1995 article.[12]

The future requires broader ambitions. The universal faith in cutting costs needs to be broken. Some are taking the initiative – look at Kodak chairman, George Fisher. "When I came here the mental set was that this is a slow-growth industry, and that the way you keep going is you keep cutting," he says. "The new mind set I think we've succeeded in establishing within the company is that there are

153

tremendous growth opportunities; we have to go develop them."[13] Easy learning RIP.

Low Difficulty/Low Value

Easy solutions are fool's gold. Over the last generation, managers and organizations have embraced the easy-to-learn material. It was not only Union Carbide which was content to rest on its laurels. On the surface at least this is something of a surprise. After all, executives are more highly trained than ever before. They know more. Unfortunately, while the level of business education has been unprecedented, this has simply resulted in most large organizations having access to similar information. Low Difficulty learning is more effectively disseminated and so, consequently, its value is correspondingly reduced.

Low Difficulty/Low Value describes the things you have to do just to stay alongside your competitors. Unfortunately, when an idea or product is fairly new, then it tends to be trumpeted as a breakthrough and a route to becoming more competitive. Think again. Actually, these are the things that if you don't do, you simply hand over advantage to another organization.

Low Difficulty/Low Value activities may previously have been Low Difficulty/High Value. The temptation is to believe that because this is where they originated this is where they will stay. The introduction of the fax machine, for example, allowed organizations to communicate as never before. But is your fax a significant aspect of your competitive edge? Once, possibly in the very early days, it made a difference. Probably not now, but you wouldn't want to be in a business without a fax, would you? (See figure 4.3.)

The Low Difficulty/Low Value option does not offer competitive advantage or, if it does, only temporarily – and for shorter, and shorter times. The advantage quickly evaporates, no matter what you do. But not keeping up to date with Low Difficulty/Low Value activities is like not keeping up the maintenance on your car or your factory machinery. It may save you time, money and trouble in the short term but will cost you dear in the long term.

Under this category come the me-tooisms which companies relentlessly pursue. Take the fashion for customer loyalty cards. With their array of "smart" cards, credit cards, incentives and various

Figure 4.3
MOVING ARENAS

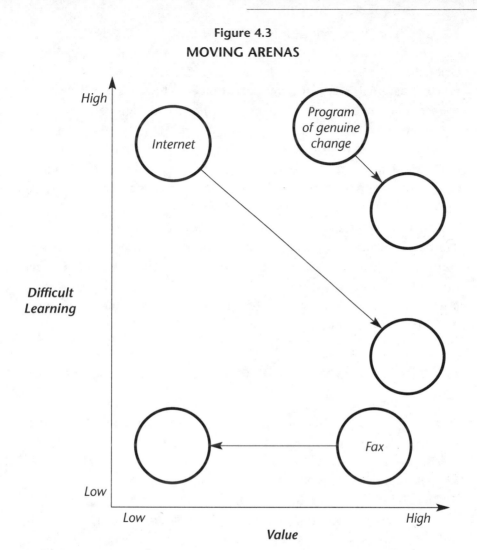

promotions, petroleum retailers are at the front line in the battle for customer loyalty. All offer some sort of loyalty program. This particular loyalty battlefield has become a treadmill of endless promotion rather than an efficient means of loyalty building. The scenario is familiar. Companies are locked into a cycle of defensive actions and have to respond continually to the initiatives of their competitors. And each additional promotion eats into their profit margins. There is no escape. Loyalty programs and a continuous stream of promotions have become a requirement to do business. Consumers expect them and which company is brave enough to break the cycle?

"There is a danger of pinning all your faith in a loyalty program, treating it as the cure for all known organizational ills," says Mark Uncles of the UK's Bradford Management Centre. "Companies glibly talk of sustainable competitive advantage. While it is an attractive phrase, it is in danger of becoming a Holy Grail and may well be equally elusive. I prefer to think of *evolving* competitive advantage. This is what organizations are constantly doing – changing the way they do business and what they offer to customers to add value and create competitive advantage. If customer loyalty is regarded in these terms it is a powerful competitive weapon."[14]

Low Difficulty/Low Value means airlines fiddling with the size of their seats. It means constant discounting (the end result: customers wait for Chrysler to discount because they know it will). It means easy option after easy option. It keeps people busy but to what purpose? Low Difficulty inevitably becomes Low Value and is no longer a competitive option.

High Difficulty/Low Value

No one aims to be in this arena, in the same way as no one intends to be in a bunker when playing golf. But in the same way that a promising golf swing degenerates into a hook or a slice, a promising high value initiative can often degenerate into the High Difficulty/Low Advantage outcome.

Take the introduction of Total Quality Management (TQM). Many organizations took up TQM during the last decade with the fervor of religious converts. TQM, like most major change programs, contains some components which are hard to learn – such as genuine changes in behavior and real concern for quality. But it also has components which sound good and are easy to learn – such as suggestion schemes. Unfortunately many organizations head straight for the easy-to-learn parts without recognizing that they can only achieve superficial change. They start using the language of TQM, having short seminars not supported by any serious attempt to change operational behavior, introduce suggestion schemes but don't act on the suggestions, show videos to everyone without listening. All of these activities are easy to learn and probably in the short term produce some improvement in performance, but in the longer term they have little significant effect on competitiveness.

"For the last 18 months we have been working on TQM," said one executive we interviewed. "It is terrible to think of TQM as an interruption but there is no doubt that the way we have done it or the way it was done corporately was not the right way. It has interrupted many of the things we were doing and changed resources around. . . . We did it but there was a degree of cynicism or uncertainty within the organization from me downwards."[15] Research conducted at Ashridge Management College suggested that 70 per cent of CEOs felt that TQM has failed to fulfill its promise within two years of the start of the program.[16]

There are always several current examples of the latest good idea being given lots of time by companies. All of these ideas will produce some short-term advantage, however minimal, and a few will sustain long-term development.

With equal access to the learning available, only organizations that are able to take on difficult learning will be able to gain sustainable advantage from their implementation. This goes against the received wisdom that you find a short-term competitive advantage, use it until others catch on, then abandon it and find another.

Look at what has happened with reengineering. A few companies took the gamble and tried to reengineer themselves. The result, after a great deal of disagreement, disillusionment and confusion, was usually a compromise with part of the organization being reengineered and other parts left alone. Or, worse still, the organization being reengineered apart from the management. Companies which took the lead were quickly followed by others claiming to be reengineered. James Champy begins his second book on reengineering

> **There are always several current examples of the latest good idea being given lots of time by companies.**

with the startling revelation that more than two-thirds of reengineering attempts have failed to meet the very high standards that the reengineering movement had set for itself. He then goes on to lament the failure of companies to reengineer their management.

Most forms of failed change initiative fall under this category. This does not make them bad ideas. It simply means that in isolation they will not be a source of competitive advantage.

High Difficulty/ High Value

Finally, there are things that are difficult to learn but which are useful to the business. These are the ones that give an individual and the organization genuine competitive advantage – such as making customer service really work or developing an innovative patentable product.

It is often the case, although not always, that if something is difficult to learn, then it will also be difficult for competitors to learn. If one can persevere and acquire the learning, it gives an advantage which may sustain for some time. Competitors are put off by the steepness of the learning curve. On a personal level, it also represents development, growth and change. It is reassuring that a growing number of organizations now seem to appreciate the need for difficult learning and are moving towards it.

In *The Competitive Advantage of Nations*, Michael Porter cites the development of the tulip industry in the Netherlands. As Porter points out, it is not the ideal country to begin a flower growing industry. It is cold and space is at a premium. The Dutch have overcome this through specialized breeding, handling and preservation techniques, auction houses, labor and academic skills. Confronted with a problem of their own invention, the Dutch have utilized all their intellectual resources to turn High Difficulty into High Value.

As an example, look at the program of radical change achieved by British Airways. After the arrival of new chief executive, Colin (now Sir Colin) Marshall, BA developed a set of corporate objectives which pinned the company's future on the development of service excellence throughout its operations. BA's seven central objectives identified were:

- **to provide the highest levels of service to all customers, passengers, shippers, travel agents and freight agents**
- **to preserve high professional and technical standards in order to achieve the highest levels of safety**
- **to provide a uniform image worldwide and to maintain a specific set of standards for each clearly defined market segment**

- to respond quickly and sensitively to the changing needs of our present and potential customers
- to maintain and, where opportunity occurs, expand our present route structure
- to manage, operate and market the airline in the most efficient manner
- to create a service and people-oriented work environment, assuring all employees of fair pay and working conditions and continuing concern for their career.

The opportunity was clear. Research showed that two-thirds of recent airline passengers thought that BA was neither better nor worse than other airlines. This presented an opportunity for BA to achieve a vital competitive edge through service. Neutral responses could be turned into positive experiences and support.

The first step was the staff awareness program, "Putting People First." This program, launched at the end of 1983, was initially aimed at the 15,000 people in direct contact with customers. Its success was such that it was extended throughout the airline. Initially it was criticized by some as being too American – though in fact it was developed in the UK by a Danish company. The program lasted two days and the groups were up to 180 strong. Colin Marshall made a point of personally closing as many of the program's seminars as possible. They ran for two and a half years and he closed 40 per cent of them.

"I was conscious when we embarked on the program that it couldn't be a one-off," recalls Marshall:

> "It had to re-focus the organization, changing it from a company focused on operations to one which was led by the marketplace and one which recognized the needs of customers. I thought it would take at least five years, but more likely a decade to really carry it through. To achieve genuine culture change takes time, effort and the overriding concern to get at the values involved. The reason so many companies seem to achieve a useful change in culture and then slowly disintegrate over the passage of even short spans of time is that one suspects they confuse the appearance of culture change, the presence of the symbols, with the needed solid change in values and their acceptance."[17]

"Putting People First" was only the beginning for BA. It was accompanied by "Managing People First" which focused on how to lead, to be willing to take risks and raise your head above the parapet. This one-week training program aimed to help managers deal with the transition and to manage their people through the process of change.

BA has now completed the fourth of the total employee programs. The second, entitled "A Day in the Life," focused on what the company actually does in its day-to-day operations. The third program, "To be the Best," focused on the competition and the fourth, "Winners," on quality and customer service. A fifth is now being developed to be launched in 1996. BA tackled difficult learning, shifted the organizational culture, and continually moves up through the gears.

In the USA the modern blueprint for the organizational revolution can be seen at General Electric (GE). When chief executive Jack Welch arrived

> **The bigger you are the more you are getting things wrong. How's that for a paradox for the 1990s?**

in 1981, the company was cumbersome and underperforming. Welch has since succeeded in overhauling and realigning it in a way which few thought possible. Between 1981 and 1990 GE cut the average number of management layers between Welch and the very front line from nine to four. Its headquarters was slashed from 2,100 people to fewer than 1,000. The number of senior executives across the company was cut, first from 700 to 500, and between 1990 and 1994 by another 100. The overall workforce was almost halved, from 404,000 to 220,000. Yet GE's revenues more than doubled through this period, from $27 billion to $60 billion (they have now risen to $70 billion).

Welch has stripped hierarchies away. When he arrived GE had an average of five or six people reporting to each manager. By the late 1980s this average had doubled and is now at about 14 – with some units reaching 25 or more. With more people to manage, managers have to manage in a different way using new skills and, increasingly, enabling others to do jobs once the sole preserve of management.

What Welch is achieving is about more than cost cutting. He believes the process of improvement can continue into the future. Its energy does not come simply from financial performance. Nor is it measured solely in financial terms. "Who runs out of ideas?" asks Welch. "If you never had another idea, you might as well quit your job. Every day we wake up, there's another basket of opportunities. When you're a $70 billion company, you're doing so many things wrong that the amount available from improvement is literally infinite. Our improvements are getting greater with time, not diminishing."[18] The bigger you are the more you are getting things wrong. How's that for a paradox for the 1990s?

What BA achieved and GE is tackling is not easy. Both have eschewed the easy option of improving by degrees or paying lip service to the latest ideas. They are not alone. Difficult learning comes in a huge variety of forms, but is a corporate necessity. It can involve eating humble pie, admitting that a diversification was not a good idea or that the company simply doesn't have the expertise to make something work (such as Kodak selling off its drugs operations).

Difficult learning is about innovating, risk taking, breaking free and being upfront. Take Gilbert Trigano's speech at the ClubMed annual general meeting in 1992:

"I spoke a year ago of how hopeful I was about our involvement with Minerve and Air Liberte. I was mistaken. I do not usually look for excuses and I shall not now. I have been unable to unite these companies, neither their management, nor their shareholders."[19]

Difficult learning is not an automatic answer. Eventually, as your people leave for other companies, medicines and machines go off-patent, or others have success in the Difficult Learning/High Value arena, your Difficult Learning/High Value becomes lower in difficulty and eventually lower in value. Then you must start again by seeking out new areas of difficult learning. Only if this is achieved time and time again – if you genuinely renew and create a true learning organization – will an organization achieve competitive advantage and move beyond the temptation of easy learning.

Table 4.1

DIFFICULT LEARNING AND YOU

Having identified the five skills, we have been working on the question of how to assess and develop them in individuals and organizations. In the earlier stages of our research we developed a series of audit questions and checklists covering the five skills which we have used during our presentations and to aid our consultancy. These included an Ambiguity Preference Scale and an Organizational Checklist.

The Checklist contains some "push the boundary" suggestions and a few "out of the box" suggestions, ideas that are not yet common but which extend an organization's ability to embrace uncertainty. These are listed in full in the Appendix, together with the original interview agenda we used for the structured interviews from which we quote during the book. We have now developed a more detailed and statistically robust inventory to assess skill levels. This is in the final stages of testing. At the end of each skill section, we have included a table with the latest findings from the questionnaire results. A more complete discussion of the inventory and a list of all the current questions is contained in the Appendix.

- Are you embarrassed when you make a mistake? (In our survey of 566 US managers at all management levels, ironically only 20 per cent of respondents answered never or seldom to this question.)

- Are you concerned if a problem has several solutions? (75 per cent of respondents said seldom or never.)

- Do you wish life were simpler? (Fully 77 per cent responded in the affirmative.)

2 MAXIMIZING ENERGY

Liisa Joronen runs a Finnish cleaning and waste management company, SOL. She has turned a dull and dirty business into something special. In 1992 Joronen's father split up the family business, a national laundry chain called Lindstrom. Joronen took over the company's cleaning operations.

> **"There I was on January 1, 1992 with 2,200 people and 2,500 customers not knowing quite what to do. The economic situation in Finland was really bad. Fortunately, some of the best people at Lindstrom took a personal risk and followed me. We moved very quickly, changed the name to SOL and adopted a completely new identity based on the philosophy that employees must be given the chance to perform at their best."**

Joronen challenged conventional culture. She sloganized – "Kill routine before it kills you", "Freedom from the office." She abandoned traditional Finnish working hours and introduced teamworking. SOL weathered the

The masters of uncertainty seem to have energy to spare.

recession and now has a turnover of $50 million and is growing at an annual rate of 20 to 25 per cent. Joronen has injected fun, energy and enthusiasm into a moribund business.[20]

A common feature of people who handle uncertainty well seems to be an easy access to energy, both in themselves and in others. The masters of uncertainty seem to have energy to spare. Managing uncertainty requires abundant energy. When data are not clear or certain, there is often a need to adopt an experimental trial and error approach to a large proportion of the workload. This can be very wearing and uses a lot of physical, intellectual and emotional energy. It takes more energy to seek out a difficult learning solution than to provide the easiest one available.

Leaders are energetic. They have to be. Margaret Thatcher slept four hours a night and rose to pore over yet more government papers. IBM's Lou Gerstner is renowned for his energy (and sleep) levels. Top executives travel constantly and yet still emerge from the arrivals lounge looking fresh, armed with a report they've just written somewhere over the ocean. David Campbell of the Center for Creative Leadership finds over and over that effective leaders and high energy go hand in hand on his Leadership Inventory.

> **Quality is vital; quantity is no longer a competitive advantage.**

Energy is a prerequisite for the job. "One of the things I look for most in people is energy levels," says Robert Devereux, CEO of Virgin Group. "I won't employ people who don't have high energy levels, because they won't last. Because people with energy, they're self-motivated, they get going, they get things done." [21]

But, is this all there is to energy? Are these people just plain lucky, with metabolisms to match their ambitions and lofty status? Yes and no. They are fortunate to some extent. Part of being more effective is to pay more attention to the whole idea of energy – what it is, what its source is and how it is regulated. But energy is more than another word for physical stamina. After all, who wants a marathon runner when you are running the 100 meters?

Maximizing energy is more than running fast or working harder. Anyone can work 16 hours a day. The world is full of hard-working executives who have mortgaged their future health against their current working day. But how you spend your time, how you enthuse others is more important. Quality is vital; quantity is no longer a competitive advantage.

In fact, executives who pin their faith simply on working harder are taking a route to burn out and disenchantment. "What happened to me is that I had 16 direct reports in four different locations and five different levels. The organization was flat enough so I had to develop relationships with everyone and they required intense relationships. But I also had to relate to peers, the board and customers. It was an overwhelming diversity of constituents. Working at such an accelerated pace restricts your range of emotions," says one chief operating officer (COO) who has since left the organization in an effort to simplify his life and rediscover his frayed emotions.[22]

We believe that slowing the pace will expand your range of emotions. Explaining his departure from the organization he led, the same COO said: "My activities took me away. I allowed the pace and breadth of my work to drive me away. I didn't have the time so celebrating breakthroughs was a luxury I couldn't afford. I became the proficient superficiality. I had the awful sense of being the 15-minute man and part of the fun as a professional is to spend time. 15 minutes is too short."[23]

> **Leaders have to dig deep and deeper and deeper still.**

In many cases, people like the COO quoted above are channeling their energy into reaching a neat and linear solution. They are seeking out consensus when none exists or is likely to exist. In uncertain situations it is easier to drive towards a point that looks like it's a direct linear solution and accept it rather than carrying on the search for other things which may be far more complex.

In white water, energy must be channeled effectively. It must drive you beyond the existing situations, solution or compromise. You must always want more. (And that does not mean always doing more.)

Energy leads you to question what others assume. "Don't assume you understand the core issues. You will probably run into issues you are not at all prepared to deal with. Can you even define the problems? I would walk into this opportunity fraught with difficulty. We had been briefed, but we didn't allow the knowledge to enter into the planning," said one CEO.[24]

A retail manager explained the sources of his energy as "my desire for success, my inability to feel comfortable with failure and wanting to explore as many options as possible to get the best solution. And that will get me the extra hour or two's energy which will make me go a bit deeper into things."[25]

Leaders have to dig deep and deeper and deeper still. Take an apparently mundane example. One of us had a malfunctioning answerphone and rang the local store. They were uninterested and provided an immediate solution: buy a new one from our store. Great idea for them; poor value for us. So, we tried a local repairman. The first conversation didn't sound very promising. He couldn't immediately say what was wrong, but he knew quite a number of things which could possibly be wrong. He came to the house to have a look. Slowly, he started examining the possibilities. Gradually he became excited as he explored and then narrowed down the options. He found the idea of seeking out a solution exciting. Eventually, after trying various possibilities he found the fault.

The repairman who sorted out the problem accepted that there were a wide range of possibilities. The store may have thought as much but discounted them and came up with the instant solution – a solution, but one which was not to our benefit. The repairman came to a solution without cutting out the myriad of choices. He was prepared to say there are a number of possibilities – they might be unlikely but they are still possibilities. He went through a process and came up with a solution. He was energized by the possibilities. This is energy.

> **What gives you energy and pleasure? . . . the answer is simple: the job itself provides a reservoir of energy.**

"I have always had lots of nervous energy. Even when in school, the classic things were I talked too much and didn't apply myself. I have always been an enthusiast. I am a very keen card player and I play the game. I enjoy any form of games, particularly intellectual games. I want to apply my analytical mind. I actually like solving problems and sometimes you look for problems to solve," said one interviewed executive.[26] You must look for problems to solve. And then there is another problem, and another. Listen to Bill Gates: "Your products are always gonna be obsolete so you'd better enjoy doing the next version. It's like pinball – if you play a good game, the reward is that you get to play another game – there is no ultimate gain."[27]

Generating energy

If there is no ultimate gain, no quick sale, what gives you energy and pleasure? From the executives we interviewed and many more whose behavior we have examined, the answer is simple: the job itself provides a reservoir of energy.

A vice-president for developing new drugs at a major pharmaceutical company observed:

> "I think there are two sources of energy. The first is probably the reward one gets from playing a key role in a large international organization and the interface with different types of people – pure R&D people, researchers one day, marketing people the next day, commercial people, operational managers, very often the same day, so from a functional view a wide diversity and from a cultural view the same diversity. That diversity and the willingness to integrate that in one structure and one function is a source of energy. The second source lies in building something important and exciting. I strongly believe that the energy invested in your job is closely related to the output you receive."[28]

The job matters

Why else is Jack Welch running GE after a triple bypass or Michael Eisner still at Disney after his heart attack? Listen to a senior strategic planning manager we talked with:

> "I think it's a question of looking after yourself. I look after myself emotionally – not exactly physically, I'm not fit, my diet is appalling so when I need sleep I by and large sleep. If that's what I feel I need then that's what I do. There are various other ways of looking after yourself. You can pamper yourself, basically I do that. I think that eating the food that I want is one way. The other is satisfaction from the job, it's enormous for me – I like doing things well; I like the variety of things to be tackled; I like fixing things; I like being used as a resource; I like thinking about things; I like planning things then seeing them through. They all have their different satisfactions and maybe a competitive edge. I like doing my job a little bit better than I think most people do. The job satisfaction means a lot to me."[29]

For these leaders, financial motivation is limited. They are not angelic figures who regard financial rewards as unimportant. They expect to be well rewarded, but look beyond the narrow motivation of money alone. Paul Allen, Microsoft founder, recalling the day he and Bill Gates realized they had shipped one million copies of BASIC, says: "We were marveling that, wow, a million people were using our code to do God-knows-what number of interesting things. That was such a gratifying thing to realize, that you have been able to affect other people's lives in a positive way."[30]

Affecting lives in a positive way is what the leaders we studied and talked to thought it was all about. They believe in what they are doing or trying to achieve. It sounds corny, but has anyone ever done a good job if they weren't committed to doing it? Perhaps once, but not day after day.

> **This just means you have to find another dollar for the pinball machine.**

"When I used to drive up in the morning I felt this was my organization, I owned it psychologically. As the 1980s wore on I felt less and less that way. That to me is a central part of the excitement – take your work and feel real wondership," recalled one such executive.[31] This childlike enthusiasm appears widespread. The leaders are perpetually amused and enthused by the range of possibilities and the sheer potential of their organization. In a world of doubters, they are true believers. A project manager on a huge IT project said: "I think we got energy through a belief in the outcome, a belief that we would have a good system and that we would be proud of having been part of it. We all had a feeling of working on something really big and sort of pioneering because it was such a big project."[32] The project failed but, as Bill Gates would say, this just means you have to find another dollar for the pinball machine.

Liberating energy in others

This belief and desire to change things gives leaders energy. In white water the true leaders find energy where people thought there was no energy. They go through a tedious task and find a way of making it enjoyable not just for themselves, but for others too. We talked to a former linen porter. It was, he admitted, not a particularly exciting or mentally stimulating job. He filled his time thinking about how he would make life better for linen porters when he was their manager. He wasn't a linen porter any more, he was researching the ground for being a great manager of linen porters. The linen porter is now an entrepreneur restaurant owner, Denis Quaintance. Denis has developed

> **In white water the true leaders find energy where people thought there was no energy.**

his thoughts to how to continually make the dining experience better for everyone – chef, patron, business person, wait staff and the people who fill the role of linen porter. His chain of restaurants in North Carolina continues to grow.

High performers discover energy from the mundane, from the routine. They extract ideas to generate enthusiasm. They invent different approaches and try new things. They generate energy from themselves and stimulate energy out of those they work with. They attract people with energy. They stimulate energy in others.

The most obvious manifestation of their energy is their sheer enthusiasm. It is something they carefully cultivate and nurture. And it is highly infectious. Go to a Tom Peters seminar and even if you do not remember a single idea, you will remember that Peters is an enthusiast who can transmit his enthusiasm so that people begin to believe in their own potential. Leaders transmit energy. This might not come naturally. "I have tried to develop as a person to get enthusiasm, to make it infectious so that you can stand

> **High performers discover energy from the mundane, from the routine.**

back and let that filter through the organization and only dabble where it is needed to top it up a little bit," said an area manager in a railroad company.[33]

In many cases, enthusiasm and energy were areas where CEOs and other leaders believed they added value. How do you add value we asked one CEO? "By bringing my experience to bear on problems that will help others in the organization solve the organization's more significant needs. Also by attracting and motivating people to join the organization and to sustain the enthusiasm."[34]

Adding value in this way actually gets things done. We asked a banking executive about why things sometimes don't happen. His reply was quick – he had seen apathy and caution kill many projects and bright ideas stone dead: "When I look at why things don't get done it's because people without much inward direction are looking after them, because senior people take their eye off the ball, because there's no fun, joy or sense of kudos attached to the work."[35] So, his job was to make sure there was fun and kudos, that people remained focused. He also knew who he wanted on the team: "There are those who don't seem to be able to do very much. Others do things that really suit themselves but no one else. And then there are those who are prepared to do something new, something different, something interesting. They are most likely to respond to challenges."[36]

Paradoxically, energy and enthusiasm are not hard work. Really effective energy doesn't look as if it is energy at all. It looks energy-less. Great energy slows time – look at great athletes. They have all the time in the world – or so we think.

This is not dreamland. The bottom line is that energy means listening and involving people. We talked to the anesthetist of a hospital who also worked as the director of a clinical unit. We asked how she created a sense of energy in people?

"What you've got to try and give them is where their bit fits in. It is looking at the jigsaw, so that they can see that in itself, although it may seem unimportant, what they do is actually critical to the functioning of the whole machine. If you can give that then when they achieve it and see it move forward, they can say if it wasn't for me it wouldn't have happened."[37]

Esa-Pekka Salonen, principal conductor with the Los Angeles Philharmonic, says:

"The main thing is to motivate – to try to release the energies and passion in different individuals in order to make them feel free, to create the illusion that they are actually doing what

they are doing and not being led by somebody. That is when the best results happen. In the best possible case, the illusion of freedom becomes true. They are free."[38]

Putting your faith and trust in people produces energy from them. The anesthetist gave a good example:

"We now have a dedicated theater porter for the day theater – we used to get someone different sent down every day and of course there was no loyalty to the unit. Now he actually does far more than just the theater porter job. He looks at the list and will come in and say you've got two kids to go and this one is screaming why don't we get this one down first? He interfaces with the ward and will say this lady is nervous and nobody minds at all though it is not really his job. But it works. He feels tremendously valued. Of course, the traditional anesthetist would not take kindly to a very lowly theater porter – perhaps the lowest paid medical staff in the hospital – coming and saying do you fancy changing the order of your list? They may not even dare to say it, but the fact that he could both say it and see it acted on means that he won't worry about coming to say it again."[39]

Sometimes the message fails to be transmitted. An executive in a telecoms company tried to generate enthusiasm by encouraging a particular team "to play more." "They are a new team and seem very cautious, isolated sorts of individuals. They have built barriers around their desks and don't seem to talk to anyone. They are working on a particular topic and I said look we've got this equipment which you can demonstrate it on – go and put it together, see how it works, make sure you understand how the wires all fit together – go and have some fun doing it." The response was unenthusiastic. "They just sat at their desks and did nothing," recalls the executive. On other occasions his enthusiasm has gone against the prevailing conservative culture. "I got someone to build a demonstration room. He didn't have to do it, it was an extra on top of all his other responsibilities. So I got a brass plaque and we named the room after him. All the other rooms are B, X, Y, Z. It was slightly out of tune with the culture, but it was a reward for him."[40]

He was struggling hard to transmit and generate enthusiasm. It can be done. We can't all be Tom Peters, but one major US auto manufacturer even carries out training in enthusiasm!

Percy Barnevik – Energy Generator

If you want an archetype of what we mean by energy look at Percy Barnevik, CEO of Asea Brown Boveri. ABB is one of the corporate success stories of the 1990s and Barnevik is rapidly attaining mythical status. ABB is involved in the energy business; Barnevik epitomizes the leader who maximizes every ounce of energy in himself, his colleagues and his entire organization. The genesis of ABB began in 1987 when Barnevik, at the time chief executive of the Swedish engineering group, ASEA, announced what was then the world's largest cross-border merger

> **Barnevik has rigorously rooted out and extinguished any vestiges of bureaucracy in ABB.**

between ASEA and the Swiss company, Brown Boveri. When the two companies merged, Barnevik established the new corporation in a mere six weeks. What followed was as dynamic as it was dramatic.

Since then ABB has acquired over 70 more companies, assembling a corporate monster worth $30 billion. Its engineering markets include electric power generation and transmission equipment, high speed trains, automation and robots, and environmental control systems. ABB has set unprecedented standards. Its ability to change itself continually impresses and concerns commentators – and ABB managers – in equal amounts. By 1994 ABB's turnover reached $29 billion and productivity had increased by about six per cent a year since the merger.

Barnevik has rigorously rooted out and extinguished any vestiges of bureaucracy in ABB. His straightforward and much quoted rule is that 30 per cent of central staff can be spun off into separate and independent profit centers, another 30 per cent can be transferred to the operational companies as part of their overhead, another 30 per cent can be eliminated as superfluous to requirements and the remaining 10 per cent can be kept on as the minimum required. At

ABB, Barnevik reduced the number of employees at head office from 2,000 to 250. Barnevik's revolution is based around a number of simple precepts (though their implementation is often highly complex):

- **Identify the skills required of executives and identify a small number of key executives** (250 in ABB's case) to carry changes through. Barnevik sought out "people capable of becoming superstars – tough-skinned individuals, who were fast on their feet, had good technical and commercial backgrounds and had demonstrated the ability to lead others."[41] ABB's leaders are resilient, smart and truly global in outlook.

- **Eliminate head office bureaucracy.** Barnevik reduced ABB's head office to a relatively meager 250 people.

- **Develop a matrix structure.** With its 250 top managers, ABB split itself into a federation of 5,000 profit centers with defined product segments. Alongside this is a Top Management Council (70 executives who meet three times a year) and the Konzernleitung (Barnevik and seven others).

The matrix seeks to utilize the company's global presence with local knowledge and speed. It confronts one of the great paradoxes of contemporary business. "ABB is an organization with three internal contradictions. We want to be global and local, big and small, and radically decentralized with centralized reporting and control. If we resolve these contradictions we create real organizational advantage," says Barnevik.[42]

The final phrase – "organizational advantage" – sums up the aims of the merging new model organization. Instead of regarding structure as a means to an end – increased production – how a corporation organizes itself can have an impact on all aspects of its performance and its values. Interpreted in such a way, it becomes an infinitely more dynamic process than a pyramid shaped chart on an office wall. Barnevik's personal dynamism has been translated into organizational dynamism and energy.

Table 4.2
MAXIMIZING ENERGY AND YOU

- Do you learn more from your failures than your successes? (In our survey a small number said they never behaved this way while 17 per cent said always.)

- Do you try to make work fun for others? (Only 2 per cent of our sample said they never or seldom behaved this way.)

- Do you attempt to make the tedious parts of your job exciting? (55 per cent said they always or often tried to do this.)

- Would people describe you as enthusiastic? (75 per cent of the 566 managers responded often or always.)

3 RESONANT SIMPLICITY

Pythagoras' Theorem contains 22 words; the Christian Lord's Prayer makes do with 76; the Gettysburg Address has 267; and the Preamble to the Constitution restricts itself to 52. Many of the great documents of history possess what we call resonant simplicity. They work and last not because they are beautifully phrased, though some may be, but because they strike a chord with people – and continue to do so long after the personal impact of their authors. They are accessible, yet communicate important, sometimes profound, messages and information.

Communicating through resonant simplicity is the first of the channels to white water leadership. Resonant simplicity is not sound bytes. It is not a formulaic mission pinned on the wall. It is not frivolous or insincere. If simplicity doesn't come from deep within the culture it will lack resonance. And, if it lacks resonance, it will fail to communicate any goal, aspiration or value.

In the technological age, clear and effective communication is vital. Sustaining high quality communication at all times is a vital part of any leader's job. Without clear communication good ideas disappear into the corporate ether. As we have seen, choice and complexity can overwhelm. The supply of information and opinions which leaders receive is incredibly complex. Every hour 100 million telephone calls are made using 300 million lines across the world. It is predicted that this figure will treble by the year 2000. Despite the flood of calls, letters, faxes and e-mail, white water leaders can make sense of it and extract the important details from the vast bulk of paper and input from a wide variety of sources. No matter what, they keep communication as simple as possible while still discovering resonance within people and the organization as a whole.

> **In the technological age, clear and effective communication is vital.**

"You concentrate on the few points that make the product innovative and competitive against what exists on the market," said the vice-president of a pharmaceuticals corporation. "Even with our very sophisticated communication tools and we have all of that – voice mail, e-mail, videoconferencing – talking to the people and trying to see whether they understood a number of things is quite essential. It is really putting yourself in the shoes of one who has to receive information from you."[43]

Communication is still about people. "Despite the internationalization of markets, despite air travel, despite information technology, there are still things that are done best by people who find themselves frequently in the same room," says London Business School's John Kay.[44]

Think of great sportsmen and sportswomen. Often, we reflect that they are good because they make the game look so simple. We watch and believe it is simple. We watch Pete Sampras serve a ball at 130 miles per hour and go out and buy his brand of racket. A golf swing like Fred Couples? Buy his brand of clubs.

Their simplicity convinces us. This brings us back to childlikeness. Children cut through the nonsense, the veneer of sophistication by asking simple but profound questions, often beginning with why? Leaders must do just the same. They must inspire us by simplifying the complex – without being

> **Communication is still about people.**

simplistic. Their message must resonate. Executives must go beyond rigid but regular communication with people in the organization. Instead, they must strike a chord which resonates with people no matter what their role in the organization. But, how?

● Make it dramatic.

● Make it small, make it clever.

● Link communication with your values.

● Resonant simplicity is a reference point.

● Brilliance is simplicity and truth is beauty.

Make it dramatic

Munich Reinsurance, the world's largest reinsurance company, is being forced to transform itself from a stumbling colossus to a more nimble, light-weight organization. Outside its newest office it has a fifty-foot white statue – a featureless walking man which symbolizes its new strength and mobility.[45] It is a bold and necessary ambition and a symbol which acts as a constant mental reminder.

Not everyone is turned on by artistic images; instead they turn to the potency of language. We have already looked at the plethora of new images emerging in the business world – corporations as amoebas, ever present butterflies. The nature of the imagery is changing. "Organizations used to be perceived as gigantic pieces of engineering, with largely inter-changeable human parts. We talked of their structures and their systems, of inputs and outputs, of control devices and of managing them, as if the whole was one large factory. Today the language is not that of engineer-ing but of politics, with talk of cultures and networks, of teams and coali-tions, of influence or power rather than control, of leadership not man-agement," observes Charles Handy in *The Age of Unreason*.[46]

White water leaders seek out new, fresher and clearer images. Some have highly developed metaphors to describe their own orga-nization. An oil company executive was trying to persuade others to look at the organization anew.

"I view our business as a jewel, a diamond. We were going to look at the diamond from every possible direction, and in every

direction another picture would emerge. We looked at the business against just about every variable that we could think of. It was a hell of an effort. But we were forcing people to look at the world, our place in it, the competition and our position relative to them."[47]

Others use images as a means of getting things past their boss. "I've used analogies and word pictures to take him gradually on-board," said one insurance executive describing how he gained support from his boss.

"The mental image I have is of rolling countryside. The journey we've got to do is up and down those hills, but, if you go too far, you disappear out of sight into the next valley. And, if my boss can't see, he has no point of reference. So I can only take him a certain distance at each stage. I take him that distance then invite him to look back at where he's come from so he sees where his point of reference is. Then I say, 'Now look forward. You see the hill up there, that's the next point we are going to get to.' Then I take him on again. In between he's going to lose sight of me and what I am trying to achieve. But I've got to keep moving."[48]

Make it small, make it clever

Imagery, for some, is too prosaic. They prefer the straight talk. Small and clever. Executives at Corning Glass label really important ideas, issues and objectives as "the critical few." "Say you have a meeting and someone goes home at night and the next day there's a ten-page memo that's crisp in evaluating the ideas – that's a smart piece of work. In software, it's not like ditch-digging where the best is two or three times faster than the average. The best software writer is the one who can make the program small, make it clever," says Bill Gates.[49]

It is easy to lose sight of the essential simplicity of what you do. "1995 is about remembering who we are and focusing on what we do best. This is the company that makes yellow boots," says Jeffrey Swartz, chief operating officer of Timberland. Compare this with the company's mission statement:

> **"The Timberland boot stands for much more than the finest waterproof leather. It represents our call to action. Pull on your boots and make a difference. With your boots and your beliefs, you will be able to interact responsibly and comfortably within the natural and social environments that all human beings share."**[50]

Simplification is a necessary evil. If you are to sell an idea in a complex environment the choice is often between achieving resonant simplicity or simplifying or disguising it to such an extent that it becomes untrue or inaccurate. A project manager on a major IT project explains:

> **"If you undertake a computer development of that size and complexity, you don't actually know much about it when you start out. You don't know how long it's going to take. You don't know what it's going to cost, but you're expected to know both of those things and you've got to say that you do. Otherwise you don't get permission to proceed. There's a sort of mutual conspiracy to silence between senior management and people who do things. Senior management has to take the decision. They know the basis on which they want to take decisions and want their decisions to be clear-cut and easy. They don't want to be in the position of being blamed if they take the wrong decisions. But the people who are doing the things know that there are all sorts of risks, problems and unknowns. But, if they come clean about them the decision makers will take fright and not let them do it."**[51]

Link communication with your values

What you say has to resonate with what you do and with what others in the organization feel, value and do. The changes Percy Barnevik has introduced at ABB have been driven by simple, evocative communication. ABB continually states, communicates and evolves clear values. The ABB values – meeting customer needs, decentralization, taking action, respecting an ethic and cooperating – are reinforced through intensive in-house programs of executive education, in which Barnevik and other members of the top management team invest a great deal of time. The prime values, from Barnevik's point of view, are meeting customer needs and decentralization. ABB emphasizes human contact. It is what its executive vice-president Goran Lindahl has labeled "human engineering."

> **What you say has to resonate with what you do and with what others in the organization feel, value and do.**

When the USA invaded Panama in 1989 the operation was given the code name Blue Spoon. Colin Powell changed it to Just Cause – "You do not risk people's lives for blue spoons," he explained.[52] Resonant simplicity may demand discipline. We've been told that at National Semiconductor presenters on its special presentations can use no more than three overheads.

Resonant simplicity is a reference point

At best, resonant simplicity crystallizes ideas. It is always easy to make things complicated; far harder to make things simple. "Simplicity means figuring out how to hide complexity. That takes a lot of code," said Compaq

> **High concepts are managerial shorthand, and more.**

marketing director Dave Hocker back in 1993.[53] In the 1980s, BA's Nick Georgiades poignantly described the work of cabin crew as "emotional labor." Similarly, Disney's Michael Eisner came up with the phrase "high concept" to describe a brilliant idea which can be condensed into a single persuasive sentence. (The writer of the screenplay *Twins* reputedly condensed the film into six words – "Arnold Schwarzenegger, Danny de Vito, twins" – to persuade studio moguls to back it: they did.) Leaders must continually develop their own high concepts.

High concepts are managerial shorthand, and more. Pierce Brosnan, the latest James Bond actor, cannot wear a dinner jacket in any other movie – his contract forbids it. The dinner jacket is Bond – more than the stunts, the glamorous locations and beautiful women.

Resonant simplicity acts as a constant reminder of why you are here and why you are doing something. The area manager of a railroad used a simple refrain "Are we winning?"

> **"What I try to do is get a set of structured meetings with the key managers. Are we winning? I ask. We focus on the key things that we must achieve and that have been collectively agreed by the team. . . . 'Are we winning' is broken up into key components. Identify the key components and then put in a couple of measurables on each one. I've found this helps considerably. It also helps ownership. They have agreed what the key ones should be, the basket of measures, and we go through and stick to the same ones. There are one or two we have added but basically the same measures are steered through so people actually see the process and start targeting things where necessary."[54]**

Resonant simplicity provides a route through complexity. It is a ready source of reference and, sometimes, inspiration. It is an abstract measure for increasingly abstract times.

Brilliance is simplicity and truth is beauty

It is not simply a matter of communication. Ideas can possess resonant simplicity. Their timing and their pitch are perfect. They are right for the times.

A senior planning manager may not be John Keats, but he knows the kind of message he needs to find and get across:

> **"You have to get the whole complexity on board because if you don't what you end up with is simplistic rather than simple. You then need to pick out from it those things which are going to mean something to the people you are talking to and what you do to do that is to match up what you know of their world, their language, their concepts and see where this idea might**

fit, how it might gel and then you also know something about how you can add something."[55]

The great business ideas cut through perennial problems or situations with devastating ease. And good ideas can strike at any time. In 1950 Frank McNamara was dining in a Manhattan restaurant. When the bill arrived he realized he had no cash. McNamara rang his wife to get him out of the embarrassing situation and began thinking how he could solve the problem. Within a few months he had persuaded 27 restaurants to join a credit card scheme under the name Diner's Club. Within a year the billings exceeded $1 million; the credit card was born.

> **Brilliant ideas are about timing.**

Others take lessons from nature. After a day's hunting and with many burrs stuck to his clothes, Swiss engineer Georges de Mistral developed the idea of Velcro – a way of fastening fabrics firmly while leaving them easy to unfasten. Brilliant ideas are about timing. So, too, is the communication of messages which contain resonant simplicity. Generally, they are notable by their absence. There aren't many business examples because managers are poor at coming up with brief inspirational statements which are not sound bites. They are often masters of the pithy phrase which might mean something to a coterie of top executives but little to anyone else. In white water, they must spread their message far more effectively and imaginatively than is now usually the case. It must be understood by everyone in the company as well as your customers, suppliers and investors. (See table 4.3.)

Table 4.3
RESONANT SIMPLICITY AND YOU

- In foreign environments, do customs fascinate you? (In our survey, 87 per cent of respondents said this was always or often true.)

- Can you explain complex subjects so that a child can understand? (Only 7 per cent said they could always do this.)

- Do people get you to explain complex things? (In the survey about the same number, around 6 per cent, say always as say never or seldom.)

- Do you believe there are few certainties in management, only probabilities? (Around 20 per cent of our sample act as if management is about certainty.)

4 MULTIPLE FOCUS

There is a great deal of discussion on the role of focus in the modern organization. Corporate clarity is one of the business themes of the 1990s. Downsizing and ridding organizations of peripheral investments have kept managers and consultants busy. Overnight, AT&T becomes three separate businesses. Others follow suit in search of focus and clarity.

Frederic Escherich, a corporate finance manager at investment bank JP Morgan, has created an index measuring corporate focus on their core businesses. The index awards scores from 20 for a widely diversified conglomerate to 100 for a "pure investment play," a company with only one or two activities. Escherich measured the business clarity of 830 US firms with a market capitalization of over $500 million at the end of 1994: 429 had multiple businesses spread among 54 broad industry groups. Between 1988 and 1994, it was found that there was a trend towards clarity. For every firm that diversified, two became more focused. The number of pure plays leapt from around 30 to 40 per cent. The overall clarity index rose steadily from 76.1 in 1988 to 79.1 in 1994.

Escherich found that when firms narrowed their interests, their shares outperformed the market by an average of 11 per cent in the next two years. Firms that diversified and thus lowered their clarity score underperformed the market as a whole by around four per cent. "Investors want managers to focus on a few things and do

Focus is good, but focus on what and how?

them well, thereby increasing the odds of good share-price performance. What could be clearer than that?," commented *The Economist*.[56]

The problem is that doing things well is often interpreted as doing the things you already know how to do well, rather than doing new things well. It is an encouragement to live in the known world, not the unknown. The temptation is to avoid uncertainty and not take risks and so not to learn. A handy short-term recipe is a dubious long-term one.

Clarity works but that does not mean it is easy to make a clearing in the corporate jungle. Focus is good, but focus on what and how? Corporate clarity has to fight its way through the unfocused and conflicting focuses of those in – and around – the organization. Corporate clarity does not emerge from the skies. There is no thunderbolt spinning off peripheral activities or telling you what to focus on, when and where, but there is plenty of thunder.

Corporate clarity clearly comes from individual clarity – and resonant simplicity. A company with a clear statement of intent may require that different people have a different focus. The question then is how well this is articulated and communicated. The trouble is that people yearn for a single, simple focus which does not change. The commonly held view is, "If I only could do one thing at a time." Focus is routinely interpreted as tidiness. It is one-dimensional. In reality, reducing things to a single dimension means you will miss many of the most important components of the debate. You need to focus on multiple things at a time and still create corporate clarity.

In some jobs focus and objectives are shared (air traffic controllers, for example) but rarely in management, and certainly not in leadership. Think of focus at a personal level (figure 4.4).

My key objective is your distraction.
Your key objective is her distraction.
Her key objective is my distraction.

Figure 4.4
THE DISTRACTION CHAIN REACTION

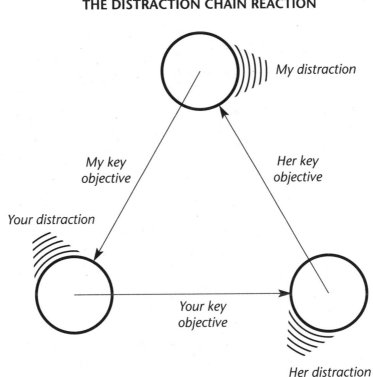

My agenda is not your agenda. Your objectives are unlikely to be identical to those of your colleagues. Yet, this flies in the face of the standard texts on vision and mission. Their logic is simple: you work for the same organization; you want the same things. However, in reality, no matter how well-crafted and all-embracing your vision, and whatever your focus is, it is always in a state of flux and will rarely, if ever, correspond with my focus.

When bosses complain about subordinates not being focused what they probably mean is subordinates not being focused on the things bosses think they should be focused on. In all likelihood subordinates are focused on the things they think they should be focused on. But between boss and subordinate there is no exchange going on.

Focus is not a linear phenomenon. Instead, it is often a matter of persuasion and advocacy – you have to persuade others to put your focus on their agenda. "If it reaches me, then it must be important, at least to the person who raised the issue," said one CEO.[57] This goes completely against the last few decades of time management teaching. It was assumed that an absolute priority existed and could always be imposed. Yet, executives listening for faint signals may need to accept the multiple focus, multiple priority acknowledged by this CEO:

"Someone else may have an insight into your business which you don't have. You give them time and explore the new and uncertain, but if you allow too many other things to creep on your agenda you risk steadily becoming less and less focused yourself."[58]

The constant introduction of new initiatives is a matter of focus. A manager seeks to exhort his or her focus on the rest of the organization. It does not work, so another initiative is introduced. Focus becomes overlaid by another focus and another. The process tends not to be dynamic. It needs to be. Focus needs to be about exchange. People need to handle a number of areas of focus and be involved in a constant process of exchange. Focus must be about making things happen.

Listen to the finance director of a TV company: "It's about focus, not staring at a complex problem, worrying about how complex it is but diving into it and trying to see what the elements that make it up actually are. Paralysis by analysis is about sitting with the problem and just looking at it and worrying that it's too big to deal with and you've got to kick start. Start moving, start doing." We then asked him what he focused on? What were his criteria? "The honest answer is does it sound like fun, is it interesting, does it grab my attention. If not, what the hell do you want?"[59] It was a disarm-

Focus needs to be about exchange.

ingly honest answer. Many executives use the same criteria and feel the same when their focus is challenged or disturbed – of course, they may not admit it.

Too often focus becomes inflexibility. In the service economy how many times do you receive inflexible responses from companies which claim to be focused on customer service? So, focus must remain flexible and steady. But, while a football team can only score one touchdown at any one time, a company can actually hit ten goals at the same time – whether they are market share, return on assets, environmental safety, product quality. And almost always, by definition, these are going to be at the expense of other objectives – such as safety or costs. Only at the very top of the organization are the multitude of objectives held together by the CEO. Further down, each executive probably only carries one or two of these objectives and regards other executives as a nuisance taking up so much time with their objectives. Focus is shifting. It means prioritizing, reprioritizing, changing, shifting, moving. And yet it must remain steady. The horizon must be the only stable thing and yet that too is constantly evolving. From prioritizing we have moved to global positioning.

Our organizational worlds are full of multiple and conflicting objectives. The uncertainty induced by a set of conflicting objectives begs the kind of difficult learning that brings competitive advantage. Two decades ago, improved quality and reduced costs were seen as self-evidently conflicting objectives. Now they are seen as perfectly compatible for those companies that have learned how to focus effectively on both.

All the corporate disasters of recent times have a shared characteristic – mutually exclusive focus. Tankers go through treacherous straits to save on fuel and end up on the rocks. Ferries sink because their owners espouse safety but won't spend money on meeting the highest possible standards. The QE2 leaves the dock only partially refitted. In such cases, people seem to be trying to use their creativity to resolve one or the other side of the dilemma, not find ways to handle both.

The downside of the channels

Executives are on a knife edge between focus and narrow mindedness. Commercial strictures and expectations can become a creative straitjacket. Obsession is when focus and energy get out of hand. Focus can become obsessional. The leader continually brings things back to a core objective. The challenge is to be highly focused without becoming blind. The balance between focus and obsession is a precarious one.

"Obsession doesn't guarantee success. On the other hand a lack of obsession does guarantee failure," writes Tom Peters in *Liberation Management*.[60] In the hyper-competitive 1990s, obsession is a managerial necessity, but a dangerous one when individual focus is so fuzzy and changeable.

In the business world, obsession takes on many different guises. Managers obsessed about their sales targets, obsessed with reengineering, obsessed with corporate politics, or obsessed with their latest great idea for boosting performance. And, more questionably, there are the managers obsessed with tidy desks, car parking spaces and the company's consumption of paper clips.

Focus can become obsessional.

Take Victor Kiam, the man who famously liked the company so much he bought it. In his biography, Kiam says: "Business is a game and eight hours don't afford you enough time to score the deciding run." As a youthful and obsessive salesman, Kiam stalked the USA seeking out every advantage possible. "When a snowstorm hit my region it wasn't an obstacle: it was an opportunity! It was amazing how receptive a buyer could be when the snow outside his door was waist deep and climbing, and you were the only friendly face he had seen all day." In business, such obsessiveness is not a curious foible. Often it is not even regarded as strange or unhealthy. People don't lose their jobs for being workaholics or devoting every moment of their lives to meeting sales targets.

The business world does not, however, have a monopoly on obsession. Educational systems encourage children to be obsessive and sport is dominated by obsessives who think of nothing else but crossing the line first, jumping higher or hitting the ball harder. Coaches encourage this form of obsession (though they call it focus) in the same way as a boss is liable to encourage the obsessive traits of a young manager who works 16 hours a day and lives for the business.

Similarly, the acting world attracts obsessives. Indeed, actor Alan Bates has observed that "everyone who's any good is obsessive." This explains why Robert De Niro gained pounds in weight to play the aging Jake La Motta in *Raging Bull* – and then trained demonically to transform himself into the younger boxer at the peak of his career. Films also tend to be about obsessive characters. Indiana Jones travels the world in obsessive pursuit of ancient treasures and James Bond always faces obsessives intent on ruling the world.

There is culturally acceptable obsession – musicians who practice 12 hours a day – and unacceptable obsession. In organizational life we expect and demand obsessional behavior from managers. Yet, later in their careers if they take up more senior positions we expect them to throw off obsessional qualities to adopt a wider view.

All pervasive obsession is regarded as a good thing. Its connotations are so positive that there is even a perfume called Obsession. In the less fragrant business world, there is a fundamental belief that obsession motivates. The chief executive works days, nights and weekends not simply because this is what gets the work done. He or she believes that this is what motivates others to do the same. Leading by obsessional example means that managers work longer and longer hours. The question of whether these extra hours make them more productive is rarely addressed.

Obsessive managers can point to a lengthy list of like-minded individuals who reached the top. But, what happens if you don't want to take part? "Obsession is where commonsense bites the dust," says a manager who has worked for two bosses he identifies as obsessive. "I did not go along with the obsession so I was quickly shown the door. But the people I worked with carried on working obsessive numbers of hours and did not question the boss's demanding habits. To the obsessive boss no one else's world matters. If you point out, as I did, that their decisions are not rational but based on obsessive prejudice, you can guarantee fireworks."[61]

Even so, obsession is sometimes essential. The downside has an upside. If you are starting your own business, tepid enthusiasm is not enough. You have to live for your bright idea. The bank manager demands obsessive commitment and belief that the business will work. Nothing less will do. "If it is your own business, your own product, your own idea, obsessed is the only way to be," says consultant and author, Tim Foster. "The trouble is that few people share your level of obsession for a particular project. It is difficult to retain your obsessiveness when you are continually confronted by a lack of enthusiasm and commitment. The trouble is, to succeed, you have to."[62]

Similarly, if you are leading a Total Quality Management initiative keenness is inadequate. Obsessional behavior can set new standards of customer service. Companies such as McDonald's and Marks & Spencer are built round an obsessive commitment to giving customers quality service. McDonald's founder, Ray Kroc, used to pick up litter from car parks and was discovered one Saturday morning cleaning the muck out of the holes on a mop bucket with a toothbrush. The crew handbook which all McDonald's workers receive lists strict dress codes based on hygiene considerations and is prefaced by the words "Cleanliness is like a magnet drawing customers to McDonald's." This is where obsession shapes entire organizations – positively, constructively and profitably. (The trouble is that, taken too far, obsession can blind individuals or the organization to the faint signals suggesting that change is required.)

"If they are controlled, obsessions can actually change ingrained ways of behaving," says account management expert Ken Langdon. "If a manager targets a particular activity and develops a short-lived obsession to eradicate it, this will often work. The new behavior becomes internalized and the manager can relax. The only danger is that if the obsession continues it can become an excessively bureaucratic rule causing more problems than it solves."[63]

A common current obsession is with breaking down functional divides. At one company a senior manager developed an obsession with eliminating long-established barriers. In the middle of an interview, to prove his point, on a walk round the company's factory he asked everyone he met what they did to "functional silos." The replies were uniformly aggressive. His obsession had got an important point across.

The trouble is that obsession can lead managers and their businesses down potentially costly blind alleys. Henry Ford fervently believed that all people wanted was a low cost, uniform car. He delivered it to great acclaim and then sat back (as his Difficult Learning/High Value became low value) as General Motors sped past with constantly changing models in different colors. Ford's obsession was too rigid and unbending to take his company forward. Similarly, IBM developed an obsessional belief in mainframes and then stood bemused as upstarts eroded its markets.

Any psychologist will point out that obsession is dangerously unhealthy. As a result, managers are engaged in a precarious balancing act. When does the stock market dealer who energetically and constantly pulls off deals become an obsessive Gordon Ghekko-like figure discarding any pretense of ethical behavior? When does commitment and enthusiasm become obsession?

> **Obsession is a potent force which needs to be harnessed to the organizational good rather than being allowed to gather pace by itself.**

"It is a question of being obsessed about the right things," says Robert Matthews, development director of Discovery Expeditions which organizes expeditions to far-flung corners of the globe for jaded executives, among others. "You can't let obsession with achieving goals and targets cloud your judgment. We are obsessive – you have to be if you are organizing a major event like an expedition – but you also have to maintain the ability to step back and take in the total picture."[64]

There is a dividing line between commitment (healthy and outward looking) and obsession (unhealthy and inward looking). If obsessive managers took a step back it would be easy for them to recognize the unhealthy side of the obsession. It dominates their life to the detriment of family, friends and fun. Obsession is a potent force which needs to be harnessed to the organizational good rather than being allowed to gather pace by itself. Managers spend huge amounts of energy in obsessive search for promotions and engaging in corporate politics. If this energy was set free and channeled a potentially enormous corporate and individual resource would be unleashed.

Managing obsession successfully so that it brings personal and corporate focus involves:

- recognizing obsessive qualities in yourself and channeling and directing them to the organizational good;
- recognizing obsessive qualities in others and focusing their energies where most effective;
- identifying the divide between healthy and unhealthy obsession (ensuring, for example, that TQM does not develop into obsessive form filling);
- questioning corporate assumptions and long-held obsessions whether they be with particular people, products, strategies or markets;
- using obsession as an inspirational example.

Clearly, obsession is a fact of corporate and managerial life. The constant question must be whether managers allow it to control their behavior or control obsession for the benefit of themselves and their organization, and to bring focus to their own and the organization's activities. (See table 4.4.)

Table 4.4
MULTIPLE FOCUS AND YOU

- Do you stick at a complex problem until the solution is clear? (Only 19 per cent of people in our survey always did so.)
- Do you think that team members should always be doing the same task? (Only 2 per cent felt this was always or often necessary.)
- Do you manage your time ruthlessly? (Only 4.2 per cent said they always did and just over 9 per cent said they never did this.)

5 MASTERING INNER SENSE

Management was once tangible (or so we were led to believe), and when it wasn't managers tried their damnedest to make it so. They produced reports, budgets, strategic plans, memos, directives, rules and minutes. It didn't work. There was – and is – something more. As we have seen, corporate life is more intangible than ever. The decisions are bigger, the information more complex and the timescales shorter. If you're in white water, a report may be the baggage that sinks the raft and reading it may be more of a distraction from the approaching rocks than a navigational aid.

The vice-president of a pharmaceuticals company attempted to put this into historical context: "Due to the complexity of society, one has to make choices that are probably as difficult as the ones Archimedes or Plato were supposed to make so many years ago. They didn't have a lot of choices because everything they detected was really new."[65]

Given the nature of this choice and complexity it is little wonder that, instead of executives and professionals, we now have the emergence of knowledge workers. Indeed, some organizations have taken to heart Peter Drucker's message that knowledge is "the only meaningful economic resource" and have job titles incorporating the "k" word. In the late 1990s, rumor has it that Vice-President Knowledge is an actual job title, though it remains harder to explain at social events.

Despite the popularity of the concept of knowledge, it is still inextricably linked to hard facts. We may all be knowledge workers but we haven't stopped producing exhaustive reports which achieve little or dispatching data and statistics with gay abandon around the organization. Two Japanese academics, Ikujiro Nonaka and Hirotaka Takeuchi argue that Western companies remain caught up in "explicit" knowledge while the Japanese thrive on "tacit" knowledge.[66]

Tacit knowledge is more elusive, based on gut feeling, idealism and skills. To utilize such knowledge fully, Nonaka and Takeuchi advocate three things. First, companies must ensure that employees share experiences. This revolves around shifting flexible teams. Second, using middle managers as a conduit of information between the factory floor and the boardroom creates information flow. Third, they suggest that organizations must structure themselves as "hypertext" organizations. This unites traditional hierarchy with freer creative teams both based on a third element, the tacit base of knowledge in the organization. In their work on tacit knowledge, Richard Wagner and Robert Sternberg have developed the Tacit Knowledge Inventory for Managers. They identify three kinds of tacit knowledge used by successful managers:

- **tacit knowledge about managing oneself** refers to knowledge about self-motivational and self-organizational aspects of managerial performance. An example of tacit knowledge about managing oneself is knowing how best to overcome the problem of procrastination;

- **tacit knowledge about managing others** refers to knowledge about managing one's subordinates, peers and superiors. An example of tacit knowledge about managing others is knowing how to convince a skeptical superior of the worth of one's idea. The importance of tacit knowledge about managing others is suggested by the fact that inability to get along with others is a frequent reason for derailment of fast-track executives;

- **tacit knowledge about managing tasks** refers to knowledge about how to do specific managerial tasks well. An example of tacit knowledge about managing tasks is knowing how to get your main point across when making a presentation.[67]

We call our interpretation of tacit knowledge, **inner sense**. This is the final of the three enablers of white water leadership. Inner sense takes in intuition, gut feeling, instinct and much more which executives fail to understand but utilize continually during their careers. It is as elusive as it is all-embracing. Executives have difficulty in explaining learning; when it comes to inner sense they are rendered speechless rather than inarticulate.

Most executives can't and won't talk about this inner sense. Shareholders and institutional investors are particularly unimpressed by intuitive decisions and judgments. As a result, annual reports and the like have become works of incredible fiction. If a chief executive hits on a brilliant idea while in the bath, it is not something he'll proclaim at the AGM. If he sacked the finance director for the simple reason that his instinct told him that he was the wrong person for the job, he won't tell everyone this was the reason. Instead, he will pretend that the decision was the culmination of months of exhaustive analysis or came, regrettably, after close examination of the manager's performance. We asked many executives whether they used inner sense – more than 80 per cent said they did, but fewer than 30 per cent said they would admit it in the boardroom.

If they admit to using inner sense, but won't talk about it, we will. The truth is that for all the flow charts, neat diagrams and carefully constructed hierarchies, no executive can escape or avoid it. Indeed, with growing emphasis on the speed of decision-making, inner sense is likely to increase in importance. Uncertainty breeds intuition and vice versa. Things now happen so fast that managers rarely have all the information they might need to make a decision. They have to rely on their inner sense if they are to seize the opportunity. "You don't have to discuss things. You can sense it. The tingle is as important as the intellect," argues Sir David Simon, chairman of British Petroleum.[68] One CEO told us: "I'm sometimes driven by something that makes me say, 'I'm not sure I can explain this but I'm pretty sure that it is right.' And it's not come from talking with other people and it's not come from gathering data, it's come from inside."[69]

On his decision not to elevate Jeffrey Katzenberg to president, Disney chief Eisner said it was down to "a lot of very logical reasons and also for some intuitional reasons." Does this explain the decision or does it sound like a smokescreen? Explaining a decision by citing the unexplainable, often appears a cop-out. We demand real explanations, based on statistics, strategies, something solid, not nebulous. Western culture and society remains data driven, yet often limited data are available or they simply can't be trusted. In these circumstances the only source of data may be inner sense.

When Michael Dell told his parents he wanted to leave school, not surprisingly they asked him what he wanted to do. "Compete with IBM," was Dell's famous response.[70] Is this inner sense, adolescent arrogance or pure luck? We don't know but you can't write off a feeling which so many executives encounter and act on. This is not revolutionary. Management and leadership have always relied on the inexplicable, the feeling that a decision is right or wrong, an instinctive judgment of someone's personality or likely next move. Yet, we don't usually admit to it.

Increasingly, inner sense is making its voice heard. "Once I have a feeling for the choices, I have no problems with the decisions," says IBM chief Lou Gerstner.[71] Or take this description of Michael Eisner by Barry Diller, formerly Eisner's boss at ABC and Paramount:

"Michael looks like Goofy, and he often acts like Goofy, and he's definitely in the body of Goofy! But he's got one of the most smartly spirited minds that I've ever come across. You can see the electrical charges moving from one point to another in his brain. Spectacular instincts. Of course, he's not always right, and when it comes to that he has a somewhat tractionless memory."[72]

An article in *The Economist* on Bill Gates commented that: "His genius has never consisted in seeing further than anyone else, but in seeing the near-future more clearly, and understanding much better than his competitors how to exploit it. Time and again, Microsoft has recognized the potential in someone else's idea and simply done it better."[73]

The executives we interviewed encountered and utilized inner sense in a variety of ways. Some were mundane: "I have a sort of well-developed sixth sense for when something isn't quite right," said one CEO. "I can go through a batch of 20 invoices almost subconsciously and pick the only one which is wrong which infuriates everyone like hell. I think I can read my people reasonably well as to when things aren't right and you get all sorts of different signals. The information I get there is a lot of control information which merely points you to go and look in another area." But many cited inner sense as a constant influence on some of their most important decisions.

The inexplicable is a constant factor – no matter what the business. "One of the things that is confusing and almost intoxicating when you are growing a business is that you really have little way of determining what the problems are," observes Michael Dell.[74] In Europe there is a sports car manufacturer called TVR. It defies all the logic of the marketplace and has survived since 1947. It is very small, making less than 1,000 cars a year, and competes with the giants. Yet, it is highly successful. The media occasionally examines the company hoping to find out how it does it. Hard-nosed City writers usually retreat scratching their heads. The design of the TVR Chimera was helped along the way when the managing director's dog bit the end off a clay model of the prototype design!

TVR developed a new model called the Griffith. Its total development budget of around £200,000 was less than Renault spent developing the heating system for one of its new models. When it was exhibited at the London Motor Show in 1993 it took 48 orders immediately. Even then the price was a matter of debate. The managing director, Peter Wheeler, explained: "We've said it will be £29,000 and a bit, but we don't really know because we haven't built one yet. What we tend to do is build a car, work out how much it cost us, and then add a couple of hundred quid." It seemed gloriously amateurish until you learnt that the Griffith is actually faster than a Ferrari.[75]

> **Inner sense can – and inevitably will – encourage you to go against the corporate rule book.**

Mastery of inner sense partly explains the success of Microsoft. IBM, DEC and other multinationals had all the data, the facts, at their fingertips. But it didn't help them spot how the market was likely to develop or how they could play a part in its development. Microsoft picked up the faint signals: "I remember, from the very beginning, we wondered, 'What would it mean for DEC once microcomputers were powerful and cheap enough? What would it mean for IBM?' To us it seemed that they were screwed. We thought maybe they'd even be screwed tomorrow. We were saying 'God how come these guys aren't stunned? How come they're not amazed and scared?' By the time we got to Albuquerque to start Microsoft in 1975, the notion was fairly clear to us that computers were going to be a big, big personal tool," recalls Bill Gates.[76]

Inner sense can – and inevitably will – encourage you to go against the corporate rule book. One executive we interviewed was in the middle of a complex situation in which he had clearly breached the way things were done. "I was going against the internal rules. In most situations those rules were acceptable and understood. But, in this situation, they were giving me the wrong answer. It would have been very easy to say to the client 'No, those are the firm's rules and that's it,' but I felt so strongly that I made the decision. I had to inform the senior partner and he backed me. Other people interpreted the rule book and said you can't do that."[77] We are not saying abandon data, reason and logic, but we are saying that there is a huge hidden truth in many of the decisions made by organizations. That inner sense is there, alive and influencing. Yet, we don't acknowledge it. By failing to acknowledge it, for example, by simply asking someone who is wavering "What would make you more comfortable about this decision?" – we miss the opportunity to explore the uncertainties that will lead us to breakthroughs and insights. Many of the major technological discoveries that affect our lives have come into general usage because someone followed their inner sense when at the time there was insufficient supporting data.

Inner sense denies any rule book. It feels right, so right you have to do it, however unconventional. Barrington Jones was a well-respected don at Oxford University. He had also taught philosophy at Princeton. Then, in 1981, he resigned to become a plumber. He wanted to solve problems and he wanted, along the way, to find truth. He died in 1993, true to his inner sense and, who knows, perhaps nearer to truth.

Faint signals

One of the clearest uses of inner sense is in picking up on suggestions, patterns and trends in the organization and in the marketplace. "What all the wise men promised has not happened, and what all the damned fools said would happen has come to pass," observed nineteenth-century British Prime Minister Lord Melbourne. And, a century later, futurologist Arthur C Clarke commented: "When a distinguished but elderly scientist states that something is possible, he is almost certainly right. When he states that something is impossible, he is almost certainly wrong."

Don't write anything off. Everything is on tomorrow's agenda. Learning to adapt, to cope with the market and the environment is important – but that is learning about what is already there. The other kind of learning is an increased curiosity about what isn't yet there, seeking out what we label **faint signals**.

Executives make a great many decisions based on faint signals. It happens all the time. In November 1995 it was announced that a subsidiary of Italy's state-owned Finmeccanica engineering group had agreed to buy a unit of Mannesmann of Germany. The German company wanted to concentrate on its core businesses of engineering and telecoms. It was reported that the price of DM1 billion ($700 million) "far exceeds analysts' expectations."[78]

We often read such reports. Corporations are prepared to pay more for an intangible factor which defies the analysis of corporate valuation experts. It doesn't add up, but it makes sense in the boardroom. Why? We believe that in such cases executives are backing their inner sense. They are picking up faint signals from somewhere – it could be over lunch with an analyst, in conversation with their production manager who has an idea, a sense of what makes for a good deal.

Faint signals apply to people. They can enable you to spot potential. The hospital anesthetist we interviewed identified potential in a porter: "I suppose he had some sparkle that you pick up. If you are sensitive you can pick up the vibes from people who want to give a bit extra and they are just looking, itching to do a bit more. They have got something to give."[79]

Inner sense is picking up a scent and then following it. "Here at head office, we don't go very deep into much of anything, but we have a smell of everything," says Jack Welch of GE. "Our job is capital allocation – intellectual and financial. Smell, feel, touch, listen, then allocate. Make bets, with people and dollars. And make mistakes."[80]

Peter Senge has developed the concept of **generative learning** which he contrasts with the alternative **adaptive learning**. Generative learning occurs when people start looking at the world in new ways. Building on inner sense and faint signals requires this sort of different thinking. Faint signals often challenge conventional orthodoxy. Acknowledging truths that contradict previously held views may lead to major business opportunities, but can be painful. In *Managing on the Edge*, Richard Pascale tells the story of how Honda decided to launch its bikes into Los Angeles, as part of a grand strategy to sell into the USA.[81] Honda sent some people to California expecting to promote its larger bikes. In order to get around town, the sales people used some of the newly developed small 50cc bikes. These attracted a lot of attention wherever they went. Eventually the sales team received inquiries, not from motorcycle dealers, but from sports shops and other retailers. It seemed that fewer people were interested in the large machines, and against Mr Honda's and the American team's expectations the 50cc bikes were to become the biggest seller. They opened up the USA market to Honda, and within four years Honda was marketing almost 50 per cent of all motorcycles sold in the USA.

This is a much-quoted example, but it is interesting to look at the readiness of Honda's managers to learn rather than criticize. For instance, the team in the USA did not call Tokyo to say that (as Toyota had found previously) the strategy for launching the larger machines into the USA was failing. Instead they offered the alternative idea that everyone wanted the small machines. Yet, here was an organization that had spent a lot of effort in putting together a strategy to sell a product into a major market. A variety of alternative actions might have been taken – the sales people could have been fired for incompetence because they failed to sell the big bikes; a different sales strategy involving more or different advertising could have been adopted; and so on. Many organizations would have been loath to let go of their hard fought for strategy, especially on account of a few comparatively junior people several thousand miles away, in a market that had not yet proved itself.

Some of the best managers are adept at picking up weak signals from the environment. Their very faintness makes them occasionally inexplicable and usually unexplainable. We talked to the production director of a printing company. He had recently seen inner sense in action:

> **"As we are a small company we don't have the time to justify everything. We have just spent over £300,000 on a new printing press. We didn't know whether we could justify on paper that we could fill that press. The MD took a gut decision that there was a lot of work out there and bought it and he proved dead right. I was looking at what he'd seen in the marketplace and I couldn't see where we would get the work. I could see it being a white elephant. He just knew that the way the business was going that there would be more work coming our way."**[82]

Inner sense is a belief that, one way or another, you are right. It is a leap into the unknown and often the possibility of a safe landing place or any landing place is doubted by most others in the organization. The sensible advice is don't jump. But if your inner sense says go for it and you do then you will redefine your target area for yourself and for everyone watching.

Inner sense is about spectacular instincts: the right answers which come from somewhere which only you can explain – but probably can't. Virtually every leader we spoke to had reached a critical decision when they had flown in the face of opinion. The data were uncertain, but they felt and knew it was right to move in a particular direction. Richard Branson recalls his decision to go into the airline business in 1984: "It was a move which in pure economic terms everybody thought was mad including my closest friends but it was something which I felt that we could bring something to that others were not bringing."[83]

> **Inner sense comes from inner strength.**

Self-awareness

Confucius used a Chinese guide to leadership. "Radical changes require adequate authority. A man must have inner strength as well as influential position. What he does must correspond with a higher truth," it advised. "If a revolution is not founded on such inner truth, the results are bad, and it has no success. For in the end, men will support only those undertakings which they feel instinctively to be just."

Though by its very nature, inner sense is abstract, it is built on the more solid foundation of self-awareness. Inner sense comes from inner strength. And it is this strength that can protect you from corporate madness when all around people are losing their grip. The leaders we interviewed were often strikingly aware of their own strengths and weaknesses – and were frank and honest about them. Compare this with a *New Yorker* cartoon of a fortune teller with her crystal ball giving the bad news to a client. "You are fair, compassionate and intelligent," she says. "but you are perceived to be biased, callous and dumb."

"I'm very quick to see my weaknesses. As part of an appraisal, I drew up a long list of weaknesses and a short list of strengths. I think that came across very strongly, even from my boss, the chairman. He marked me fairly highly on a number of areas. I can't be complacent, there were certainly areas where he felt I could improve, particularly with team interaction. I still sometimes think that I've got to prove something and go out and show I can do the business to prove something maybe to myself," the CEO of an insurance company told us with commendable honesty and insight.[84] Such self-awareness provides a vital reference point. It provides confirmation, the resilience so that you can maintain energy in the face of opposition. It confirms why you stay focused on a particular objective.

Indeed, acceptance of inner sense involves acceptance of risk. Inner sense is far from infallible. Look at Steve Jobs' career after he left Apple in 1985. He launched NeXT which was as ostentatious a start-up as Apple had been modest and unheralded. The aim was to produce a computer as black as Henry Ford's Model Ts which would capture the higher education market. With money aplenty (Ross Perot weighed in with $20 million) and Jobs' previously unbeatable inner sense it seemed a guaranteed winner. Canon put in $100 million to help it on its way. When asked if Microsoft would develop software for NeXT Bill Gates reputedly said: "Develop for it? I'll piss on it." In February 1993 NeXT stopped production and moved to selling software. Jobs was proved wrong. It was an expensive mistake.[85]

Inner sense is fallible, but such is the strength of self-awareness that white water leaders persist. Jobs may have failed with NeXT, but he has succeeded by following faint signals elsewhere. While struggling with NeXT he acquired Pixar, a computer-animation company, in 1986. To date, Jobs has invested $60 million in Pixar and the company is now into film-making (including *Toy Story*). Jobs admits that he was buying into a dream of creating computer animated films. "I believed that computer graphics were going to be very important in the future and I saw the potential of what was happening at Pixar," he explained. Once again, Jobs was right. His 80 per cent stake in the company is now worth nearly $1.2 billion. But, would you bet that sort of money on a belief?[86]

Venture capitalist Robert Drummond, former chairman of Grosvenor Venture Managers, agrees. "Intuition is all about flexibility – being tuned into what's going on and being prepared to change direction." By its very nature, venture capital relies on hunches about whether a business is likely to succeed or fail. According to Robert Drummond, it is not simply a question of backing winners. "It is no good following rigid rules in business. Successful people not only make the right decisions, they have a grasp of timing. Being a venture capitalist is all about being opportunistic, using your intuition to identify changes in society and to invest in areas which meet new needs."[87]

To a large extent, it appears to be a question of confidence – or perhaps arrogance. Nevertheless, managers seem to agree that hunches are more likely to be proved right as you become more experienced. "As you do more and get better at it, you need fewer instruments," said one. Less experienced, younger managers are therefore unlikely to have the necessary intuitive skills to make instant decisions. Inner sense comes from a base of knowledge.

A finance director we interviewed recalled having an intuitive feel about a franchise bid. He suspected that the sole competitor would bid high but would fail the quality threshold required – therefore, there was no point in bidding high. "Occasionally I will feel the adrenaline surge. It's always quick – let's try that, no big analysis about it. You've got to have knowledge. You've got to understand what you're doing and what the background is. Emotion comes into it. Sometimes the ideas stay inside because the time isn't right or there's too much risk attached. I don't have intuitive insight into things I don't know anything about. I don't see how you can."[88] And he was right – the competing bid failed to provide for the quality standards required and his company won the franchise for a minimal cost.

Too often, however, experience overpowers inner sense until it is completely negated. Executives become used to ignoring their instincts and placing their trust in analysis. Inner sense must incorporate the key notion of learning from and through experience and is invaluable if there is inadequate data to analyze.

Building inner sense

Increasingly, inner sense is seen as a skill which can be learned or, at the very least, appreciated and used more effectively. Research carried out for the book *What Do High Performance Managers Really Do?* suggests that managers who use their inner sense effectively and continuously are likely to have a number of characteristics:

- they take decisions quickly and confidently. They are willing to back their judgment and don't spend large periods of time weighing things up;

- they use data only when necessary. Not for them the computer printout containing every single statistic available;

- they recognize inner sense as a skill, part of their managerial armory;

- they accept and encourage ideas, whatever their source or apparent usefulness, at every stage;

- they act on intuitive judgments, rather than questioning them;

- they accept no rigid or right method of doing things. If something feels, looks or seems right, they will do it (not to be confused with ethical valuations!).

How do you develop a more useful inner sense? (See table 4.5.)

1 **Find your own inner sense and listen to it.** "It is something that leaves you on a little razor edge all the time and you think on the night might be all right," explains actress Judi Dench.[89]

2 **Acknowledge the existence and value of inner sense in others.** This inevitably makes life more complex. How do you utilize or learn from something so intangible in yourself and even more intangible in others? One of the executives we interviewed had been particularly influenced by a more senior manager. We asked: "Did you learn anything from watching this person in action?" "I guess getting down to the basics and he seemed to identify fundamental questions even if he didn't have the answers," he replied. "How do you think he picked out what were the fundamental

questions or issues?" we asked. "I'm not sure I know the answer to that." The senior role model defied emulation – but through listening and appreciating that inner sense was being used, the younger executive was already learning a valuable lesson.

3 **Find or create an environment in which you can explore the first two.**

Table 4.5

INNER SENSE AND YOU

- Are you on the lookout for the faintest of signals? (A staggering 95 per cent of our 566 respondents said they were sometimes, often or always.)

- Do you find it easy to make predictions for the future? (20 per cent said never or seldom; 35 per cent said often or always.)

- Do you have a sixth sense about the correctness of a decision? (No one said never and over 68 per cent of our sample said often or always.)

- Are you most at ease with familiar problems? (45 per cent said they always or often behaved in this way.)

Notes and references

1 Quoted in Sherman, S, "How tomorrow's leaders are learning their stuff," *Fortune*, November 27, 1995.
2 Quoted in Van Clieaf, MS, "Executive resource and succession planning," *American Journal of Management Development*, vol. 1, no. 2, 1995.
3 Author interview.
4 Grove, AS, "A high-tech CEO updates his views on managing and careers," *Fortune*, September 18, 1995.
5 Author interview.
6 Cram, T, *The Power of Relationship Marketing*, FT/Pitman, London, 1995.
7 Quoted in Jackson, T, "Chemical formula," *Financial Times*, November 3, 1995.
8 Quoted in Trapp, R, "Off with their overheads," *Independent on Sunday*, December 10, 1995.

9   Bennett, A, "Downsizing doesn't necessarily bring an upswing in corporate profitability," *Wall Street Journal*, June 6, 1991.

10 Noer, D, *Healing the Wounds: Overcoming the Trauma of Layoffs and Revitalizing Downsized Organizations*, Jossey-Bass, San Francisco, 1993.

11 Dougherty, D and Bowan, E, "The effects of organizational downsizing on product innovation," *California Management Review*, Summer 1995.

12 Ghoshal, S and Bartlett, C, "Rebuilding behavioral context," *Sloan Management Review*, Autumn 1995.

13 Quoted in Gowers, A and Jackson, T, "Kodak develops a brighter outlook," *Financial Times*, December 18, 1995.

14 Interview with Stuart Crainer, November 1995.

15 Author interview.

16 Binney, G and Williams, C, *Making Quality Work*, Economist Intelligence Unit, London, 1992.

17 Interview with Stuart Crainer, February 1995.

18 Quoted in Jackson, T and Gowers, A, "Big enough to make mistakes," *Financial Times*, December 21, 1995.

19 Quoted in Binney, G and Williams, C, *Making Quality Work*, Economist Intelligence Unit, London, 1992.

20 Tillier, A, "A fresh wind blows in Finnish business," *European*, October 5–11, 1995.

21 de Vries, M Kets and Dick, R, *Branson's Virgin: The Coming of Age of a Counter-Cultural Enterprise*, INSEAD, Fontainebleau, 1995.

22 Author interview.

23 Author interview.

24 Author interview.

25 Author interview.

26 Author interview.

27 Quoted in White, L, "Net prophet," *Sunday Times*, November 12, 1995.

28 Author interview.

29 Author interview.

30 Schendler, B, "Bill Gates and Paul Allen talk," *Fortune*, October 2, 1995.

31 Author interview.

32 Author interview.

33 Author interview.

34 Author interview.

35 Author interview.

36 Author interview.

37 Author interview.

38 Advertisement in *Fortune*, September 18, 1995.

39 Author interview.

40 Author interview.

41 Arbose, J, "ABB: the new industrial powerhouse," *International Management*, June 1988.

42 Taylor, W, "The logic of global business: an interview with Percy Barnevik," *Harvard Business Review*, March–April 1991.

43 Author interview.

44 Kay, J, "Is there a competitive advantage of nations?," *Siemens Review*, 5/95.

45 Atkins, R and Fisher, A, "A giant step for reinsurance," *Financial Times*, November 27, 1995.

46 Handy, C, *The Age of Unreason*, Harvard Business School Press, Cambridge, MA, 1992.

47 Author interview.

48 Author interview.

49 Quoted in White, L, "Net prophet," *Sunday Times*, November 12, 1995.

50 Quoted in Summers, D, "Boots made for the global path," *Financial Times*, October 12, 1995.

51 Author interview.

52 Powell, C (with Persico, J), *My American Journey*, Random House, New York, 1995.

53 Quoted in "When the boat comes in," *The Economist*, October 2, 1993.

54 Author interview.

55 Author interview.

56 "In a clear light," *The Economist*, November 11, 1995.

57 Author interview.

58 Author interview.

59 Author interview.

60 Peters, T, *Liberation Management*, Alfred P Knopf, New York, 1992.

61 Author interview.

62 Interview with Stuart Crainer.

63 Interview with Stuart Crainer.

64 Interview with Stuart Crainer.

65 Author interview.

66 Nonaka, I and Takeuchi, H, *The Knowledge-Creating Company: How Japanese Companies Create the Dynamics of Innovation*, Oxford University Press, Oxford, 1995.

67 Wagner, R and Sternberg, R, "Street smarts," *Measures of Leadership*, (Clark, K and Clark, M eds), Leadership Library of America, West Orange, NJ, 1990.

68 Quoted in Hosking, P, "The leader's leader," *Independent on Sunday*, December 31, 1995.

69 Author interview.

70 Quoted in Jacob, R, "The resurrection of Michael Dell," *Fortune*, September 18, 1995.

71 Quoted in Cornwell, R, "The iconoclast at IBM," *Independent on Sunday*, August 1, 1993.

72 Quoted in Huey, J, "Eisner explains everything," *Fortune*, April 17, 1995.

73 *The Economist*, November 25, 1995.

74 Quoted in Jacob, R, "The resurrection of Michael Dell," *Fortune*, September 18, 1995.
75 Clarkson, J, "Small wonder," *Sunday Times*, November 21, 1993.
76 Schlender, B, "Bill Gates and Paul Allen talk," *Fortune*, October 2, 1995.
77 Author interview.
78 "Business and finance," *The Economist*, November 4, 1995.
79 Author interview.
80 Quoted in Jackson, T and Gowers, A, "Big enough to make mistakes,"*Financial Times*, December 21, 1995.
81 Pascale, R, *Managing on the Edge*, Viking, New York, 1990.
82 Author interview.
83 de Vries, M Kets and Dick, R, *Branson's Virgin: The Coming of Age of a Counter-Cultural Enterprise*, INSEAD, Fontainebleau, 1995.
84 Author interview.
85 Stross, R, *Steve Jobs and the Next Big Thing*, Atheneum, New York, 1993.
86 Kehoe, L, "Patience of Jobs pays off," *Financial Times*, December 2–3, 1995.
87 Crainer, S, "Instincts that point to success," *The Times*, September 2, 1993.
88 Author interview.
89 *South Bank Show*, London Weekend Television, November 1995.

"Gaining and maintaining competitive advantage depends upon the ability of individuals at all levels of the organization to learn and adapt quickly to changing business realities."

GARY L TOOKER
*VICE CHAIRMAN AND CEO,
MOTOROLA*[1]

"People go through four stages before any revolutionary development:

1. It's nonsense, don't waste my time.
2. It's interesting, but not important.
3. I always said it was a good idea.
4. I thought of it first."

ARTHUR C CLARKE
FUTUROLOGIST

MAKING UNCERTAINTY WORK

✳ The water is engulfing us.

✳ How do we get back on board?

✳ How can we get back into the white water?

Uncertainty is here and here to stay. Industries once regarded as stable and slow moving are now beset by the bubbling white waters of change. Amid the confusion and messiness, some corporations and some leaders are seizing the new uncertainties and are making them work.

The logic we have mapped out begins with the acceptance that management and leadership have traditionally sought out certainty. They have thrived on answers and solutions. Then we argued that leaders must embrace uncertainty as this is the new reality of business life. In Chapters 3 and 4 we described the five skills we believe are essential to white water leadership and emphasized the importance of leveraging learning – both organizationally and personally – if true change is to be achieved.

Case studies are orderly; our message is messy.

Now, in this chapter we look at the organizational challenge, the reality of uncertainty and how the skills of white water leadership need to be utilized.

If we were to follow conventional wisdom we would present five or six case studies of organizations which have been able to move towards uncertainty and have reaped the benefits. Yet, few organizations are seeming to demonstrate an ability to move towards uncertainty. Even if there were many to choose from, a neatly defined case study defeats our point – there is no resting place, no ideal situation where all the corporate demons have been slain. Case studies are orderly; our message is messy.

Uncertainty has been circumvented, put on hold, but like water pouring through a crack, you can only hold it back with your finger for so long. The longer you wait, the wetter you will become.

We are going to look at the uncertainty evident in three industries – retailing, accounting, and pharmaceuticals – and which of the five skills these most clearly demand from leaders. We are not suggesting that the five skills need to be continually and universally applied. There is no universal panacea. Instead, they need to be utilized in different ways at different times.

In these three industries some, although not all, of the skills are being applied, and even inside the same industry different players are applying different skills. In the future we will be able to look back and assess who applied the skills effectively, and who didn't. Uncertainty has been circumvented, put on hold, but like water pouring through a crack, you can only hold it back with your finger for so long. The longer you wait, the wetter you will become.

THE RETAILING REVOLUTION

Retailing is one of the major industries of the 1990s. Its success stories have become the benchmarks for innovative management in many areas. Retailers lead the way in developing customer loyalty. They often lead the way in harnessing new technologies to improve performance through customer service. The excellence of the few is celebrated and copied – whether it is WalMart, Nordstrom or Europe's Marks & Spencer. They are the high achievers during a period of huge turbulence where cut-throat competition is the order of the day.

There is no escape from the maelstrom of change, innovation and fear. Impregnable giants are being challenged and sometimes slain. Innovative companies such as Body Shop are sweeping the world. WalMart is crushing KMart, costing the CEO his job. Brands are being extended, globalized and cannibalized. Retailers are becoming financiers and financial institutions are discovering retailing.

Choice and complexity, change and uncertainty – and the omnipresent forces of uncertainty come in many forms.

Upstart competitors

Competition can come from anywhere at any time. GM moves into credit cards; grocery retailers move into clothing; KMart experiments with groceries in order to save itself; GE moves into broadcasting.

Look at cola. Until 1994 the Toronto-based Cott Corporation was not a well-known name in the retail world. It propelled itself to the front pages through challenging two of the world's biggest brands – Coca-Cola and PepsiCo. The result was what quickly became labeled the cola war. By the end of the year, the two goliaths weren't out for the count, but they were groggy, on the ropes, waiting for the bell to ring. Cott, the chirpy but unfancied challenger, had danced circles around Pepsi and Coke – though whether it will continue to do so is open to question.

Cott may have called the shots in the cola war, but its roots lie in the increasing power of large retailers. The battlefields are the world's cola shelves in the supermarkets; but the war goes far beyond. The story is simple: Cott makes cola concentrate which it sells to supermarket chains and other retailers. They then market the cola under their own brand name. It may not be the real thing, but it is cheaper. Retailers can undercut the premium brands – Coke and Pepsi – while still extracting a bigger profit margin. The Cott concentrate costs as little as a sixth of that for Coke or Pepsi and the logistics allow retailers to make an extra 15 per cent profit. Neat logic – though less appealing if you work for one of the dominant duo.

The commercial attraction was simply put by Cott chairman and CEO Gerald Spencer: "The bottom line is that our product sells to retailers at around $3.25 a case and theirs sells for $5 a case or more. If the products are of equal quality, why should retailers pay more?"[2] The additional benefit for Cott is that its agreements with 90 retail chains worldwide don't involve it in any expensive advertising. Contrast this with the vast amounts spent by Pepsi and Coca-Cola in promoting their products. Coke sponsors the US National Football League while Pepsi picks up the bills for celebrity advertising – basketball star Shaqille O'Neal, and more.

With minimal marketing costs and a world apparently full of willing purchasers, it is little wonder that Cott's sales and profits are soaring. Its sales have mushroomed from C$43 million in 1989 to C$665 million in 1993 – and, by June 1994, its sales were up 66 per cent and profits 67 per cent on the previous quarter. Cott's insurrection is truly international. It sells to the largest US retailer WalMart, Sainsbury's and Safeway in the UK, and Ito Yokado, one of Japan's biggest retailers. The retailers simply add the brand name of their choice. WalMart sells Sam's American Choice; Sainsbury's has Classic Cola (whose packaging too closely resembled Coke for the giant's liking); and in Canada there is Royal Crown Cola (RC Cola to its admirers).

The threat from Cott has already dramatically affected the financial fortunes of the cola giants. In June 1994 Pepsi's share price fell by 16 per cent in New York in 10 days. Coke's Canadian bottling subsidiary closed eight of its plants and 62 of its administration offices. In some areas, Coke and Pepsi have lowered prices and increased the margins for retailers. The cola war demonstrates that financial might and traditional strength in the markets count for very little, and may underscore why so many CEOs and senior management teams feel at risk over short-term performance. Combined Coke and Pepsi sell more than 50 per cent of all carbonated drinks consumed in the world – that is a lot of fizzy flavored water. Yet, despite their huge advertising budgets and their traditional leadership, customers appear to have little brand loyalty. Even if this is just a storm in a cola container, Coke and Pepsi have lost a large amount of money. If this is a long-term change in the market, they are looking at vastly diminished returns.

The cola wars also brought home the fact that the balance of power is shifting to a small number of large retailers. Retail chains have considerable, and increasing, power. In the past they were loath to exercise it, as they concentrated on their geographical and physical development, and nurtured their brand. Now, many have exhausted geographical expansion and their brands are strong and established. The new emphasis is on extracting increased profits from the shop space they have and on using their private label brand within the shop as effectively as possible. Every single item they sell must justify its existence, it must fight for shelf space. If they believe that their private label product will make more money, they will stock it at the expense of the established brand.

Of course, this is where the uncertainty comes in. The very success of private label products may lead to the retailers marketing their brands in a similar way to the likes of Coke and Pepsi. If private label brands become locked in a cycle of outmarketing each other, then their price competitiveness may soon disappear. What happens then?

Our view is that this is a good time to seriously contemplate some difficult learning. The conditions are right in that no one has been there before and although there will be some tempting remedies from the past – advertise more, discount more, offer more and bigger promotions – these are so easily copied that they won't, and can't, last for long. Something new is needed and the most likely route is when a company takes it seriously enough to set up a program of exploration and trial and error to learn how to do something that no one else has been able to do before. The challenge is to move towards difficult learning. Moving to the High Difficulty/High Value arena is the only way to survive.

Another point is made by Cott's Gerald Spencer: "Consumers are smarter now than they were 20 years ago," he says, adding the punchline, "You can only pay so long for an icon."[3] Customers are more sophisticated and more demanding than ever before. More of the same is no longer enough. Their expectations are continually increasing. Companies must move to meet them – otherwise they face certain disaster.

In the case of Coke and Pepsi familiarity may, in the end, be breeding discontent. They are so successful and dominant that there is the risk of appearing dull and unexciting. Indeed, recent years have seen the steady rise of competition to cola. While in the late 1980s cola accounted for 63 per cent of the US soft drinks market, by 1993 this figure was around 58 per cent as consumers experimented with new products. Interesting, isn't it, that when new Coke was introduced and promptly flopped, we all agreed that it was just a stunt to gain greater shelf space (facings) to display Coke products.

The cola wars have shaken up Coke and Pepsi. The end result will probably benefit the two giants and consumers – prices are likely to remain lower and Coke and Pepsi are likely to have become more competitive. Coke's chief marketing officer, Sergio Zyman, has promised faster and more frequent new products and has summarized the company's aim as "aggressively addressing growth opportunities wherever they exist."[4] The company's mission remains: "To put a Coke within arm's reach of everyone in the world."

Old responses no longer work

Coke pins its faith on being faster. Remember Quicker, Faster, Better? But even that may not be the answer. Speed can precipitate disaster as companies attempt to square the circle. A more balanced rationale was given by former Pepsi president, Andy Pearson, in a 1989 *Harvard Business Review* article. Pearson suggested that for leaders and their organizations to be successful they must demonstrate higher order skills grounded in basic values. He saw:

- a commitment to "giving customers better value than your competitors do" (as competitiveness);

- a reasoned approach to investment, not "spending cash as though it belonged to someone else" (as judiciousness);

- the idea that one should look for "the simplest ways to do things" (as efficiency);

- an understanding that you can get the most impact by "concentrating on a few things at a time" (as selectivity).[5]

More of the same no longer works. We've looked at cola wars, but 1994 also saw soap wars between two of the world's largest companies which set new records for bitterness and launched a European industry worth £6 billion into unprecedented turmoil. It is a painful reminder that there are no guarantees for a company attempting to gain advantage through difficult learning. As with most wars, the seeds of the discord were apparently negligible. In fact they are barely discernible to the uneducated eye – minuscule crystals of manganese. But these pink crystals led to an expensive and long-running war between the Anglo-Dutch giant Unilever and its traditional rival Procter & Gamble. The chairman of Unilever's UK business, Sir Michael Perry, later called it "the greatest marketing setback we've seen."

Unilever claimed that a new product (labeled either Omo Power or Persil Power in different European countries) was a huge technological leap forward: "We always knew it would start a washing revolution. We just didn't expect it to start a war," a statement from the company later observed. Unilever saw the new product as the way of striking back at P&G's growing pre-eminence in the market for fabric detergents. Unilever had been slow to exploit growing demand for concentrated products and required a major technological development to regain lost ground. Power was seen as a dramatic means of breaking through the mass of products on the market. Unilever claimed that it could clean more effectively and at lower temperatures. In financial terms it represented a £200 million stake from Unilever to recapture the initiative.

The crucial crystals in Power were manganese, which P&G had tested and found could attack fabrics and accelerate bleaching. It had, as a result, put a stop to its research. So far, so good. Here was a definite opportunity for difficult learning. If Unilever could carry on where P&G had stopped, there was a chance to achieve genuine competitive advantage. Unilever was optimistic that it could eventually find a solution. It thought it had done so – in the new products manganese was used as a catalyst to increase the cleaning power of the detergent.

The launch of the new product did apparently give Unilever the leap forward it needed. P&G's new detergent – Ariel Future – was not scheduled to be launched until later in 1994. And, the Power detergent appeared to be highly effective in removing stains. P&G quickly began examining the ingredients of the new Unilever detergent. Its research suggested that the new Power products created holes in clothes after repeated washing. "Only Ariel washes so clean yet so safe" ran P&G's advertisements in newspapers. If this was not controversial enough, P&G also claimed that the manganese was actually retained by the clothes so that even if washed in other detergents the effect would continue. P&G's claims sparked war.

Power was a disaster. It sought to defy the increasing segmentation of the market by offering a stronger and better product which could be used for a wide variety of clothes at low temperatures. This was a tough objective and one which should have given enormous advantage to the company. But in trying to be all things to all people, it turned out to be, as P&G relentlessly pointed out, too good to be true. Power is now downgraded to a specialist detergent for whites and use on heavily soiled clothes. In December 1994 it took less than 1 per cent of the UK detergent market. In February 1995, Unilever wrote off £57 million of stock thanks to the soap war. So this particular piece of High Difficulty/High Value learning became more like High

Difficulty/Low Value. Should that stop a company like Unilever? Should it stick to the familiar retail formula of quicker, faster, better? Silly question. Of course it must continue the struggle to develop new and better products, but it has also had an opportunity for a different kind of difficult learning in coping with this problem internally. For an organization with high visibility and high internal self–esteem, Unilever has to squeeze dry this source of learning so that it is not vulnerable to a much bigger corporate threat – downscaling its readiness to continue to take risks and to continue to seek competitive advantage through difficult learning. Our information suggests that it has learned the lesson well and has become stronger, not weaker, as a result. Watch out P&G.

Customers don't help

The dilemma facing Unilever is not as straightforward as we have so far presented. There are customers to add further complexity. In developing Power, Unilever assumed it was giving customers what they wanted – perhaps it was. But, increasingly, customers are behaving in paradoxical, even contradictory, ways. We are told that customers want relationships, personal contact. They want to be loved and rewarded. The trouble is that we are constantly led to believe that customers are also more fickle than ever before. Love them today and they may well be gone tomorrow. "Going fickle, ephemeral, fashion," proclaims Tom Peters in *Liberation Management* in his robust shorthand. In the age of the consumer, they know what they want and will speedily change brands when their expectations are not met. Customers for frequently bought brands are likely to buy competing brands almost as often as they buy their favorite brand. This is the kind of information which gives brand managers sleepless nights.

Indeed, the term loyalty is often a misnomer – on average the most frequent business travelers are "loyal" to three different frequent flyer schemes. And this pattern is repeated across products as diverse as petroleum retailing and coffee. Loyalty is not easily bought, or even understood. In the new world order with hyper-competition and globalization, complexity, choice and confusion lurk at every turn.

If you can't increase your profitability through developing better relationships with customers there is always geographic expansion – more stores in more towns. The trouble is that many big name retailers are nearing the end of geographical expansion. They are in all the major markets and can no longer rely on regular store openings to boost turnover. Some, like WalMart, are actually buying up smaller regional competitors and closing them down. They have to look elsewhere for new products and new approaches to old products and markets. (Gas stations serve as the latest outpost for fast food franchises.) The growth of the last decade appeared self-perpetuating, now they find it is faltering.

Others have wooed analysts with brilliant use of new technology. They know that technology cuts costs and can attract customers. But how long can people be cut and customers satisfied? (CBS News on December 26, 1995 suggested that the five millionth US worker would be cut in 1995 by New Year's Eve!) Retailers are seeking every available easy source of competitive advantage, however minuscule and fleeting it may be. UK supermarkets even battle over exotic fruits. As one celebrates the introduction of Vietnamese dragon fruit, another begins selling longans. The novelty value of exotic fruit sums up their desperation and its shelf life is the duration of whatever competitive advantage it had.

The choices are hard and enormously varied. Does the company consolidate – and risk losing the excitement, energy, verve and enthusiasm which allowed it to grow in the first place – or seek out different markets? There are no easy answers, indeed often there appear to be no answers. But to get nearer the answers retail organizations and their leaders must use **difficult learning**.

PepsiCo and Coca-Cola could sit back and relax knowing that Cott's incursion cost them a relatively small amount of money. Or they can seek out lessons from the experience and ways forward which break consumer boredom with their products. Instead of being shaken by the markets, they have to do the shaking. Instead of seeking out easy learning – throwing more money into the marketing budget or more me-too cost cutting responses – they must seek out difficult learning. Unilever will fill shelves with newer and better detergents, but in the aftermath of Power, it has also learned to think beyond Quicker, Faster, Better.

In such cases Difficult Learning may mean broadening horizons and changing perspectives. This can bring with it a huge people challenge. People who work with them have experience in their specific area and little else. What if Unilever's brand managers were carried away by their own desire to get a new product onto the market, rather than broader considerations – such as does the product work, what will the competition do and say? How will the marketplace – our customers – respond? Difficult learning will mean breaking free from the stranglehold of what always worked in the past.

Cott struck a blow because its message was persuasive to retailers and consumers. Its message was far from complex – so why didn't the giants see it coming? Why didn't they take preemptive action? The only conclusion is that they chose not to as recognition would have demanded the kind of learning they were not prepared to undertake or even contemplate. They ignored the signals – and they weren't exactly faint – and carried on.

Leaders must pay attention to **faint signals** and long-term possibilities while at the same time paying attention to quarter-to-quarter profits. It's not enough to win at today's game – look at the large beer brewers in the USA. They had market share and forgot to be on the lookout for the next hot trend – microbrewers. Now that microbrewers are all the rage, the big brewmasters are playing "me-too."

Faced with new competitors, organizations have to go through difficult learning to achieve (or regain) competitive advantage. They must resist the temptation to do something which is easily copied and they must resist the temptation to copy, to allow the competitive race to become a series of copycat initiatives. We believe that companies in such situations need to find difficult learning in the area they want to move into, to seek ways of expressing it simply and then to apply energy to sustain trial-and-error learning in preparation for the launch of new ideas, products and services.

To do so, organizations and their leaders must **maximize energy**. Doing things which are new or different increases the likelihood of mistakes, failure and defeat. Energy and enthusiasm can be the response that sustains members of the organization as they engage in difficult, mistake-prone, new learning.

Generating and sustaining such energy requires **resonant simplicity**, a particularly potent weapon in retailing. Simple phrases can sum up what an organization stands for and how it behaves. Coke sticks with its aim of putting a coke within everyone's reach. It is understandable and it works. But what if it has already largely achieved this? If the only place you might struggle to find a coke is on top of a mountain or a deserted island. Is it still an inspirational and valid phrase?

The paradox is that companies have to reinvent themselves without losing the things that made them successful in the first place. (Remember the Sigmoid Curve?) The danger is that by changing the business to live in the new environment, what helped to make the business successful in the first place will be forgotten.

One organization to have pulled this off is the Virgin Group which has moved with minimal fuss (and maximum public fanfare) from record stores to airlines to selling pensions and cola. Yet, we still think of Virgin in the same way. "We've never bought companies, we've always built companies, so we've always been a small person taking on a big person. When we started retail we were the first people who discounted records against the big retailers," says Richard Branson.[6] Virgin may be a multimillion dollar business but it is still behaving and thinking like David against Goliath.

Keep it simple and paradoxically have **multiple focus**. Retailers must accept the paradoxical demands of a wide variety of stakeholders with wildly different agendas. Who does Pepsi aim to please – its stockholders who want dividends no matter what's going on in the markets, its consumers who can buy a similar product more cheaply elsewhere or its distributors who can get higher margins elsewhere? Somehow, corporate leaders have to keep everyone satisfied.

NUMBERS CRUNCHING

Auditing appears to inhabit a world of quintessential certainty. But, as elsewhere, the certainty is skin deep. Occasionally it flares to the surface – at the end of 1995 over 90 members of an international auditing firm in Madrid deserted the company to join an arch rival across the road. Such drama is unusual as auditors have established an unspoken, conflict–averse culture which few break free from or even disturb. Auditors live in something of a twilight world. Their product has become a commodity. There is a captive market – companies need to buy their product – which has proved highly lucrative. Indeed, it is such a cash cow that major firms have used revenues from their auditing business to fund other parts of the organization.

Ironically, it is difficult to establish the true nature of this as the auditing partnerships are not required to publish accounts giving the same details as public corporations. The published information simply gives total fee income or total billings – not for auditors public revelations of Return on Investment or profitability. The companies even grow at a similar rate – look at the 1994–5 figures in table 5.1.[7]

Is there another industry in the world where the performance of the dominant businesses is so similar? There are a small number of huge players and plethora of minuscule partnerships. Undoubtedly, auditors are good at providing a particular service. Their technical training is excellent and, notably, involves a great deal of learning on and from the job. So, where in this lucrative world, does the uncertainty lie?

First, auditors do not leverage every kind of learning. Learning is localized (and blame is globalized). Learning is measured and packed into the early part of a strictly mapped out career path. Aspiring auditors cram learning in and then appear to stop. There is a myth of mastery – acquisition of knowledge leads to promotion and the route to partnership involves negotiating rites of passage, the late nights with the text books, working 80-hour weeks.

Such certainty narrows perspectives. Partners are responsible only for an immediate circle of clients and staff. Their focus lies in a narrow product range, sold to a small number of clients and delivered by a small team of staff. The atmosphere is claustrophobic. Partners are conflict-averse. The emphasis for wannabe partners is on keeping your nose clean, getting on with the job safe in the knowledge that one day a partnership could be yours. From an individual perspective it makes sense. You know where you are going and how to get there. It is easy to forget what you (and the organization) are missing along the way.

Table 5.1

GROWTH OF MAJOR AUDITING COMPANIES, 1994–5

Firm	Revenue 1994–5 $billion	Revenue 1993–4 $billion	Growth %
Arthur Andersen	8.1	6.7	21
KPMG	7.5	6.6	13
Ernst & Young	6.9	6.0	14
Coopers & Lybrand	6.2	5.5	13
Deloitte Touche Tohmatsu	6.0	5.2	14
Price Waterhouse	4.5	4.0	12

Organizationally, this climate of certainty makes no sense at all. These huge organizations employ large numbers of highly trained, intelligent people, who do a professional job to a generally high standard. But they don't do any more. All too often the auditor doesn't seek to develop a relationship which goes beyond auditing.

Ask any auditor how they add value to their organization. They will say that they do so by nurturing long-term relationships with clients which earn the organization fees. True. Ask them how they could add more value to their organization and you will in all likelihood draw a blank. They do what they perceive as their job and no more. Auditors talk about selling their firm's consultancy services, but when you enquire what the percentage is of auditors that have made career moves across into consultancy and back again, the answer is usually very small. The plain fact is that there is little or no active communication between the auditing and consulting arms in many audit partnerships. Each regards the other as holding the organization back in some way. By not communicating, the possibility of conflict is minimized. The rationale is that auditors are suppliers of certainty and experts in it. Their customers expect solutions, answers, certainty.

Some partnerships are dynamic. They target smaller businesses or particular segments of the market. They set up multidisciplinary teams which, if they really can operate in a multidisciplinary way, have huge potential. These are exceptional and sometimes don't fulfill their promise because they are perceived as sophisticated ways of selling on, rather than leading towards integrated solutions. Most auditing firms are unsure how to change, yet change they must.

Change when it comes is usually tinkering at the edges. It is Low Difficulty/Low Value. All of the major firms have invested heavily in training over the last few years. They have their training centers and universities, they use the best business schools. But talk to some of the people who teach at these centers – how do they describe their students? "Arrogant," "time pressured," "short attention span," "clever but very focused" are the types of phrases used. Are these students monsters? No, of course not. But they do work in a system that measures, marks, assesses and rewards them by the billable hour. Every billable hour. Time off for training and development can easily be seen as just that. Time off equals time unbilled and that equals time wasted. This is what the system tells them and in this case the medium probably still is the message.

The trouble is that customers are becoming increasingly more selective. They demand value. They know more about the suppliers and their products and the markets into which those products are sold. The customer is now better placed than ever to demand and critically assess value. One definition of when a product becomes a commodity is when the customers know almost as much about the product, its price and its quality as the supplier does. Expensively trained and remunerated audit partners don't like the thought that they deliver a commodity (like coal, wheat, electricity or sewage disposal). They don't compare themselves to miners, farmers or water treatment managers. Maybe they should. Software and expert systems have helped turn auditing into a commodity. Maybe that is where the difficult learning could start. Certainly the market is now cutthroat with upstarts offering lower prices and the Big Six being forced to come down in price in the hope that the competition will be a momentary blip and hourly billing will soon be back up in the stratosphere.

It won't happen. Not while the auditing companies remain addicted to the front of the fridge. They expand services and cut prices. Easy options. They bolt on related business expertise. The trouble is that such expertise – which usually comes in the form of consulting – is also becoming a commodity.

The audit firms face one of the hardest kinds of difficult learning encountered by any organization – to do something radical when things are still going well. And things are still going well – look back at Table 5.1. So, it is easy to cry wolf and be ignored within the organization. But we believe the faint signals are already there, indicating that for this industry doing nothing is now the high risk strategy. Audits will always need to be done, and auditors will always need to make moderate changes in the way they work. The prospects for those who can change radically could be considerable. But for those who can't, the long-term prospects are bleak.

Inevitably the issue is **difficult learning**. It needs to be acknowledged and tackled. For auditors, difficult learning always used to be climbing the mountain that led to excellence in technical knowledge. But the huge body of knowledge that once offered competitive advantage is now just the entry ticket. In reality, the difficult learning is going to be getting close to customers in ways that they value. With that will probably come the recognition that different customers will need to be treated in very different ways in order to create value, even though the basic principle of the audit and its legal requirements are the same.

Audit firms have to learn how to maintain their reputation and technical competence, meet legal compliance requirements and become sufficiently creative and insightful at a corporate level so they can create value for their various clients in appropriate forms. The creative auditor! Even the term sounds a little dubious. And that dubious reaction gives one clue about just how much difficult learning there has to be. For if the public finds the concept difficult, then think how much competitive advantage there is to be had from convincing clients by demonstrating that it is possible. Think how hard the other audit firms will have to work to make the changes in their own organizations.

Sometimes difficult learning produces a difficult message. The "We try harder" slogan of Avis emerged from several days of scouring for some – any – competitive advantage over Hertz. If a difficult message has to be conveyed then it had better be simple and it had better be clear. These things take a lot of work because they need to be more than slogans and glossy advertising, although that may well be necessary. We are talking about the whole organization asking itself what it really wants to say to its customers and clients. What it can really deliver and what it is prepared to do to demonstrate its commitment. Reinventing the way you work is more than changing job titles.

Auditors have traditionally been marathon runners. They need enormous reservoirs of physical energy to move up the career ladder. The energy is channeled into more and more billable hours and little else. There is no trial and error learning. Make a mistake and your fear is that you will be shown the door. Energy is not channeled into developing relationships with other parts of the organization or in seeking out new ways of doing things.

Energy will also be required elsewhere. Auditing has thrived and grown by being single–focused. It now must encourage people with **multiple focus** to work in a multiple focus world. By channeling energy and focus into different areas, auditing firms would be undertaking difficult learning. Both would be obstructed, criticized, dismissed and regarded as destructive.

The trainee auditor is taught to be rigorous and always to provide evidence for assessments and decisions. It is an irony therefore that the most skilled and experienced partners, while still retaining the expectation that conclusions must be proven by data and evidence, will often talk about a feeling that they had on going into a business for the first time; how in the early stages they just knew that something was not quite right with a set of figures well before they uncovered the detail.

If auditors can use their **inner sense** to good effect for their clients then we hope they can use it for good effect for themselves and their industry. Because one of the few things that can be guaranteed is that the way ahead for those who want to survive in the long-term will not contain clear markets with all the data necessary to make a decision. Signals that were faint only a few years earlier have now become strident – the risks associated with the legal liability of the partnership structure, ever more sophisticated software and expert systems, and the changing needs of clients. The audit firms are going to need all the inner sense they can muster to give them the insight to find their way between these major obstacles and turn them into opportunities, as well as listening out for the next generation of faint signals. For example, as knowledge transfer becomes electronically easier and easier, why do we need big organizational structures? Why not lots of small very well connected ones? There are lots more faint signals out there to be navigated during the next decade of difficult learning.

PHARMACEUTICALS: BETTING ON THE FUTURE

In 1988 Eastman Kodak bought the drug company Sterling-Winthrop for $51 billion. For six years Kodak wrestled with the complex world of pharmaceuticals and then surrendered – in 1994 Sterling-Winthrop was sold for $1.7 billion.

Riddled with complexity, the pharmaceuticals world is well used to uncertainty. Little wonder that Kodak failed to make sense of it. Years spent on developing a product can be wasted or lead to competitive advantage which lasts for months rather than years. (It takes 11.5 years for the average drug to go through basic research to approval by the regulators.) The pharmaceutical giants also have to contend with the vicissitudes of stringent and ever-changing government regulations. "The average amount of data included in the submission to regulators is up four-fold over the past decade," says Peter Farrow, senior director of European clinical development for Pfizer.[8] And, to add further uncertainty, interlopers are entering associated markets from a perplexing array of different angles. Try a few of the many angles – Northrop Grumman, which makes the B–2 bomber is working with the US Defense Department and Johnson & Johnson to fund an MIT project designing the operating theater of the future; consumer credit rating company Equifax has bought six small healthcare firms; Toshiba's medical systems division generates $54 billion a year from selling body scanners – what will Toshiba move into next? Where will the competitors of tomorrow come from? What will happen to the competitors of today?

Over the last decade, the level of uncertainty has moved onto a different plain and different pharmaceutical companies have made different bets. Some have integrated horizontally by becoming bigger. They have played corporate pacman by gobbling up smaller firms and moving into different markets with different products. Sometimes they have consumed major players, partly because nearly all the smaller players with a market value of between $5 billion and $12 billion have already been consumed. In 1989 there were the Bristol/Squibb, SmithKline/Beecham and Marion/Merrell Dow mergers. And 1995 saw another flurry of activity with FHP International spending $1.1 billion on TakeCare, United Health Care paying around $520 million for GenCare Health Systems (using some of the $2.3 billion it had received from a sale to SmithKline Beecham) and a host of other combinations, purchases and mergers. Despite a history of organic growth, Glaxo spent £9.1 billion on Wellcome (and then said it was looking at "savings" it could make in R&D – a low difficulty option if ever there was one).

Others, more interestingly, are trying to integrate vertically as well as horizontally, broadening their perspectives to take in healthcare generally. Some are repositioning themselves as full-service healthcare organizations (the unspoken colloquialism for this strategy is "womb to tomb") so that in the future they could well own and run their own health centers.

The attraction is clear – the US hospital industry has a turnover of $800 billion. The vertically integrating giants are moving in. SmithKline Beecham has announced its intention to become a "mega-company", anticipating a world dominated by a few huge corporations and has bought the pharmacy benefit manager, Diversified Pharmaceutical Services, enticed in part by the attraction of a large patient database.

The UK drug company, Zeneca, paid $195 million for LA-based Salick Healthcare in 1995 and through it now controls the cancer wing at the Mount Sinai hospital in Miami Beach and plans further expansion in the USA, Europe and Asia. Zeneca is the number two cancer drug supplier in the world, but is the only large pharmaceutical company to have moved into direct patient treatment – so far at least. "The cost of drugs is 7 per cent of total US healthcare spending," says Zeneca CEO, David Barnes. "Salick gives us the opportunity to reach the other 93 per cent of the healthcare market."[9] The significance of this statement is not lost on other pharmaceutical CEOs.

Zeneca's move clearly represents difficult learning – a process made even more demanding by the ethical questions raised by a cancer hospital being owned by a producer of cancer drugs. Elsewhere in the pharmaceuticals world, there is growing recognition of the need for change, though most organizations have yet to transform recognition into achievement. The immediate response tends to be more of the same, but faster. In trying to respond to uncertainty, companies have speeded up the discovery and delivery process – one corporation has reduced its product development model from 5,000 days to 2,500. But much more is needed.

The stakes are enormous. In the year 1994–5 sales through pharmacies in the USA totaled $403 billion, up 10 per cent. Americans spend around $1 billion a year on over-the-counter remedies to control stomach acid. Pravachol, a drug to lower cholesterol, developed by Bristol-Myers Squibb, generated sales of $35 million during its first quarter on the market. Given the prizes, it is not surprising that R&D budgets in excess of $500 million are not unusual.

The business is lucrative, but pharmaceutical companies have discovered that the fundamental proposition of their activity has changed. As Eli Lilly tells it, it was once a process of find it, make it, sell it. The uncertainty lay in finding the product in the first place. If they could find it they might be able to make it and, if they could make it, they knew they could sell it. Now, even research is being contracted out. Contract research organizations are growing rapidly – according to Boston Consulting Group their sales are rising at 15 per cent a year and 1996 revenues of $1.8 billion are anticipated.

Now price is an issue. Strange as it may seem, this is the biggest nightmare imaginable for the pharmaceutical giants. Some companies, such as Sandoz Pharma, are already positioning themselves as lower priced competitors. And corporations have to consider how they will deliver; what the competitors are doing; and what markets they are actually in. Instead of rushing to market they now have to consider timing of entry – addressing questions such as when can they start selling an improved, more expensive drug when they have a cheaper, but less effective one still on the market? Or, if they have a drug that might be more efficacious yet more costly, how to get governmental agencies to allow reimbursement on factors other than cost alone when the new therapy is $1.30 a day versus 30 cents a day?

These issues have to be tackled on a global scale. The global–local issue is predominant. "Competitive success depends on timely, efficient, large-scale development conducted simultaneously in major markets throughout the world," says SmithKline Beecham chairman, Henry Wendt:

> **"The company must conduct sizeable clinical trials on a global scale while involving leading clinical experts in important local markets. Such strategically effective clinical trials require extensive global planning, intensive input from local markets, and a rigorous determination to follow the plan without adding extraneous activities. Execution makes great demands on the company's global communications network and data-management system. Ultimate success depends on skillful planning, disciplined follow-through, and the ability to manage data quickly and accurately."[10]**

We would argue that success depends on detecting the faintest of signals. Tomorrow's leaders in pharmaceuticals will be attuned to faint signals in a way never previously envisaged. They will have to make bets on the future of products and markets continually. Then, having made their bets, these sprawling, complex and huge industrial operations, must communicate the complex in as simple and evocative form as possible. The range of stakeholders that they have to address is expanding rapidly. Their message has to resonate. While the definition of exactly who is and who isn't a customer is in flux, the fact remains that customers are more demanding, the media clamoring for any misadventure and governments more stringent. Brand strength will have to be nurtured among a variety of groups rather than, as was previously the case, targeted solely at buyers.

Everyone in the organization and in their various markets has to understand what they are doing and why. Look at the care taken when Glaxo acquired Wellcome. The deal was presented more as a merger than a takeover. Gerrit Aronson was appointed the new group HR director, having previously been the HR director at Wellcome. "From the start, priority was given by Sir Richard Sykes (deputy chairman and CEO) to a process designed to make sure that senior people from both companies had a good shot at all the top jobs," Aronson reported. The focus of the company could not simply move to that held by one or the other of the companies, it had to include both. Of course, there was uncertainty among the combined workforce of more than 60,000 but the company did its best to minimize the problem (and thus restore focus) by completing the integration process as quickly as possible while wanting to get it right.

Companies – even if they are highly profitable giants – are tiptoeing forward, scared to give offense. Their fear is understandable. The old paradigm – find it, make it, sell it – no longer fits. Discovering the new paradigm demands difficult learning – move into healthcare by all means, but it will only work if you take on difficult learning rather than simply applying what you already know or what works elsewhere. The companies must reorient themselves, develop new and changing focus for their operations, and then develop more. The test for global pharmaceutical players involves not only their ability to engage in difficult learning, for they have been doing that for many years. The question is: can they make the right bets? This is a test of inner sense. At the same time, the pharmaceutical business is becoming the healthcare business – involving more complexity and testing focus and simplicity in an already uncertain future.

WELCOME TO THE NEW WORLD

These industries – retailing, accountancy and pharmaceuticals – are not exceptional. Uncertainty dogs every industry and every business no matter where it is. Leaders the world over are struggling to accept this is the case or are struggling to do something about it.

The new era of uncertainty, the one we label white water, will not come to an end. It is not a blip. It is here to stay. This means that leaders and their organizations will be involved in a continuous and tempestuous journey, moving with, through and down the rapids. The future is upon us. Change is rapid and never complete – new roads to somewhere are always being built. A survey of 200 senior managers in the UK found that 40 per cent of them said they would need to restructure their business every six to 12 months; and 41 per cent said this would have to be done every two or three years.[10] Remember the line from Will Rogers: "Even if you're on the right track, you'll get run over if you just sit there."

Change is accelerating. At home roles continue to evolve and change. At work we are asked to do more and more with less and less. Columnists and thinkers are asking whether the pain of reengineering is really worth it. Does organizational performance improve after such drastic steps? Since beginning to share our ideas across the Atlantic five years ago, much has happened. We have not only seen a panicky flurry of downsizing and the concomitant calls from middle-aged, mid- to senior-level executive job seekers, but also many new start-ups. We have seen the dawning of the information explosion with everyone and everything on the Internet. We have seen computer software billionaires predict the future and one information age billionaire running for President of the USA.

> **The new era of uncertainty, the one we label white water, will not come to an end. It is not a blip. It is here to stay.**

We have also seen and experienced, through our teaching and counseling work with senior managers, the struggles to cope with the enormous amount of change while continuing to perform at the highest levels possible. Unreasonably, but understandably, the highest level of executive performance is expected by stockholders, boards, analysts and everyone else with a direct stake in the corporation no matter what. In fact, organizations holding large blocks of stock are now routinely invited in to take a look round and voice their opinion about policies and how the company is or should be run. If any trend continues unabated by the new harsher realities, it is the intense pressure to perform, to provide increasing levels of knowledge, goods and services to produce increasing profit margins with fewer people and other resources.

Most managers we see are just plain tired. It's hard work. "My boss doesn't have the slightest idea what it takes to perform at this level," is a typical lament. "We all know we need to change, but who has time?" is another plea increasingly heard in corporations. And, of course, the fear factor is very much in evidence in many US, European and, unthinkably, Japanese organizations – the fear of failure. So, trying to do something different, something risky, like the things we discuss in this book, is tantamount to high treason – "We're doing so well, why mess up a good thing?"

While there is broad and growing recognition that we need to behave differently, the world remains wired together in such a way to encourage old style – front of the fridge – behaviors. So, you not only have to fight with yourself to change but also with the rest of whatever social system you find yourself in. It is a lesson we remind all of the managers we encounter as they leave full of energy and enthusiasm to make the behavioral changes they realize the world now demands. You can change your behavior, but at the same time you're practicing the behavioral changes, you must also deal with a system that wants you to stay the way you were. Then, at least you were predictable. When you change you introduce instability into the system and systems don't like instability.

> **"We're doing so well, why mess up a good thing?"**

233

Our notion of leadership – to seek out uncertainty and move towards it – is fraught with risk. One way to balance that risk is to learn new behaviors and skills which are neither easily diagnosed nor taught. Yet, they are the building blocks for dealing with the higher order leadership issues faced in complex ever-changing societies. And, who knows, there may be other behaviors even more critical for leadership effectiveness. We are willing to believe that there are, but only those leaders and organizations attuned to learning, risk-taking and moving towards uncertainty will discover their identity. And then, having made that discovery, they must move on.

We therefore leave you with our organizational uncertainty checklist. It is something we use at our presentations to spark dialog with and between our participants.

Table 5.2
ORGANIZATIONAL UNCERTAINTY CHECKLIST

In this list, which we have used in our presentations and consultancy, we have rated people's reaction to the ease of adoption of the ideas. In the assessment scale we have used, **S** means it should become standard behavior soon. **PTB** means pushes the boundary and is a rather more adventurous approach. **OOTB** means out of the box, and is a high risk, potentially high reward, and probably high adrenaline option to introduce. You have been warned!

Learning

S	Every job interview contains a question on learning from failure.
PTB	Learning reviews at the end of every meeting.
S	Appraise on ability and willingness to learn.
OOTB	Reward people for first-time error; then make the person who made the error responsible for educating the rest of the organization and be critical of that person if anyone makes the same mistake again.

Energy

S   Audit tasks and projects to assess "fun" level.

S   Make energy generation a company competency.

S   Assess energy pull as well as push.

PTB Hire energy consultants – such as court jesters, a Falstaff for every division.

Simplicity

S   Review statements on:
  - vision
  - policy
  - values
  - competencies.

S   Are they short and clear?

PTB Documents thrown back if not simple and clear.

PTB A project in a sentence: not approved unless it can be summarized in one sentence.

OOTB A project from a sentence. (Just the sentence given to the approvals committee. Only if they can reconstruct key aspects of the proposal from the sentence is it clear and simple enough to explain to everyone.)

Focus

S   "Vital few" feedback:
  - what I need from you
  - what you can expect from me.

S   Projects checked for unsuspected side effects.

PTB Interaction table created for every project.

Inner sense

S   Identify data-rich and data-thin assignments.

S   Assign people to both.

PTB Place developing executives with coaches who are "gut feelers."

PTB Help executives learn that inner sense is an art and a science. Encourage public discussion of what drives inner sense of key decision-makers.

Notes and references

1 Quoted in *Fortune*, September 18, 1995.
2 "Cola warriors identify new enemy," *Financial Times*, June 11–12, 1994.
3 "Cola warriors identify new enemy," *Financial Times*, June 11–12, 1994.
4 "Tonic for fickle tastebuds," *Financial Times*, August 24, 1994.
5 Pearson, AE, "Six basics for general managers," *Harvard Business Review*, August–September 1989.
6 de Vries, M Kets, *Branson's Virgin: The Coming of Age of a Counter-Cultural Enterprise*, INSEAD, 1995.
7 Kelly, J, "The show goes on despite some backstage bickering," *Financial Times*, December 21, 1995.
8 Green, D, "Testing times," *Financial Times*, January 11, 1996.
9 Green, D, "UK drugs group takes Salick's growth treatment," *Financial Times*, December 21, 1995.
10 Wendt, H, *Global Embrace*, Harper Business, London, 1993.
11 *Shaping the Workplace for Profit*, Workplace Management, 1995.

POSTSCRIPT

We see this book not as the culmination of a project, but as the beginning of a continuing dialog about leadership in complex, rapidly changing social systems. And we'd like to involve others in our work. We would like to gather examples of difficult learning where any or all of these behaviors were used or are being used. We would like to find examples of these behaviors used effectively and also situations where they were ineffective. Obviously, we all want to know about the successes so that we might try and tease out what is replicable in our own situation. But we also want to explore the negative to find out what went wrong and why, because there is rich learning in failure when we take the time to study it. We hope that you want to share your story as we all attempt to ride the rapids just ahead and report the successes and failures to those who will follow.

In the USA contact:

Randall P White
RPW Executive Development
1821 Lendew Street
Greensboro
NC 27408-7016
USA

Internet:
randy@rpwexdev.com

In Europe contact:

Philip Hodgson
Ashridge Management College
Berkhamsted
Herts
HP4 1NS
UK

Internet:
Philip.Hodgson@Ashridge.org.UK

APPENDIX

Most leadership research has a single source of data, a set of interviews, a questionnaire administered to 1,000 people, or something similar. This study is different in that there is no single source of data. In fact, data for *The Future of Leadship* were collected in a variety of ways and at different points in time from executives and others on both sides of the Atlantic. When people hear that we are doing work on uncertainty, they go quiet for a moment, then grin, and then ask how we can be certain that we can finish a book on uncertainty. There have been times when we've wondered as well. So, probably the best way to understand each source of data and where it fits into the project is to take a chronological look at the project's chequered history.

The roots of this project go back to 1991, when Phil Hodgson took a short sabbatical from Ashridge Management College. During this time he visited Randy White at the Center for Creative Leadership and attended his strategy course for senior managers. The idea was to give a critique of the course and suggest ways it might be changed. During conversations after the course, Randy and Phil discussed how people came to strategy courses looking for things that were not offered or were false dichotomies. For example, participants often wanted to spend time making distinctions between their role as strategists and leaders or wanted to know when you did strategy. It was as if strategy was a separate entity, something that happened on a Friday afternoon and was divorced from everything else the leader did. Research by Phil Hodgson and Stuart Crainer in the UK found striking evidence that even in the literature this distinction persists – a run through a database found 17,076 articles on strategy, 2,344 on leadership and a mere 49 which mentioned both strategy and leadership. The resulting book, *What Do High Performance Managers Really Do?*, examined the roles and skills of high performers. It again emphasized that the distinction between strategy and leadership is a false one.

Meanwhile, Randy White was taking on a director level role at the Center for Creative Leadership – managing other managers and carrying out policy and strategic planning activities – and exploring what executive learning and growth entail through participating in the action learning research project, APEX™ (Awareness Program for Executive Excellence). APEX is a project where senior level executives undergo a round of extensive 360-degree feedback – from bosses, peers, subordinates. It can and often does include feedback from family and friends, as well as responses to a battery of tests taken by the executive. These interviews – and cases taken as a whole – represented an early insight into the role of leaders actively dealing with uncertainty, complexity and the bottom line. Though we have not focused on any one case, we have used ideas generated from these case discussions as the basis for some of the examples in *The Future of Leadership*.

In parallel, in the UK Phil Hodgson was engaged in action learning research projects. While the data collection was not nearly as elaborate, it also generated stories and ideas which illustrate many of the major concepts in this book. These processes (not reproduced here) continue to be provided by Ashridge Management College as well as the Center for Creative Leadership.

In 1992, an attempt to convert the ideas into a children's fable failed to capture the imagination of all but our own families. At various speaking engagements the audience looked slightly entertained. In an effort to make sense of what we thought we were seeing, we examined the literature on leadership, strategy, chaos, and now uncertainty and ambiguity. We plowed through hoping to find the link between the theory and the reality we were increasingly encountering in our interviews and discussions.

To explore more fully how executives handle uncertainty, Randy and Phil conducted a series of interviews during 1993 and 1994 with senior executives to elicit which of the five skills they used. The sample was convenient rather than representative, but provided many interesting avenues and personal insights later explored in the book. In the text, these 28 interviews are denoted as author interviews.

UNCERTAINTY RESEARCH: STRUCTURED INTERVIEW QUESTIONS

Fear of failure/difficult learning

1 When did you try something and fail? What was it and what did you learn?

2 Probe for risk – were you aware of risk? How did you approach risk? Was risk an important factor in perseverance?

3 As a result of this what do you do differently/what did you learn?

4 What has tested your resilience most when you made a "mess of something" and recovered?

5 What has brought out the fight or flight reaction in you – when were you fearful that if something wasn't done you'd lose face/your job?

Finding energy/fun

1 What gives you your greatest kicks/thrills/energy in doing your job? How much of your time do you spend like that? If a high percentage of time, has it always been like that? If not, how have you increased that amount of time?

2 What are the tough things (things you don't want to do) in your job? How do you bring yourself to do them?

3 What do you do to create fun/enthusiasm in those who work for you? How do you get people excited about what you/your boss is doing? What do you look for to know if people are excited? What do you look for (what signs) if they're not?

Resonant simplicity

1 Who have you worked for who made the complex simple? What did they do? How did they do it? What have you taken from them?

2 Walk through one complex problem. How do you come to grips with a complex problem? How did you explain the problem to others?

3 How do you read your environment? When you shifted to this job, how did you learn to read this environment?

Focus and concentration

1 How do you evaluate whether something is an interruption or a piece of your agenda? Tell me about a time when you were wrong and (a) it was an interruption that you treated as part of your agenda (b) it was part of your agenda but you treated it as an interruption.

2 What are your foci now? What are you trying to achieve at the moment? (Probe for static versus fluid answers – want to achieve five per cent growth versus want to increase generally versus want to learn about that market.)

3 What distracts you? Tell me a story about when you were distracted from achieving an important objective.

4 How rapidly do your foci change? What causes this change (please give examples)? How do you express the foci to self? To others?

5 How do you add value?

Inner sense

1 Tell me about a time when you did something in the face of opposition, contrary advice, or opposing data. Why? What did it feel like? How did it turn out? What finally gave you the confidence to go ahead despite the opposition?

2 Tell me about when you listened to your gut and (a) you were right (b) you were wrong. What did people say? How did you feel? What is the difference? Who was involved?

3 Have you seen this tendency (to go ahead in the face of opposition) in others? How do you explain it? Do you respect it? How do you feel about it?
Tell me about someone else (boss, subordinate, colleague) who does the same as in the example you gave about yourself. What were your reactions and the reactions of others?

4 To what extent do your organization, culture, circumstances, encourage or discourage disclosing statements about gut feel, inner reference points, etc?

On the basis of this interview study and a first attempt to write up our findings we made a presentation to the American Society for Training and Development in June 1994. The reception at this and other meetings during 1994 and 1995 in Germany, Switzerland, Canada, the UK and the USA was warm and warming. This encouraged further development of our questionnaire which, thanks to Jane Hodgson and Katie White, has now become a more sophisticated self-scoring instrument.

In 1995 Stuart Crainer joined the project to develop the ideas into a coherent whole. At the time Stuart had just completed editing *The Financial Times Handbook of Management*, a massive undertaking which had involved him interviewing many of the most eminent management theorists of our time.

At the Human Resources Planning Society International Conference in Orlando, Florida, in April 1995 we launched our data collection effort for the Questionnaire and also began testing it out at the Harvard/Pilgrim Health Care (an organization undergoing merger), First Data Corporation, management classes in the USA and UK, a conference of Certified Public Accountants and Financial Planners, a conference of senior HR practitioners, a group of senior public utility managers, a group of women serving in state houses and the senate and the class of an advanced management program in the USA.

After getting rid of partial and unusable responses, 566 responses remained for the factor analysis of the five skills. Prior to factor analysis, the Questionnaire had 48 items divided into 5 skills (reverse coded elements are in italics).

QUESTIONNAIRE

Difficult learning	$\bar{X}$	SD
I give up when I can't see the solution to a complicated problem.	4.00	0.73
I'm embarrassed when I make a mistake.	2.80	0.89
A crisis is an opportunity to learn.	4.16	0.80
When I am in a foreign environment, I am fascinated by different customs.	4.39	0.81
When mistakes happen it's somebody else's fault (always was not selected).	3.45	0.69
I like to have someone from another field explain their work to me.	4.04	0.72
I wish life were simpler.	2.94	0.91
I prefer to modify a solution I have already used rather than inventing a completely new one.	2.91	0.75
I'm open in telling people about the mistakes I make.	3.70	0.78
I learn more from reviewing my failures than my successes.	3.79	0.80

Spearman-Brown reliability coefficient = 0.60

Energy

	$\bar{X}$	SD
I try to make all my work enjoyable.	4.22	0.69
One of my roles as a manager is to inject enthusiasm into the workplace (never was not selected).	4.44	0.63
I try to make work fun for others.	4.10	0.76
I get energy from my work.	4.14	0.74
Difficult problems energize me.	4.09	0.78
I enjoy the challenge of my work (never was not selected).	4.34	0.68
I tolerate the dull and tedious parts of my job.	2.61	0.92
When work becomes a grind, I grit my teeth and get the job done anyway.	2.04	0.80

Energy	$\bar{X}$	SD
People describe me as enthusiastic.	4.01	0.83
I look for ways to make even the tedious parts of my job exciting.	3.61	0.86

Spearman-Brown reliability coefficient = 0.69

Simplicity		
I believe that every problem has one correct answer.	4.12	0.79
When I've made an important decision, everyone understands the consequences.	3.41	0.75
I can explain complex subjects simply enough for children to understand.	3.52	0.76
People ask me to explain complicated things to them.	3.58	0.73
I keep working at a complex problem until I have a clear solution.	3.93	0.72
I try to capture my business strategy in a single sentence.	3.15	1.05
It bothers me when a problem has potentially more than one right answer.	4.05	0.84
I find it hard to explain complex subject matter to someone not in my field.	3.68	0.82

Spearman-Brown reliability coefficient = 0.65

Focus		
I manage my time ruthlessly.	3.19	1.01
I incorporate interruptions into my work pattern.	3.94	0.81
I usually know what I'm trying to achieve at any moment.	3.86	0.71
Distractions can be managed into productive outcomes.	3.63	0.70
At the end of the day, I wonder what I have achieved.	3.17	0.80

Focus	$\bar{X}$	SD
I accept that colleagues may have different priorities than I do.	4.30	0.66
I identify the short-term decisions that also bring long-term benefits.	3.79	0.69
I can see how the smallest detail of a plan connects to the big picture.	3.83	0.73
I prefer to work on several linked ideas rather than concentrating on just one (never was not selected).	3.87	0.81
People on a team should all be doing the same task.	4.16	0.74

Spearman-Brown reliability coefficient = 0.47

Inner sense		
At work I usually know where I am going, even if I do not know precisely how to get there (never was not selected).	4.00	0.61
I have a sixth sense telling me about the "correctness" of a business decision (never was not selected).	3.76	0.73
I find it easy to make predictions about the future.	3.19	0.85
There are few certainties in management, only probabilities.	4.05	0.78
When faced with a complicated situation, I wait until an answer feels right.	3.25	0.82
When I look back at a decision I have made some time ago, I want to change it.	3.33	0.68
I feel most comfortable when I'm dealing with familiar problems.	2.68	0.94
I'm on the lookout for even the faintest signs of what the future might bring.	3.88	0.85
Knowing accurately about what my competitors did this year is more important than speculating on what they might do next.	3.60	0.89
When I'm traveling I can find my way.	4.37	0.77

Spearman-Brown reliability coefficient = 0.52

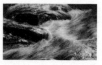

INDEX